SPIRITUALITY
IN THE MOTHER ZONE

SPIRITUALITY
IN THE MOTHER ZONE
Staying Centered, Finding God

TRUDELLE THOMAS

Paulist Press
New York/Mahwah, N.J.

Scripture extracts are taken from the New Revised Standard Version, Copyright © 1989, by the Division of Christian Education of the National Council of the Churches of Christ in the United States of America and reprinted by permission of the publisher.

Cover and book design by Sharyn Banks

Library of Congress Cataloging-in-Publication Data

Thomas, Trudelle.
    Spirituality in the mother zone : staying centered, finding God / Trudelle Thomas.
      p. cm.
    Includes bibliographical references.
    ISBN 0-8091-4298-8 (alk. paper)
  1. Mothers—Religious life. 2. Motherhood—Religious aspects—Christianity. I. Title.
    BV4529.18.T46   2005
    248.8′431—dc22

                                       2004028241

Published by Paulist Press
997 Macarthur Boulevard
Mahwah, New Jersey 07430

www.paulistpress.com

Printed and bound in the
United States of America

Contents

Introduction 1

BEGINNINGS

1. Stranded in the Mother Zone 13

2. The Crisis of First-Time Motherhood: Matrescence 26

3. Beware: The Dangers Mothers Face 43

4. This Is My Body: Restoring Dignity to the Mother's Body................49

5. Composing Your Life: Spiritual Hunger and the Workplace 70

6. Which Way to Go? Decision Making and Prayer 87

7. Sister Miriam Dies: Losing a Mentor 97

CLASHES

8. Betrayed by a School: Talk Back When Your Child Is Hurt 105

9. The Illusion of the All-Nurturing Mother 118

10. Taming the Tiger: Coming to Terms with Anger 127

11. "I Hate *The Giving Tree!*"..148

12. In Search of Mutuality: A New Pattern for Relating 158

☞ Contents

IMAGINING A DIFFERENT FUTURE

13. A Home That Cherishes 169

14. Fresh Images of God: Mother, Guide, Friend 178

15. Everyday Mystics: Spiritual Practices for Mothers and Kids 186

16. Embracing Mothers: What Women Want from Mother Church ..199

Epilogue: Ten Years into Motherhood 220

Acknowledgments 229

Works Cited, Resources Consulted, and Further Reading 231

To Dad, Bill Thomas, 1921–2002,
who taught me to love children, the earth,
and a good joke

"I think the task of our time—and really, it's a poet's task—is to find words again that will mediate between spirit and matter. But I do not have time or skill enough to write that poem, so I'm trying to find a diction that unsettles the issues just enough to let us see them new."

—MARY ROSE O'REILLY

Introduction

On Holy Thursday, I was relieved that we'd all made it on time for the 6 p.m. prayer service. Our small church always reenacted Christ's washing of the disciples' feet, a prelude to the Last Supper. For a while I'd been out of sync with faith community, and it was good to be back. I hoped the evening would be a time to reconnect with others in preparation for the festivity of the Easter holidays.

About twenty minutes into the service our three-year-old grew restless, so my husband Bill led him out of the nave. Along the way, Bill also offered to look after another restless child. This was Gabe's first time at Holy Thursday services, and I was disappointed that they had to leave. As the hardworking parents of a preschooler, it had been years since we'd both been able to fully participate in the services leading up to Easter. But soon I was caught up in the timeless rite of Jesus' final evening with his disciples. Lights were low and the sanctuary felt cozy and inviting. The ritual foot washing helped all of us to reconnect more closely. My soul was parched for the nourishment of my Christian faith; I savored the loving rituals of foot washing and communion.

Afterwards, my spirit was soaring as I caught up with Bill and Gabe in the parking lot.

Just then a woman from the church descended upon me. "I can't go home without telling you how angry I am about all your commotion."

I was caught off guard. "What commotion?"

"I could hear those kids upstairs running around and making noise. I was completely distracted! They ruined the service!"

"I'm so sorry, Donna. I didn't hear…"

1

"You have no business bringing a child to a service like this!" With a fierce look, she hurried off.

I fumed all the way home. Didn't Gabe have a right to be in church too? When he was baptized here, everyone had promised to help raise him in the faith. We had no "cry room," so Bill had taken him into an upstairs meeting room even though that meant they'd both miss out on the service—what more did she expect? And why was she yelling at *me,* not Bill?

That was the last straw, I decided. I was foolish to think we'd all be welcome at church.

That weekend, I wrote to Sister Miriam, my long-time mentor. I was fed up with organized religion, I told her. That night wasn't an isolated incident. Time and time again over the past three years I'd left church services feeling out of sync. I could never keep Gabe quiet enough, the sermons often seemed irrelevant, and I felt unfairly judged by uptight people. Church was once the place I'd felt most at home, I wrote, a part of the *family of God.* But in recent years I'd changed, and church had grown less and less welcoming. Since becoming a mother I was acutely in need of spiritual nourishment but too often I left church feeling more jangled than ever.

When Sister Miriam wrote back, she mailed a book: *She Who Is: The Mystery of God in Feminist Theological Discourse.* Her note described the author, Elizabeth A. Johnson, as "a brilliant theology professor at Fordham University in New York City." For many years I'd trusted Miriam's guidance. It was she who had coached me back to health after the end of an abusive marriage. I was a filing clerk when we first met in my twenties, and Miriam had urged me to go to college, then graduate school and eventually to earn my PhD. Miriam had once explained to me that the word *holy* came from the same root as healthy, hale, hearty, and whole. "Growing in holiness, is not about stuffing yourself in a girdle of meekness, it's about becoming the person God created you to be—a whole, hearty woman who can make a difference in the world." She liked to adapt St. Irenaeus's saying to me, her spiritual daughter: "The glory of

God is woman fully alive." Sister Miriam's faith in my future was a powerful healing force.

Perhaps that letter to Miriam was the beginning of this book. I needed to write to sort out my feelings. How could I feel at once so deeply spiritual and so estranged from church? Did others feel as I did?

Early on, my writing took the form of letters to Sister Miriam as I pointed out all the contradictions I was beginning to see. If Johnson was right, my alienation was not simply *my problem*—it was something much larger. *Surely there were many other mothers out there who felt just as lonely, fed up, and misunderstood.* As a professor, I had the resources to read and learn about others' perspectives. Eventually I found opportunities to interview other mothers and to meet with other scholars. For the next several years I began to read and write about motherhood and spirituality every chance I got. The contradictions began to come into clearer focus.

All my life, I'd believed in the "body and blood" of Christ. Once Gabe was born, I was more in touch with real-life bodies and blood, and I couldn't quite make the connections between religious creed and my messy life. I felt like an alien in the tradition that I had loved for so many years. Gradually I came to view myself as a "backslider"—someone who had "fallen away" from the church, from my Christian faith. But in fact I *wasn't* giving up my faith.

I began to see there were many women like me, for whom becoming a mother meant a deeper, more passionate faith. Tending children invites us to "live love" constantly and can open our hearts to a deeper love of God and others. Yet many of us find little help from organized religion.

Early one Sunday morning, I curled up with a cup of tea and began to read the book Miriam had sent: "Listening to the questions and struggles of the people of an era, their value systems, and deepest hopes, gives theology of the most diverse kinds an indispensable clue for shaping inquiry....What is distinctive [about feminist inquiry] is its specific identification with the lived experience of women, long derided or neglected in androcentric tradition" (Johnson 1). In other words, the struggles and questions of people in a given era, rather than being a temptation or a distraction from faith, can actually be the *entry point* into deeper faith. My human struggles shape the questions I ask, and asking questions, in turn, leads me to deeper understanding, a richer theology. The Christian tradition has been largely shaped by male priorities, but it doesn't have to remain that way, explains Johnson.

I thought about my disheveled home, my stretched-out body, my lovely son and husband sleeping upstairs. Johnson was inviting me to believe that *these* were as spiritual, as important to God, as anything that might occur *inside* church walls. I knew even then that her ideas would be echoing in me for a long time to come.

A Livable Faith

It took several years of living with Johnson's book before I felt ready to write my own story. Living with it has allowed ample time for reflection and comparing notes.

In time I realized that I could help make Johnson's concepts accessible to the ordinary mother who might not have time to tackle a theological tome. I could write for the tired mother who craves spiritual food but must squeeze reading time between packing lunches and late night runs to the convenience store for milk.

Johnson sets out to revise the *concepts* that shape women's religious experience. I go further by linking the concepts more fully with *stories and images,* that is, the lived experience of women. In the telling of my own story, several themes emerged that offer hope to readers. One is the belief that, if you are discontent with your lot, *you're not alone.* Vast numbers of women are struggling to reconcile the realities of motherhood with the script we've received from society and religion. We're finding ways that we can embrace motherhood *and* full personhood; we're discovering the freedom to bring our whole selves to God. Paying attention to our experiences as mothers is an integral part of the process of authentically encountering God.

But this perspective isn't just for mothers. By naming "She Who Is," we can also find new ways to pray and to teach our children and others to pray. With patience, we are developing new metaphors for thinking about church and helping it to evolve in ways that will serve our daughters as well as our sons. As we grow into greater spiritual wisdom, we will become more capable of contributing to a society and church that values women as well as men, children as well as adults. Just as women have moved into fuller participation in other areas of society, it is time for us to move into full participation in our churches too. It is important that we bring our whole selves along—including our mother-selves. Discovering Sophia will help us to find a livable, workable faith.

Discovering She Who Is: Sophia

Because I trusted Sister Miriam so much, that Sunday morning I was eager to understand Elizabeth Johnson's ideas. Reading along, I learned the title—*She Who Is*—is a translation of Yahweh, the "I AM WHO I AM." She calls it a "robust, appropriate name for God...the absolute, relational liveliness that energizes the world" (245). Johnson explains the longstanding wisdom tradition of the Old Testament: A guiding spirit was present before the beginning of the world and continues to permeate all of creation. Certain books of the Old Testament—like Proverbs, Job, and Ecclesiastes—speak boldly of Holy Wisdom, and her presence is evident throughout the Bible. The New Testament often mentions the Holy Spirit in feminine terms. The Gospel of John, parts of Acts, and the Epistles all refer to a Spirit intimately involved in human affairs, promising "the peace that passes understanding."

Although this "Spirit-model" for God has always been evident in the Bible, for a long time she was overshadowed by a "monarchical model" which portrays God as a king and judge (Borg, *The God We Never Knew* 72–73).[1] Today, motivated by new historical evidence and widespread human need, theologians like Johnson are gaining new understandings of the nature of God. In a later chapter I will expand upon God as a Mother-Creator, a Guide, and a Friend. On that particular Sunday morning, it was enough simply to catch a glimpse of the Holy Spirit as Sophia, the Wise Woman.

As I read on, Johnson's words spoke to my heart: "The biblical depiction of Wisdom is…the transcendent power ordering and delighting in the world. She pervades the world, both nature and human beings, interacting with them to lure them along the right path to life" (87). As the mother of a young child, seeking order and delight were both big parts of my life; I wanted to believe that Sophia was with me, here in my home, *luring* me along the right path.

But if I was on the "right path," why did my personal life seem so at odds with the rest of the church?

Harvard Law professor Mary Ann Glendon observes that even in Christian churches, where women have traditionally played essential roles, mothers' voices have not been heard when it comes to setting priorities or making policies. Few mothers of young children can attend many meetings, she observes. "Think for a moment about all the public meetings you have attended in recent years and ask yourself what proportion of those present were mothers of children under ten?…Being out of sight, their concerns are all too often out of mind," writes Glendon (113), and therefore the pressing challenges they face are not thoughtfully considered. Religious leaders, *even those who once had small children themselves,* are too often out of touch with current realities of mothers' lives.

These "current realities" are especially challenging today, for we live in a "half-changed world" (Orenstein) in which the expectations and opportunities for women have changed, but the structures and support systems have lagged far behind. On the surface, young women today have more choices than ever. But under the surface, there's been a measurable erosion of support for child rearing and family life, huge and central parts of most women's lives.

In the face of this half-changed world, we may observe, "Never before have our struggles, once our children are born, been so daunting. We no longer step into well-defined, circumscribed roles once we become mothers....Each and every one of us must reinvent the role for ourselves" (Kenison and Hirsch 11).

And yet no one can ever really "reinvent a role" alone—it always requires cooperation. It takes a frame of reference, a common language, what I describe in chapter 1 as an "interpretive framework."

I think of this framework as a kind of essential scaffolding. Like a painter who stands on a scaffold, a woman needs a secure footing as she works to make sense of new identities. The more complete her "scaffolding," the more likely that spiritual and other kinds of growth can continue.

By introducing me to Sophia—"She Who Is"—Sister Miriam was throwing me a lifeline, a way to reconcile my Christian faith with the challenges of my life as an overworked, disillusioned woman.

In the coming months and years, as I worked my way through Johnson's dense book, I began to believe that my joys and struggles as a mother deserved a place on the map of Christian theology. No matter how mundane they might seem to others, they were important. The challenges of breastfeeding, my changed body, my gritty kitchen, my cranky boss, my love for my pediatrician and my "baby-sitter," even my frustration with church and judgmental people like Donna—all these were aspects of "the lived experience of women, long neglected and derided" in a tradition shaped by male priests, pastors, and scholars. I began to see that, far from being irrelevant, these experiences could actually *feed* theology. Paying attention to them could deepen not just my own faith but also the faith of the whole Christian community.

Overview of the Chapters

Several years have passed since I first encountered *She Who Is*. That lovely sleeping baby is now an eleven-year-old with strong opinions of his own. The following book was written as it was lived, without a map. Still, as I assemble the pieces, a pattern emerges. The first set of chapters ("Beginnings") was written mostly out of my experiences as the mother of an infant and young child (up to age three). "The Crisis of First-Time

Motherhood: Matrescence," for example, explores very early motherhood as a life crisis that leads to major changes in identity and work. "This Is My Body" considers several ways that a woman's relationship to the human body changes (her own body, others' bodies), as well as providing a new perspective on nature. These early chapters show how I—and others as well—try to find God in the everyday of the human body, relationships, nature, and work.

A second set of chapters ("Clashes") examines the friction and difficult choices that result when society's expectations conflict with mothers' and children's actual needs. For example, "The Illusion of the All-Nurturing Mother" shows the impact on real women of the cultural ideal of the mother who is endlessly accommodating and nurturing. "Taming the Tiger" explores women's anger and other taboo emotions.

The third set of chapters ("Imagining a Different Future") presents a more future-oriented way of thinking about what mothers (and others) need. These chapters articulate spiritual practices and beliefs that give shape to a richer, more experiential spirituality. For example, "Everyday Mystics" explores spiritual practices for parents and children, and "Fresh Images of God" considers new metaphors for God. The final chapter ("Embracing Mothers") in this section looks specifically at Christian churches, and suggests many practical changes that would help them more generously embrace mothers and children.

Many of the chapters end with a section called "Through a Lens of Women Flourishing" (Johnson's phrase) that offers examples of "containers" (images, practices, or structures) that both mothers and children need in order to flourish.

Sister Miriam appears throughout this book as a guiding force. It was she who led me to new names for God: Divine Wisdom, Wise Woman, Sophia—or better yet, Sophie. That Sunday morning when I first read *She Who Is* and thought about my disheveled home, my stretched out body, my lovely sleeping son, it was hard to imagine that Jesus would share my struggles.

But Sophia—*she would!*

Notes

1. The terms are taken from theologian Marcus Borg, who traces the two models (monarchical and Spirit) in the Old and New Testaments in his books, *Meeting Jesus Again for the First Time* (1995), *The God We Never Knew* (1998), and others.

BEGINNINGS

ॐ

1

Stranded
in the Mother Zone

Sister Miriam answered as soon as I rang the bell. "My dear girl, put down your things and come into the kitchen. I've been waiting for you! How was the drive out? I want to hear all your exciting news!"

I set down my suitcase to embrace her. "All the trees are starting to turn colors!" I said. At eighty-six, Sister Miriam was more beautiful than ever. She wore the same black veil and ankle-length habit that she'd worn since our first meeting—she was one of the few nuns in her community who still wore the traditional black habit. After we embraced, we smiled into each other's eyes. Then I was happy to follow Miriam to the kitchen.

"I can't race around anymore," I said, catching my breath. "I brought our wedding album to show you, but what I'm most excited about is this baby!" I settled myself into a chair. "Look at me. My due date is still ten weeks away. How much bigger can I get?"

"Now, you relax while I fix your plate." She bustled over to the stove.

"No wine this time!" I said, patting my belly. Miriam and I had a long-standing tradition—she served me warm wine at night to help me sleep and "cast aside the cares of the day."

As she assembled my meal, I brought Sister Miriam up-to-date on all that had happened over the six months: Our wedding, my pregnancy, and the classes I was teaching at the university. "If this baby's a girl, we're naming her Miriam after *you!* I'm so excited that I can't sleep at night—I just turned forty but I feel as giddy as a teenager!"

When my plate was ready, Miriam and I moved to the adjoining dining room. She sat across the table from me as I ate. "I've been praying for you since you wrote about the happy news. We must keep putting this child in God's care. It's been the desire of your heart for so long!" More than anyone, Miriam understood how much this baby meant to me.

"I've been worried because the baby hasn't moved much. My doctor says I should be feeling kicks by now but there have only been flutters. She's giving me lots of sonograms and says we need to keep an eye on things."

"Your doctor's a woman? How wonderful! Does she think you should be teaching? You wrote that you have a full slate of courses."

"I feel fit as a fiddle. I'm just tired. And nervous! I've got a few months off after the birth before I have to go back." I played with my salad. "There's just so much that's new. Will this be a boy or a girl? Will it be normal and healthy? Will I be able to handle the pain of birth? And what about juggling a baby and a job? I come up for tenure next year, you know."

"Not to mention a new husband and stepchildren!" Miriam interjected. "God is tugging you onto a new path, isn't he?"

The picture window behind Miriam revealed a tree and small lake, and beyond those a field that was turning gold and russet in the setting sun. The colors of late September framed Miriam's stalwart body as she leaned forward in her chair. Her black veil and white collar made her look old-fashioned, yet Miriam was the most forward-thinking person I knew, always so kind and *curious*.

After dinner, we visited in my guest suite. Miriam knew little about the medical end of pregnancy, but she had ideas about motherhood. "You must play classical music for the baby now. She'll pick up the vibrations in the womb, and when she's born, she'll remember. You'll be planting the seed for a love of music that could last a lifetime!"

She talked about prayer too: "You need to realize that the events of your day or week are not stumbling blocks in your search for a full life in God, but rather the way *to* it. When you go to the hospital and when you hold that baby, that's where you'll meet God. If you don't have time to sit and meditate, you can still find God all around you." Miriam's shrewd blue eyes always seemed to look right into my soul.

"You needn't be faint-hearted," she added. "You can claim your identity as a daughter of God!"

Before she retired to bed, Miriam brought out a book she'd set aside for me. *"The Continuum Concept* is by an anthropologist who studied South American Indians. She emphasizes how important it is to constantly hold and touch a newborn baby for the first several months."

I promised that I'd read it if she'd read my pregnancy journal. At nine o'clock we traded books and said good night.

It was still early, so I decided to take a walk under the full moon. The paved drive ran along the lake and across the grassy expanse where the rambling boarding school once stood, then curved around the massive stone chapel, visible in the moonlight. I loved the convent grounds at night—almost as much as I loved Miriam.

The ancient Celts believed that certain spots on the earth are "thin places" where the veil between mortals and the spirit world is more permeable than elsewhere. I discovered the motherhouse of the Brown County Ursulines fifteen years ago, when I was just twenty-four, lying face down in the backwash of a miserable divorce. Since then, the rambling boarding school had been torn down, the college had expanded, and Miriam herself had moved from her convent home of over sixty years to "Brescia," a new dwelling built nearby for the older nuns. Through these changes, this place continued to pull me back.

Sister Miriam herself had changed, too. She grew up less than a mile from here, entered the Ursuline convent at eighteen, and, except for summers away for education, had been here ever since. She was first a teacher in the boarding school, later the headmistress, and still later the dean of Chatfield, the college she helped start right here on the grounds. By the time we met, she was seventy-one and running an emergency food bank here in this rural county. Now at eighty-six she still coordinated the food bank, but more gently.

*   *   *

When I returned to Brescia, a Thermos of cocoa and a book of Renaissance madonnas were waiting outside my room.

The next afternoon Miriam and I made our way to the chapel to formally bless my child-to-be. Sitting beside me, Miriam held my hand and placed her other hand on the big mound of my belly. "Dear Creator-God, we thank you for this child who will soon enter our world. This is the child we've awaited so long—the child you have chosen for Trudy before all time. Bring her lovingly and safely into our midst, and let her know even now the vast love that awaits....Amen."

Getting into my car later, I promised Miriam that I'd write to her all about the birth, the baby, and everything that would come after. As I drove off, she waved, her black habit silhouetted against green lawn. An unlikely mentor for a first-time mother!

A week after my retreat, a routine sonogram revealed a serious complication—placenta previa—a condition in which the placenta was blocking my cervix. I needed to stop work immediately in order to order to preserve the pregnancy. I spent the next two months confined to my bed and recliner, till giving birth to my long-awaited baby. He surprised us all by turning out to be a boy. Born during Advent, we named him Gabriel (God-bearer) after the angel who visited Mary. Once he was born, the real changes began.

As promised, in the next few years I wrote many notes to Miriam. Even though this child was long awaited, I had *no idea* what I was getting into. For Miriam who'd never had a baby, I tried to explain that even my spiritual life went through a colossal change, a rebuilding of consciousness....

But it would be years before I found the right words.

The Mother Zone

A Canadian writer named Marni Jackson has coined the phrase, "the mother zone," to describe the messy, joyful, isolated world that mothers of young children often inhabit. She compares it to being a castaway on a desert island: "[A mother] is lost in the mother zone, and the husband is waving to her, with a helpful smile, from the opposite shore" (76). She speculates that early motherhood is so overwhelming and intense that it cannot be communicated, not even to a mother's closest companions.

In the first few months I would often wake in the middle of the night and nurse my baby in bed with just the nightlight glowing. Once Bill awoke to find me nursing with tears streaming down my face. I tried to explain, "I just can't tell you how overjoyed I am to have this baby. I thought it would never happen. I'm so grateful...." He shook his head, rolled over, and went back to sleep, thinking I'd lost my mind to hormones. I couldn't explain that the joy was real and powerful and enduring—he couldn't *possibly* understand!

Later came other days when Bill returned from work at 8 p.m. and I met him at the door, after being home alone all day with a recalcitrant toddler. *"Why are you so late?"* I'd whine, barely containing my frenzy. Bill would respond with that same unknowing look.

It was disconcerting to feel like a castaway from my husband and it was even worse to feel cut off from my friends. My closest friends were all busy professional women, and my colleagues at work were academic feminists who had little interest in motherhood. The urgent topics among women on campus were violence against women, sexual harassment, and lesbian rights—no one seemed the least bit interested in breastfeeding or child development. My new life was no longer on their map.

I knew a few mothers of young children, but even they seemed to be on different islands. If they felt as unstrung and impassioned as I did, they weren't admitting it. Once when I asked a neighbor if her having kids made her feel like she'd become an alien in her own life, she hurriedly changed the subject. Another time I asked Anne, an acquaintance at work, what life was like back when her three sons were preschoolers. She waved away my questions. "Oh *then*. I don't want to go *back there*. It's all a blur of exhaustion!"

Mothers sometimes joke about the fact that women forget the pain of childbirth or else they'd never go through it twice. But it seemed to me that this amnesia included the first *several years* of motherhood. Jackson writes that most mothers eventually betray their own memories: "Like a passionate affair that ends and gets redefined as a fluke, a mother learns to forget the erotic bond she once had with her baby, a perfect intimacy that may never be recaptured. All the raw extremities of emotion are smoothed over and left behind, on the island of motherhood….[The] true drama between mother and child is slowly replaced by the idealization of motherhood" (4). This amnesia causes a woman to remain silent about both the joys and the traumas of early motherhood, so that she betrays not just herself but other mothers too. Even though Anne had once inhabited the island of motherhood, now she too was "waving…from the opposite shore," not wanting to remember.

During this time I subscribed to *Working Mother* magazine. When it arrived in my mailbox each month, I often felt like an anthropologist learning about a distant, exotic tribe. Who were these stylish women who speedily advanced in their careers while raising well-adjusted, beautiful children? Superwomen "coparenting" with equally ambitious, stylish men—*who were they?*

Often such articles left me with a sick, crazy feeling. Had those superwomen never been stranded on the island of passionate, messy motherhood? Were they lying? Or had they forgotten?

Dilation of the Mind

Laura Chester uses a biological metaphor to explore the openness and changes that come with matrescence. As a pregnant woman approaches her due date, changes in her cervix are carefully monitored. When birth is imminent, the cervix softens, "effaces," and begins to slowly open up ("dilate"). This opening begins before active labor and is frequently measured—three centimeters, five centimeters—until the necessary ten centimeters, signaling that it's time to *push*. Only when the cervix is fully dilated can the womb, expanding and contracting with labor pangs, deliver the baby into the outer world.

Chester compares the dilation of the cervix to the dilation of the eye and of the mind that accompany childbirth. "When we are stunned by something completely beautiful, *the mind dilates* in order to more fully perceive. The pupils of the eye have this knowledge; they dilate when beholding the beloved. But to love is to be vulnerable to loss" (Chester 1, emphasis mine).

This "dilation of the mind" extends to a dilation of the heart and soul, and it is not limited to the process of labor. Chester believes that the change in perception, rooted in physical changes in the body, causes a change in spiritual awareness: "Giving birth is the most remarkable feat a body can achieve. We are opened up as at no other time. And when life comes through, the knowledge of *that other side* is present, sensed. When we witness that newborn for the first time, we know we are connected to *Something Larger*" (Chester 4, emphasis mine). Though Chester does not use religious language, I believe she means a nonmaterial layer of reality—the Sacred—an encompassing Spirit that is the Source of Life.

During pregnancy I was intrigued to learn that the body produces a hormone called relaxin that aids in this opening process. Its chief purpose, a nurse explained, is to loosen the bones of the pelvis and hips so that the fetus can be released more readily. Relaxin also leads to the loosening of other joints, which explains the clumsiness that many pregnant women experience.

Aided by relaxin, the body as a whole instinctively begins to relax, loosen, and open months before labor begins. This process doesn't end with birth; pregnancy is just the beginning of an ongoing process of emotional and even spiritual opening. Theologian Marcus Borg uses the metaphor of an egg hatching to talk about the process of opening the heart: "[T]he heart is like an egg with a shell around it. If what is within is to live, the egg must hatch, the shell must break, the heart must open." He goes on to say that the spiritual journey is about the opening of the self to the reality of the Spirit so that "the self at its deepest level is reoriented and transformed" (*The God We Never Knew* 114–15). In Borg's view, the "hatching of the heart" leads to a deepening of compassion and a new sense of connection to the rest of humanity. The opening of the heart liberates the individual from self-interest into a wider community of being that is grounded in spiritual reality. Borg is writing about spiritual growth in general, not specifically about women's birth experiences. However, I believe that the biological act of giving birth—and more generally the ongoing changes of motherhood—can greatly enhance this opening of the heart.

I'm not suggesting that giving birth or mothering are *necessarily* linked to changes in perception or to spiritual birth. While it does seem that a woman is in some ways programmed to relax, open up, and to love her baby (and even to gain a new appreciation for other babies), certain conditions are necessary for this process to continue beyond birth. She must, for example, have some choice in the matter; her basic biological needs (for nutrition, rest, security) must be met; and finally, she must have some way of making sense of her experiences, that is, some point of reference. In a later chapter, I develop the idea of an "interpretive framework" (or frame of reference) that allows women to freely enter into this spiritual opening-up.

Such openness is needed because a first-time mother is faced with so much to learn. In addition to the practical details of infant care, she needs to learn to interact on a daily basis with an infant—a being without language, literally speechless. This entirely dependent creature can change the mother's own perceptions and sense of self. If the mother is open, a child provides access to new experiences, a sense of wonder, a fresh perspective, and a radical questioning of her beliefs and accepted ways of doing things. Sometimes these new experiences are tedious, frustrating, and frightening. Other times they can be joyful and exciting.

This interaction with a child is a kind of interplay, a reciprocal interaction between the mother in all her individuality and her unique child. The nature of this interplay will differ from mother to mother and child to child. The Wintu Indians have no equivalent to our notion of "having a child"; a Wintu child refers to her mother as "she-whom-I-made-into-a-mother" (Nemiroff 75). Their emphasis on the child's contribution to the mother's growth hints at this reciprocal interaction. Even the process of birth is a *cooperative* effort between mother and child. Modern medicine has not yet unraveled the mysterious alchemy that causes labor to begin; many believe that the baby initiates labor and the mother's body responds.

Even in those early days I sometimes felt glimpses of insight—the sense that I wasn't as alone as I thought on the "island of motherhood."

One winter afternoon during Gabe's infancy I was carrying him through the Cincinnati Art Museum. I'd grown tired of cabin fever and was lazily strolling through the museum with my son in a baby sling across my chest, when we came upon a medieval painting of the Virgin Mary. A small triptych showed Mary nursing the infant Christ against her fully exposed breast, their eyes locked in a tender gaze.

A devotion to Mary had not been part of my Methodist upbringing. Visiting art museums over the years, I'd admired medieval and Renaissance madonnas but none had grabbed my attention the way this one did. Perhaps it was the unusually bare breast or my own dreamy prolactin-induced state of mind, but the painting of Mary and Jesus captivated me. I'd been spending several hours a day nursing Gabe, and it suddenly dawned on me that Mary had nursed Jesus for probably at least as many hours. The image of mother and nursing babe held my attention, and for a moment I felt a riveting sense of connection with Mary and with Jesus.

Standing before the triptych of Mary and Jesus, I felt an internal shift—a momentary sense of not just being *in relationship* with God but actually *identifying with* God. Mary-and-Jesus so clearly mirrored my own lived experience that for a moment I seemed to be sharing in God's work of creation, part of a grand and holy process of nurturing new life. Like the mother from pre-Christian times that Anita Diamant writes about, I felt "The baby at my breast was the center of the universe. I was the entire source of his happiness, and for a few weeks, the goddess and I were one and the same" (*The Red Tent* 228).

Reimagining Motherhood: Searching for Stories

Those first few years found me turning to books with a hunger I hadn't felt since puberty. As a teen in the days before cell phones, I lived in the country, often felt lonely, and turned to books for comfort and stimulation, greedily reading novels and poems. Again as a new mother I felt out of step with my peers, so again I turned to books.

For example, I reread *The Awakening* by Kate Chopin. Published in 1899, it's one of the few accounts of mothering to find its way into the American literary canon. Chopin creates the story of a married woman named Edna who is a mother and a member of the Southern Creole aristocracy. In her social circles, all women are expected to be mild, selfless "mother women" whose lives revolve around their children. As Edna sees it, "the mother women" never make waves or challenge authority or have any life beyond their prescribed roles as wives and mothers. The novel recounts Edna's personal awakening, an awakening of her deepest Self, which leads to artistic expression as a painter and to a heightened sexuality. She can't reconcile her awakening Self with being a mother to her two young children and eventually decides she must choose between being true to her Self and being a mother. The novel ends with Edna's suicide, as she swims to her death far out in the ocean.

My own awakening was closely tied to my son waking up to the world around him, even as I began to wake up to a fuller identity. It was so exciting to see Gabe grow, fed from my own body, to share his excitement in discovering the world, and to let myself love him with my whole heart. Author Anne Roiphe writes that becoming a mother was "the end of self as I had always known it...I was in love with my child, not sanely, nor calmly, not rationally but wholly and completely, the way people get on an airplane and give control to the pilot, to the currents of wind, and let themselves be lifted up, taken away" (4–5).

Being "taken away" often led to new ways of perceiving the world. Others have coined the terms *milk brain* and *cottonhead* to describe the altered state of consciousness that often characterizes the first months of matrescence. *Cottonhead* is "feeling unable to use the left brain or intellect for tasks such as balancing the checkbook or getting organized....We now have a chance to think with our hearts...an initiation into a whole new way of experiencing the world, a far more intuitive way...[which may] center women and help them withdraw from the world ruled by steely organized intellect" (Northrup 461). Cottonhead accompanies the approach of menopause as well as the early months of motherhood. At both times, it forces us "into our right brains and out of our former 'logo-centric' way of being" (461).

Cottonhead was part of the process of bonding with my baby. Various pregnancy guide books emphasize the importance mother-infant bonding in the hours just after birth. The idea is that mother and baby bond through loving touch, eye contact, voice, and nursing. But in fact, bonding is an ongoing interactive process that extends throughout the early years. Ideally, a mother learns to read her baby's cues over many months and, through intimate, reliable contact with her mother, the baby develops a fundamental trust in the goodness of the universe. This bonding process requires cottonhead, a powerful kind of knowing and intelligence that has little to do with reason or intellect. Bonding depends upon an opening of the heart, or thinking with the heart.

Kything

Such mother-child bonding can be deeply spiritual. During the many hours I spent with my infant son I often felt as if I were encountering the Holy Spirit in a new way—a nonmaterial level of reality in him and all around us. Gabe was so fresh from God, still "trailing clouds of glory....Heaven lies about us in our infancy" (writes Wordsworth, in "Intimations of Immortality"). I was very aware that my son was a gift from God, indeed that all children, *all human beings* were precious gifts from God. Intimacy with him also helped me see the rest of the world with fresh eyes. First bath, first taste of ice cream, first butterfly, first time I blew a soap bubble for him—all these became firsts for me too.

Much later I came to appreciate the fact that cottonhead bonding brought life skills that would stay with me for the rest of my days. Loving interaction with an infant through eyes, touch, and tone of voice can be a training ground for later relationships.

Author Madeline L'Engle coined the term *kything* to describe the spirit-to-spirit communication that she shared with her beloved husband Hugh as he lay dying of cancer (recounted in *Two-Part Invention: The Story of a Marriage*). Kything is "a loving interactive process...[that] involves three steps: centering on the mystery and goodness of oneself; focusing on the other to whom I am present; and establishing a connection or union signifying our spirit-to-spirit bonding with one another. For the Christian to kythe lovingly is to participate in the Divine Life" (Savary 49). L'Engle explains that kything is far more than telepathy because love is an essential part of the exchange telepathy; a deep, unspoken love makes understanding possible.

L'Engle believes that kything can occur even when a person is not physically present; after her husband died, at times she still felt that she was kything with Hugh despite differences in time and space.

As Gabe was growing up, several of our loved ones died, and I was blessed with the opportunity to be with them during their final weeks. Gabe had taught me so many lessons in tenderness as an infant, that I was well equipped to be tender with dying relatives. Bonding with him gave me a bodily *felt experience* of what it was to commune with a person on levels both physical and spiritual. When Gabe much later learned to read, he taught me the word "thought-speak" (borrowed from science fiction writer K. A. Applegate) to describe the our unspoken communication.

The intimacy of kything with an infant, in a roundabout way, lessened my fear of death. As a Christian, I'd always believed that death would lead to union with God in the afterlife. Yet it was hard to actually *imagine* that union. How could I remain myself and still be part of God? Kything gave me a felt experience of being a part of a transcendent, non-material spirit world even while mortal. This enabled me to find new resources in myself for coping with serious illness and grief, and for helping others cope.

Even years later, Gabe still carries strong memories of the many hours he spent on my lap or at my breast: "When I get to heaven, being with God will be like snuggling on Mom's bobo when I was a baby," he said at age seven. For me, too, the intimacy between mother and child remains a powerful image for union with God. An old spiritual implores, "Rocka my soul in the bosom of Abraham." When it came time for Sister Miriam and later other loved ones to die, I was able to accept their deaths because I believed bodily, in my cells, that they would soon be resting in God's bosom.

2

The Crisis of
First-Time Motherhood
Matrescence

"Have you seen Sister Miriam lately?" When I ran into Susan in a local shopping center, we both homed in on our shared love for Miriam. "I wish I could get out there more often, but it's hard with a toddler," I continued.

"I miss her terribly," answered Susan, pushing a strand of auburn hair back from her face. "She's been looking so frail lately. Every time I see her, I think it might be the last. Since my own mom developed Alzheimer's, Miriam's become even more important to me."

"She's definitely a second mother to me," I replied.

"She said you had any easy birth and that you're enthusiastic about breastfeeding." Susan was a childbirth educator who'd been teaching first-time parents for twenty years. It seemed strange to imagine Sister Miriam, who had never suckled a child, telling Susan about my breastfeeding. But of course she would. After all, it was Miriam who had given me Susan's copy of *The Continuum Concept,* the book that had led me down the path to breastfeeding in the first place.

"I love it! It's God's gift to women. I kept nursing when I returned to teaching full time."

Susan went on to ask me about my teaching and classes, and I told her a little about the project I'd started—collecting women's birth stories. She brought me up to date about her three grown children and the work she'd been doing lately with Tri-State Breastfeeding Advocates. Then we went our separate ways.

After that chance encounter, books and articles began to appear in my mailbox from time to time. Susan's handwriting became familiar to me: "Thought you'd like this collection of birth stories" or "Here's a great book about attachment parenting." Susan lived in the same city neighborhood as me, yet what we knew about each other came mostly through visits with Sister Miriam, who lived fifty miles away. We traveled in different circles and seldom ran into each other. She was a registered nurse with grown children. Our differences made her more intriguing, though. I liked her red hair, strong opinions, and earthy sense of humor, to say nothing of the interesting books she sent my way.

Matrescence: A Major Identity Crisis

It was in one of Susan's books that I first discovered the wonderful term *matrescence.* In her 1976 book, *The Tender Gift,* Dana Raphael coined the term to describe what she sees as the most critical rite of passage in most women's lives. She believes that becoming a mother should be honored as a unique and important "life crisis." She writes, "Childbirth brings about a series of very dramatic changes in the new mother's physical being, in her emotional life, in her status within the group, even in her own female identity" (Raphael 1976, 19).

Raphael's ideas made complete sense to me: Becoming a mother for the first time *is* a critical rite of passage, yet our society pays little attention to this inward transformation.[1] Hoopla is made over the outward events. Friends and relatives may shower a soon-to-be mother with tiny baby clothes and nursery supplies that are dainty and sweet. And most Christian churches offer the sacrament of baptism to welcome the newborn baby into the faith.

But what about the newborn (or reborn) mother? Not nearly enough attention is paid to *her.*

I read on. While Raphael limits matrescence to the months just following birth, I think it should extend at least a few years beyond to include not just pregnancy and birth but also infant care and the reentry of the mother into her community and workplace. Matrescence is a rite of passage undergone by all mothers of infants—including adoptive mothers and stepmothers. Although the first matrescence is especially formative, variations of it repeat with each new child.

In every case the obvious events like birth and a woman's physical changes are just one part of the larger transformation. Far more significant are the changes in the newborn mother's emotional life, status, and own female identity.

As I thought over Raphael's definition, I formulated a list of my own. First come the personal changes: intense emotions that roller coaster between bliss and rage; a dramatic change in your body image; almost total loss of autonomy as you care for a completely dependent creature; the death of your sex life (hopefully temporary); dependency on others. Other changes ripple outward: changes in your relationship with your partner; the need to rework your relationship with your extended family, especially your own mother and mother-in-law, if you're married; loss of earning power and career opportunities. In time, more far-reaching changes become clear: new involvement with the health-care industry, with child-care providers, and eventually with schools and a host of other institutions.

A friend of mine speaks of becoming a mother as a colossal "shift of life-center." The impact of this shift takes years to fully register.

A recent writer believes that new mothers only gradually adopt a "motherhood mindset": "The new identity requires that…you undergo much emotional labor in bringing forth new aspects of yourself, and finally that you work hard to integrate the changes into the rest of your life. All this happens while you are nurturing a baby who demolishes your daily routines, keeps you up at night, and requires all your attention" (Stern 20).

The quality of a woman's matrescence varies with the cultural practices that surround it. In many parts of the world a period of a few years after birth is assumed to involve lactation and often is accompanied by a special diet, taboos against intercourse, and the sharing of breastfeeding among females of the tribe.[2] In more traditional (i.e., nonindustrialized) cultures, young girls are prepared for mothering with hands-on skills, and practical support is provided postpartum. In addition, in most nonindustrialized cultures, a new mother shares child care with other adults and older children.

In the United States, in contrast, many women approach motherhood with limited skills and support, so the adjustment is more difficult (Raphael 132). Most often, a new mother is assumed to be the constant and sole caregiver for the child, which can create problems. A smooth adjustment will likely lead to a strong mother and a well-tended baby. A rocky adjustment may lead to a depressed and lonely mother and a neglected child—it may even lead to child abuse and other social ills. A positive matrescence is critical not just to the mother's well being but also to her child's and to society's.

In the United States, at the very time when a new mother has the greatest need for support and for her freedom to grow, she may feel as if society boxes her in. If she has a partner, his role may suddenly diverge from hers as he focuses on breadwinning and she grows preoccupied with child rearing. If she works outside the home as well, a new mother's private life and work life often collide. Entrenched social expectations are set in motion, clamping down with the force of a powerful vise: She's expected to become at once self-sacrificing and self-reliant, always patient, cheerful, and compliant. She hears more forcefully than ever the messages of a male-centered tradition in which women play only secondary roles: "Be quiet. Try harder. Don't make a fuss!"

Cognitive Dissonance: The Cultural Scripts Don't Work

In time I began to figure out why my matrescence was so bumpy— it was so out of sync with my expectations. Like every pregnant woman in North America, I'd been steeped in a popular culture that portrays motherhood as instinctive and ever joyful. Birth and parenting manuals, advertisements, and movies all featured competent mothers for whom infant care came naturally, joyful women who were treated well by others, self-assured mothers who found child care readily.

Such images are often fantasies, pandering to the unmet needs of women who *yearn* for ease, respect, and support. Fantasies clash with reality to create a *cognitive dissonance,* an ongoing contradiction between public images of motherhood and women's actual experience. The way it's *supposed to be* simply doesn't mesh with *the way it is,* for most new mothers.

My own experience was complicated. I sometimes felt incompetent, was often treated rudely by others in ways that had never happened before, and was shocked at the difficulty of finding trustworthy child care. For example, once when Gabe was a toddler, my husband and I needed to visit my father-in-law, who was in the hospital. We decided to trade off; Bill would visit his father while I stayed with our son in the lobby and vice versa. As I waited, Gabe toddled around, babbling with delight. The weather outside was scorching and we were both glad to be in a cool place.

Then the woman at the information desk called me over. "You'll need to make him quiet down or else wait outside."

"But it's 101 degrees outside and the humidity is 95 percent. He's not yelling or crying—just babbling. He's just a baby!"

"But he's *bothering* people!" she scowled.

Early on, such rudeness was shocking but I soon came to accept it— and almost expect it.

What I never came to accept was the scarcity of good child care and the lack of respect given child-care providers. Like most mothers I know, I can tell many chilling stories about the difficulty of finding (and keeping) good child care, whether at a commercial day care center or at home. An example: When Gabe was four, I decided to hire a college student to care for him in our home. Like many universities, mine provides a large bulletin board where prospective employers post "help wanted" ads. I carefully composed my ad before bringing it to the desk of the person in Career Placement in charge of approving the ads.

"You can't post that ad here," she explained. "It's our policy to post only ads for jobs that can contribute to students' future careers. Baby-sitting isn't a real job. Ads like that just clutter up the board!"

"You mean to tell me that telemarketing and pizza delivery are real jobs but child care isn't? You don't think child care will be part of their futures?" I pressed.

"You just can't post it! *It's against our policy.*"

The rudeness, the problems with child care, and the unexpected thrills all contributed to a grating cognitive dissonance. The public images of motherhood, formed mostly by the advertising and entertainment industries, simply do not mesh with most women's actual experience.

Writing about Parenting

I began to see this cognitive dissonance in a larger context when I taught a course called "Writing about Parenting" to a group of young university students. Each student read and wrote several different pieces about family life and parenting. There were a few parents in the class but the others were mostly childless females ranging from age eighteen to twenty-two. Their papers and discussions made obvious the huge gap in perception between the parents and the nonparents.

The younger students were sophisticated—were well read, well traveled, thoughtful, and intelligent. Most hoped to become mothers someday. Yet I soon discovered that virtually all were completely in the dark about the practical realities of child rearing. They had ambitious career plans that they expected to fulfill even while raising young children. Several were adamant that they would not see themselves as successful unless they were earning at least $70,000 a year, a sum beyond the reach of most mothers of young children.

Then there was my research assistant, Jenn, a women's studies major. She was tall, hip, and passionate in her commitment to improving the lives of women and children. As she sat in my office one day, I imagined Jenn to be the woman of the future as she confidently told me of her plans to have eight children. "I really love kids and want a whole houseful of them—at least eight!"

She loved to tell people that because it sounded so outrageous at a time when her peers aspired to two or three children at most. Jenn wanted the liveliness and sense of belonging of a big family.

When I asked her what kind of support system she'd need to raise eight children, Jenn insisted she and her husband would do it on their own. She planned to move as far away from family as possible and marry a man with a good income. "I've always been an independent kind of person—why would that change just because I have eight kids?"

Again, I was struck by the dissonance between expectations and probable experience. False expectations set young women up for failure and self-doubt.

Disorientation: Where's the Map?

In light of widespread ignorance, it's not surprising that when women *do* talk candidly about early motherhood, many speak of a sense of disorientation. Like St. Paul, thrown from his horse (see Acts 9), many women are thrown completely off balance. Some are able to embrace the changes by viewing them in spiritual terms. For example, Bonnie, who once saw herself as irreligious, speaks of her first childbirth, more than twenty years ago: "My life changed the moment my daughter slid from my body and sucked my breast. My body functioned in such a miraculous way. The birth itself was a renewal of my spirituality….The mother-child relationship was the awakening of my spiritual life as an adult."

Louise Erdrich, in a diary published as *The Blue Jay's Dance*, also writes of giving birth as an important spiritual passage: [Childbirth] is intensely spiritual and physical all at once….We're taught to suppress its importance over time, to devalue and belittle an experience in which we are bound up in the circular drama of human fate, in a state of heightened awareness and receptivity, at a crux where we intuit connections and, for a moment, unlock time's hold like a brace, even step from our bodies (44). Other women speak in terms of unlocking, splitting open, breaking, and flowing.

As I encountered these various descriptions, I kept thinking of Jesus' parable of the seed falling into the earth and dying—of cracking open in order to bring forth new life. In the act of birth (and throughout matrescence, and for many years following), a woman is issuing forth new life in the form of a child but also in the form of her own new identity as a "newborn mother." She must be "cracked."

Grief and Darkness

While it's acceptable to talk about the intense love of new motherhood, mothers are often reluctant to mention the "darker" emotions that are often just as powerful. They may complain, even joke, about outward difficulties like hours of labor, sore episiotomy stitches, and sleepless nights, but few will speak candidly of the confusion, rage, and grief that may come with the territory of new motherhood and last far longer.

No religious initiation is any more intense than the deprivations new mothers face: interrupted sleep; seeing your once orderly home strewn with receiving blankets and dirty dishes; the vigilance of trying to understand a baby's unfamiliar cries; often not being able to eat, dress, shower, or even use the bathroom at will; suddenly having to learn all the practical skills of breastfeeding, dressing, bathing, and attending to the medical needs of a helpless human being.

Even amidst the joys, it is a painful time of surrendering to a new way of life, of being stripped of the familiar. This stripping occurs with even women who are middle-class—who have decent housing, food, and medical care. It is more intense for women who lack those necessities and yet must care for a newborn baby without help—or without a partner or grandmother nearby. My friend Laurie Phenix is a registered nurse who makes postpartum home visits to new mothers. She visits some low-income mothers who are home with several older children, a jaundiced newborn, and no food in the refrigerator.

When my son was an infant, I spent a few hours with a friend one evening. We sat in her stylish, immaculate living room, and she shared pictures of her recent European vacation. Aware of my own messy house, sleepless baby, and neglected husband, I yearned for my earlier carefree life. I had deeply desired my baby, but even so, a wave of grief swept through me: "My God, what have I given up? Will I *ever* have my old life back?" I'd been transported to a new and alien country and was stricken with homesickness for the old one.

All this made me very aware of my own neediness. I comforted myself by imagining that I was dough being worked by a Divine Baker, one day (I hoped against hope) to rise to the fragrance of bread.

Andrea Yates and the Mother Trap

Of course, I wasn't alone in having mixed feelings around motherhood. Several years later (in July 2001), the national news covered the tragic story of Andrea Yates, a born-again Christian who killed her five young children while in the throes of a deep postpartum depression. *Newsweek* ran a major feature article about the killings; the author was nonjudgmental of Yates, even sympathetic. Later, *Newsweek* published a dozen excerpts from the *over six hundred heated letters* they received. The letters reflected our society's ambivalence toward motherhood. One complained that *Newsweek,* by portraying Yates sympathetically, "perpetuates the notion of motherhood as a less-than-noble vocation." Another asked, "Have we romanticized motherhood so much that we can't acknowledge the harsh reality of what women actually experience?" Some letter writers felt mothers should be kept on a pedestal while others thanked the journalist for portraying "harsh reality."

This widespread ambivalence puts mothers today in a bind. Most of us deeply love our children and want to believe that motherhood is a noble vocation. Yet often others use motherly ideals to manipulate us and keep us in our place. If we admit to "harsh reality" or challenge society's definitions *in any way,* we are told we are betraying Holy Motherhood itself. Some suggest that if we can't take the pain and pressure, we shouldn't have had children in the first place.

The Andrea Yates case is extreme but it illustrates the pressures all mothers feel. Yates was a devoted Christian who was trying to be what her religion sees as a perfect mother—a selfless, ever-competent nurturer. She even home-schooled! When she fell short, Yates grew depressed and desperate, rejecting her motherly role in the most extreme way. During the court trial, she said that she killed her children to protect them from herself—that she was evil incarnate. Clearly Yates's thinking is distorted by a psychotic depression.

Still, it grows out of a contradiction at the heart of our society: Mothers must be *perfect* and selfless—or else their children are at risk.

Of course, the vast majority of mothers don't resort to such tragic measures, but desperation surfaces in other ways—for example, through the epidemics of anxiety, depression, guilt, and overeating (and other eating disorders) that afflict American women. Society's ambivalence may also contribute to high abortion rates and child abuse/neglect.

One day as I sat in my classroom watching my students write their final exam essays in their "blue books," I found myself wondering about their futures. Raising children has never been easy, but mothers today encounter an especially problematic set of circumstances. Young women face a range of possibilities their grandmothers never imagined: Will I be a "working mother" or a "stay-at-home mother"? A stepmother or a biological mother or an adoptive mother? A single mother or a partnered mother? Or some combination? Can I postpone childbearing until I'm forty? *Until fifty?* How much will I mother other people's children? Once I become a mother, how will my life be different for the next ten, twenty, fifty years? Can I count on a partner to be with me for the long haul? *Will anything in my life follow a predictable map?*

A number of trends have complicated motherhood over recent decades. Some of these seem to offer women more choices: new career options, new reproductive technologies, the "morning after pill," wider availability of abortion, increasing life expectancies, varied adoption opportunities, the delaying of childbearing. Other trends have reshaped family structures: the movement of women into the paid workforce, the shifting of gender roles, the high rate of divorce and remarriage, the epidemic of sexual violence, growing rates of birth outside marriage.

As my students wrote, I thought of my great grandmother, Mary, who was born in 1886. She had one career option: farm wife. She gave birth to six children, the first when she was eighteen, the sixth, at thirty-nine. There was no question of family planning. Except for her "egg money," Mary never expected to have her own cash. I don't envy her lack of choices. At the same time, Mary had no doubt that her work as mother and farm wife was crucial to the family's survival. She was fairly confident that her husband would stay with her life-long and that neighbors and family would help out when things got tough. What would Mary say if she could hear my students talk about their future plans? They have such ambitious plans yet so little practical support for carrying them out.

There's much talk in our society about motherhood in general, but an awkward silence surrounds many of the concrete realities. In a recent book called *The Mask of Motherhood* (1999), social scientist Susan Maushart argues that mothers themselves are partly responsible for the misunderstandings that surround motherhood. Most mothers wear a "mask of motherhood…an assemblage of fronts—mostly brave, serene, all-knowing—that we use to disguise the chaos and complexity of our lived experience" (2). According to Maushart, this mask silences, isolates, and devalues mothers. Because they won't admit to their difficulties and doubts, they can't ask for help or even make authentic friends.

The "mask of motherhood" creates barriers between mothers and everyone else, *including their children and each other.* And by hiding the "chaos and complexity," the mask actually prevents our society from realistically preparing prospective mothers. Becoming a mother is a huge "trauma of reorganization…experienced as enormous in personal terms, yet it remains socially invisible" (106). Once their children are school age, many women develop amnesia about their earliest years of motherhood.

The conditions Maushart describes struck a chord with me. In the United States, the care of young children is carried out in isolation from "the real world," and mothers function primarily as sole parents, assuming full charge of the demanding, continuous physical tasks associated with child care and domestic duties, especially in the early years. Moreover, few women in our society receive practical, hands-on preparation for motherhood; thus our knowledge base tends to be hopelessly abstract and theoretical, creating a very steep learning curve.

In addition, new mothers experience continual interruptions on a daily basis and several years of sleep deprivation. They are at especially high risk for serious depression and for marital decline. According to Maushart, all these factors contribute to "a lethal cocktail of loneliness, chronic fatigue, and panic" (120). "The lack of fit between the expectations and realities of mothering may be experienced as a personal crisis, but it is ultimately a social tragedy" (118). Yet such tragedy isn't inevitable. Spiritual resources can help mothers be more honest and courageous.

An Interpretive Framework

As I suggested in the introduction, mothers today have a pressing need for a fresh interpretive framework that acknowledges and values the many changes that come with new motherhood. We especially need a religious framework because changes in bodies have spiritual and moral reverberations. At present, we have only medical language (length of labor, type of pain relief, baby's weight) and commercial language (ads for baby products). These are inadequate ways of speaking about the powerful changes (ontological changes!) that mothers experience.

Elizabeth Johnson insists that we must be able to put religious experiences into words in order to fully claim them: "[G]race comes...as empowerment toward discovery of self and affirmation of one's strength, giftedness, and responsibility....This is a deeply religious event, the coming into being of suppressed selves. Its significance in terms of spirituality, ethical value, and articulated doctrine has yet to be fully calculated, and yet it is already bringing about *new articulations* of divine mystery" (64–65, emphasis mine). Johnson is referring broadly to women's "new ownership of the female self as God's good gift" in its many dimensions, including motherhood.

An interpretive framework is important because experience never occurs in a vacuum—it is always understood within a larger context. Our cultural context influences our expectations regarding birth and mother- hood—what it will be like, how we will change personally, how our roles in family will change. It shapes what others expect from us and what we can expect from them. We need a new (or revised) interpretive frame- work that will change what it is acceptable to talk about, what others are willing to hear, even what mothers themselves are willing to see, acknowledge, and remember.

For example, only recently did people begin to talk openly about postpartum depression. It has probably existed as long as women have been having babies, yet women have been reluctant to admit to it, and men have been unwilling to regard it as a legitimate illness. When Marie Osmond went public with her severe postpartum depression in 1999, women suddenly had a way to talk about PPD. Our interpretive frame- work for motherhood enlarged as the phrase entered public awareness.

An expanded language of matrescence and motherhood is needed in order to claim a fuller, more holistic experience of motherhood. Much of this book focuses on finding new language for mothers' experiences, because it is essential scaffolding for making sense of experience, includ- ing the inner life of the mother.

Especially important is language about God. Johnson explains that how we see God influences the kind of people we become. Johnson sug- gests that if a person views God as a Mother, Wise Woman, and Indwelling Presence, she will see her maternal work, her own matura- tion, and her inner experience as part of her faith. In contrast, if a person sees God primarily as a Father, Judge, and Lord, she will likely have a more distant, subservient, and perhaps even legalistic relationship with God. If she sees God primarily in terms of power and authority, she may identify God with human authorities and institutions, and thus believe she must adapt herself to the existing social order rather than challenge it. Overreliance on human authorities can hamper spiritual growth and make it harder to bring about change for the better. To be "leaven" in a secular society—as Christians are called to do—a person must see the need for an alternative to the status quo.

Johnson also asserts that how a person sees God will shape what she expects from family, church, workplace, government, and other institutions. For example, if a person sees God as a Wise Woman who guides her through life, she won't be likely to adapt herself to a marriage where the man is the "head," God's representative on earth. Nor will she be quick to accept a secondary role in the workplace or church. On the other hand, if she sees God as "cocreator" or "co-madre," she will expect and cultivate greater cooperation with others as well as with God.

Johnson believes that as long as female religious symbols are "underdeveloped, peripheral, and secondary" (57), women and women's work will also be underdeveloped, peripheral, and secondary. A male-centered belief system legitimizes a patriarchal society. Such a society will be lopsided, placing little value on the creating, cherishing, and sustaining work of mothers.

"Through a Lens of Women Flourishing": Birth Rituals

In her book *She Who Is,* Elizabeth Johnson offers a helpful metaphor. In a section entitled "Through a Lens of Women Flourishing," she writes about values that can help us to see more clearly various relationships, institutions, and decisions (17). I've formulated questions to help me view the world through a lens with a special focus on women's well-being: How does this impact the women involved? Does it degrade them or help them to flourish? What would it take to allow a woman to flourish in this situation? Caring, conscious attention to the changes of early motherhood can help a woman to flourish. Indeed, it can help us to strengthen our souls. I experienced this in a powerful way even during my pregnancy.

As my due date approached, a group of women from my church organized two gatherings for me. One was a large baby shower where I was "showered" with all the lovely practical things. A second was a smaller ceremony (what we called a "blessing way") during which several friends gathered to pray over me and anoint my breasts. Though the shower was fun and practical, the blessing ceremony was far more valuable.

A friend named Patsy planned the simple ceremony which we held in my living room, about eight of us sitting in a circle. First came an invocation of the presence of God, then several songs. Cathy, another friend, anointed my breasts with oil and prayed that I would have a safe delivery and a good milk supply. Then each woman presented me with a small gift and a blessing to accompany it. We closed with several songs and afterward enjoyed refreshments.

From the gathering I kept a small leather pouch: a drawstring "medicine bag" that Patsy embroidered with beads in a Navajo dreamcatcher design. In it she tucked many small gifts from my friends—a seashell, a piece of quartz, a feather, a holy medal. That simple ritual surrounded me with their love and bolstered my trust in my own body to meet the challenges ahead.

When labor began a month later, I took the medicine bag with me to the hospital, a tangible reminder of their love. I'd had life-threatening complications (complete placenta previa) during my pregnancy and my doctors were prepared for a difficult birth, probably a Caesarian section. Instead, labor proceeded peacefully and smoothly, and I gave birth vaginally to a healthy, plump boy. Just after Gabe's birth, still in the delivery room, my obstetrician actually thanked me. "It's a pleasure to bring a baby into the world when I can see that the mother is well loved too." If only she could know that I was centered and largely free from anxiety because my friends had invoked Sophia, Spirit of Wisdom, to help me. Later my milk supply came in readily. I can't help but believe that the loving blessing ceremony paved the way for all these good things!

A decade later my little "medicine bag" sits in my jewelry box, a cherished reminder of my wonderful birthing. Gabe loves to look at the objects inside and hear about how a circle of women prayed him safely into the world.

Only later did I learn that for thousands of years women have given each other talismans accompanied by blessings to promote a safe delivery and milk supply. In *The Tender Gift,* Dana Raphael mentions that thousands of plump, heavy-breasted Venus of Willendorf statues have been found throughout Europe. Predating Christianity, these small Venus statues have headdresses that resemble a woman's nipple, and their bodies are those of a mature and fecund woman. Many believe the statues are religious amulets given to new or soon-to-be mothers to promote a good milk supply in a time when breast milk was critical to an infant's survival.

A woman named Cynthia Lapp has written a book called *There's Power in the Blood: Women, Christian Ritual, and the Blood Mysteries,* which describes blessing ceremonies for menarche, childbirth, and menopause. She observes that blood is a central symbol of Christianity as well as an important part of women's life cycle. Her book offers theological context as well as a biblical ritual to mark each of these three life-events. Lapp is writing out of the Mennonite tradition but her suggestions could be easily adapted to other Christian traditions as well.

The "Ritual to Celebrate Birthing" begins with a leader welcoming all participants: "Welcome to this celebration for N. She is approaching the time when she will become a mother for the first time (or become a mother again)....She is one in a long line of strong women, of centuries of women who have given birth and who have felt the power of God within them. The power of God, the 'great womb of wondrous love,' will be with her, and our love will be with her, too" (33).

Lapp goes on to suggest particular readings, prayers, and songs that are readily available from published sources. All this leads up to a final blessing, a "Prayer for Power" for the birthing mother. The blessing is meant for childbirth and early matrescence, but it would be valuable at any stage of the mothering journey when a mother needs power. With its loving, respectful references to the female body, it echoes the theme that it has taken me years to learn—the female body is made in the image of God and continually bears and cares for God:

> *Bless my back that allows me to stand upright and that supports*
> *me through labor.*
> *Bless my round breasts that bring nourishment and pleasure.*
> *Bless my womb that nurtures and brings forth creativity and this*
> *created being.*
> *Bless my arms that they may be strong for holding close what I*
> *need and pushing away what is not necessary.*
> *Bless my mind that I may meditate on the wonder of birth and*
> *let go when I need to.*
> *Bless my breath that sustains me and allows my connection with*
> *the spirit.*
> *Bless my feet that they may carry me through sleepless nights and*
> *early morning*
> *So that I may continue my life with a new companion.*
> (Lapp 34–35)

Notes

1. A theologian would describe this as an ontological change because it is a change in the person's being, in much the same way that ordination is a change in the identity of a priest. An irrevocable inward change occurs.

2. See, for example, Judith Goldsmith's *Childbirth Wisdom: From the World's Oldest Societies* (Brookline, MA: East West Health Books, 1990) or Sheila Kitzinger's *Ourselves as Mothers: The Universal Experience of Motherhood* (Reading, MA: Addison Wesley, 1994).

3

Beware:
The Dangers Mothers Face

The Deep Waters of Motherhood

One winter afternoon Susan invited me for tea. I was eager to tell her about one of my grad students, a twenty-six-year-old named Liz who had just confided that she was pregnant.

"She's trying to decide what to do," I explained to Susan as we both sat drinking cinnamon tea. "She's been going with the guy for a couple years. She loves him but he's not interested in becoming a father, so Liz is trying to decide whether to put the baby up for adoption or raise it herself."

"Can she support a baby?" Susan always knew the important questions.

"She's scheduled to student teach this spring and start her first full-time teaching job in August. The baby is due in May—six months from now."

"So she's thinking she'll pop the baby out in May and launch right into a professional job two months later—*with no help?*" Susan looked incredulous.

"There's more. The boyfriend just approached Liz with a document from his lawyer. He wants her to sign an agreement saying that if he forfeits his parental rights, she won't expect him to pay child support—*ever.* And Liz is so mad at him, she's ready to sign it just to get rid of him."

"Oh my god! So then she'll have *no partner and no money.* What did you say?"

"I said, 'Don't sign anything till the birth, and you have a better sense of what's involved in caring for a baby—the expense and the time.' Really, she has no clue."

"Tell her it's like falling off a cliff. Or diving into the deep end of a swimming pool when you can't swim. Most women are stunned by how much they love their baby and by how much *hard work* it takes." After teaching childbirth classes for twenty years, Susan was an expert in early motherhood.

"And that's just in the short run," I added. "I was thinking you should warn women in your classes about what it's like in the *long run*— what they're signing up for when they decided to raise a baby."

"By the time they're pregnant, they don't want to hear anything negative. But they really *do* need to know if they want to make an informed decision. Both the good and the bad. Most women don't know nearly enough about the joys of mothering or the dangers."

"The dangers and the temptations. Some of the things they can control," I said. "I was reading a book by a law professor last week, and she writes about what she calls 'the deadly Ds'—disrespect, disadvantages in the workplace, destitution...."

Susan and I put our heads together and formulated our own list of "Dangerous Ds"—the pitfalls that Liz should be aware of to make an informed choice between adoption and solo motherhood. In mothering as in any new venture, we figured, a person needed to take a long look at both the potential risks and the potential benefits. If she knew the dangers, she'd be more likely to be able to deal with them; she might also join with others to press for social policies that would reduce the dangers. Susan and I got to comparing motherhood to setting out on a sea voyage where there were dragons and sea monsters lurking along the way. Later I merged our ideas with the reading I'd done. We came up with the list below.

Beware of the Dragons: "The Dangerous Ds"

1. **Depression.** Following childbirth a woman is at risk for postpartum depression. In the United States, she also faces long-term risk for clinical depression, especially in the years before children reach school age. Women who work solely at home often suffer from isolation, while women with children under thirteen who work outside the home full-time

are "the most stressed group in America" (Maushart 199). According to social scientist Susan Maushart, stress, loneliness, and years of sleep deprivation all contribute to "a lethal cocktail of loneliness, chronic fatigue, and panic" (120)—and depression!

2. **Distractibility.** With the birth of her first child, it will likely be several years before a woman can eat a meal, take a bath, or carry on a phone conversation without interruption. Valerie Saiving, a theologian, explains that a mother's "capacity for surrendering her individual concerns in order to serve the immediate needs of others [can] induce a kind of diffuseness of purpose, a tendency toward being easily distracted, a failure to discriminate between the more and the less important, and an inability to focus in a sustained manner on the pursuit of any single goal" (38). Although this can be a temporary stage, it can also become a permanent, lifelong condition.

3. **Domestic Drift.** A couple with children is likely to drift into increasingly differentiated roles. "After children the pull of traditional gender roles will exert a force that in most cases will prove irresistible," writes Maushart. The first baby is like a hand grenade that propels couples in opposing directions. Mothers change faster than fathers, taking on the day-to-day management of children's lives, including feeding, clothing, health care, homework, TV monitoring, and bedtimes. As women overfunction on the home front, fathers often begin to invest more time in employment to compensate for the mothers' loss of income or to escape from the demands of parenting.

4. **Disappointment in Marriage.** Although children can be a unifying force in marriage, they can also undermine it, especially in the early years. When they marry, couples often fail to anticipate the impact of differences in child-rearing philosophies and gender expectations. According to one recent study, 97 percent of the couples report an increase in marital conflict after the birth of a baby (Maushart 218). Married couples are *more likely* to stay together, but *less likely* to like or understand each other, at least in the early years of child rearing. Because they experience a widening gap between "his world" and "her world," the two partners begin to inhabit

SPIRITUALITY IN THE MOTHER ZONE

two different and mutually unintelligible spheres (181). There is also a "fatigue gap," with men pushing for more sex and women pushing for more sleep; men end up feeling left out and women feel unsupported. Maushart calls this the clash between "Superwoman and Stuporman."

5. **Dependency.** Not only does a mother have dependents who lean on her, she also must depend on others to meet many needs. Most obvious are the needs for financial security and child care. She also is in greater need of health care and of education for her children; these needs tie her into the larger community in ways that a childless woman can seldom imagine. In a society that prizes individuality and independence above all, this can be a rude shock, especially if a woman has been independent for many years.

6. **Disrespect.** In earlier eras, the whole society often shared the responsibility of safely raising children to become stable, contributing adults, but in recent decades, public attitudes have grown increasingly intolerant of children. Child rearing has become increasingly privatized so that today children are widely regarded as parents' private indulgences, on a par with caring for an Irish setter or raising exotic orchids. Many adults (including working spouses) have almost no understanding of how mentally demanding it is to provide for the physical and psychological needs of children on a day-to-day and year-to-year basis. Child-care workers are paid a national average of $7.90 an hour, in contrast to $12.60 for animal trainers and $7.70 for parking lot attendants (National Center for the Early Childhood Workforce. www.ccw.org/pubs/2002#compendium). Consider the word *baby-sitter* and its connotation of passivity and lack of skill.

7. **Disadvantages in the Workplace.** A woman will likely face significant disadvantages in the workplace if she chooses to give priority to child rearing. Even with just one child, she may have to don emotional armor to hide the stress involved in straddling two demanding occupations; if a second or third child is born, the "cracks in the armor" begin to show. The more children a woman has, the fewer her promotions and benefits in the paying workforce, and the less professional recognition and

job mobility. As *her* job becomes less rewarding monetarily, the job of her male partner takes more and more precedence. Women workers have grown up believing that "motherhood is not supposed to make a difference" in their needs in the workplace (Maushart 179) and don't anticipate these changes. A father who wants to play an equal role in parenting may be prevented from doing so because workplaces are so inflexible. This is especially true of professional jobs like those of doctors, lawyers, business executives, and college professors.

8. Destitution. Because of their economic dependency, mothers are vulnerable to the loss of a partner whether through *divorce, desertion,* or *death.* They are also economically vulnerable to their own or a spouse's *disability.* Women with interrupted work histories also face reduced incomes in old age. Ann Crittendon, an economist, points out that the time spent working at home is not recognized by the Social Security Administration as productive labor and thus does not lead to retirement income, even if a woman raises several children who *themselves* go on to become productive workers who pay into Social Security for the older generation.

9. Drug use and abuse. Because of their higher rates of stress, depression, and anxiety, mothers take more antidepressants and tranquilizers than their childless counterparts. Mothers of children with special needs are especially prone to alcohol or drug abuse. Moreover, because of the prevalence of drug abuse (both legal and illegal) in our culture, mothers can expect to deal with the abuse of street drugs by a spouse or child at some point in her life, probably at great financial and psychological cost.

10. Deception. Too often mothers collude with the larger culture in promoting a falsely sanguine view of motherhood. According to Maushart, mothers in Western societies wear a "mask of motherhood," which disguises both the difficulties and the pleasures of raising children. Because they hide the reality, women actually contribute to their own exploitation.

11. Divisiveness. Although motherhood can be a uniting force, too often it divides women into competing camps. This is especially true in a society like ours, where there is tremendous disagreement over the best way to nurture and discipline children. Stay at home or work for pay? Breastfeed or bottle feed? Spank or not spank? Small family or large? These are just a few of the topics that cause others to judge mothers and mothers to judge one another.

In an earlier era, parents might not have worried excessively about the impact of spanking children. But in an era of teen violence, mothers become hypervigilant about the rightness of their own actions. Mothers worry that, for example, if they spank, they will condemn their children to a lifetime of antisocial behavior. The stakes seem high, motherhood is carried out in a hothouse atmosphere, and many mothers feel very insecure. All these factors contribute to intolerance and divisiveness among mothers with different values. I know of one young mother who threatened to *shun* her doting mother-in-law for offering her precious toddler a sip of Coca Cola!

12. Disillusionment. A mother may soon lose her illusions about the value placed upon children and child rearing by the larger culture. In Maushart's study, many women reported they felt disillusioned by their employers' and spouses' lack of understanding of their needs as mothers. Many mothers also find themselves disillusioned that various professionals (such as doctors, teachers, psychologists) are more concerned with maintaining order and avoiding lawsuits than with helping children. Many schools have a "zero tolerance policy" toward aggressive behavior that leads to expelling children who don't fit the mold. Some religious institutions are notoriously indifferent to children.

4

This Is My Body

Restoring Dignity to the Mother's Body

In a book about parenting and spirituality, Myla Kabat-Zins writes: "Nursing was a huge cornerstone of my mothering....My body was an essential and completely familiar part of [my children's] landscape...a source of comfort and well-being for them [even after they stopped nursing]. You might call it soul food" (174–77). When I read this passage, I realized how much my own perspective on the body had changed in the course of growing into motherhood. In my younger years I saw few connections between my body and my spiritual life. It seemed lowly and unimportant.

My perspective changed with motherhood. For years after Gabe's birth I was shocked by my own ignorance again and again. How was it that I had gotten well into adulthood and never known, for example, that menstrual periods ceased not just during pregnancy but also during the months of lactation? That years could go by with *no period*? My ignorance of other subjects was just as great. How to build up a child's immune system, how to maintain a good milk supply, how to treat an ear infection, how to keep a love life going in the midst of this....Motherhood was a crash course in the life of the body. The learning curve has been slow, steep, and humbling.

The processes of pregnancy, birth, and lactation immerse women in the life of the body as they are forced to pay attention both to their own bodies and to their babies' bodies. This new focus continues for many years as they assume responsibility for the physical health and well-being of their growing children. In my experience, this sustained attention has led to a deep respect for the body, so that my spiritual life seems inextricably linked to it.

The physicality of motherhood forced me into a new relationship with the body in ways that have endured a dozen years later. This new relationship has greatly enriched my spiritual life, giving me a deeper appreciation of the incarnation of Jesus. This change came into focus for me when a former student gave a guest lecture in one of my classes.

Nude Photos in English Class

When I was teaching "Writing about Parenting," Angela volunteered to make a guest presentation on "Motherhood in the Trenches." Angela had been my student assistant before leaving college to marry and have a baby. By the time of my course, she was twenty-two—and back in school as a senior and mother of a sixteen-month-old daughter named Jo. Angela's offer was a great opportunity to give my students a peer's perspective on early parenthood.

Petite Angela stood at the front of my classroom, animatedly telling my students about the surprises of pregnancy, birth, infant care, and marriage maintenance. Her observations were so fresh that she might have been a traveler recently returned from an exotic land. My students hung on her every word, but the most riveting moment came when Angela held up her scrapbook.

"Here's a collection of the snapshots of my daughter's life so far. You'll see how beautiful Jo is! I also included pictures of her birth to show what a powerful experience it was. I put sticky notes on the pages with nudity in case some of you want to skip over them. I have to warn you— they're pretty graphic."

As Angela's scrapbook made its way around the room, I observed my students' reactions. Most of the males skipped the nude photos, while the females lingered over them, their eyes wide. Faces registered a range of emotions, from fascination to horror. It was one thing to see photos of a clean, smiling baby but quite another to see ones of bare-breasted

Angela nursing newborn Jo. Even more startling were the snapshots of her husband cutting the cord, Angela's thighs bloody, the baby newly emerged from the womb and still white and waxy with vernix. My students had probably seen thousands of pictures of exposed breasts, but few of nursing babies, and virtually no pictures of birth.

Angela's scrapbook drove home a fundamental change that often comes with motherhood: a dramatic reorientation toward the life of the body. Angela linked this reorientation to her spiritual life: "I felt an intense desire for spirituality but not in traditional terms. There's been a turning inward and deepening as I come to terms with my new reality. For me the crucifix has been replaced by the image of a laboring woman." Angela went on to explain that she had been raised with a deep love of Jesus, the suffering Christ, but only recently had she come to value the connection between her own laboring body and the body of Christ. She explained, "I now see giving birth and tending to Jo's little body as valuable expressions—*my expressions*—of God bringing new life and faith into the world!" Since hearing Angela speak, I have a new appreciation for the words of the Catholic mass, "This is my body, given for you." Just as the host is consecrated in the mass, our bodies are blessed as through loving service.

Our Cultural Inheritance

As Angela spoke, I found myself wondering how her young life might be different if she'd grown up with a spirituality grounded in a respect for the body. Clearly, women need (and deserve) a spirituality that values and celebrates the human body, including our reproductive capacities. Yet too often the Christian tradition views the body as merely the container for the soul—a necessary evil at best, or, at worst, a source of misery and an occasion of sin. Religious people especially are inclined to view the soul as "a bird in a tarnished cage" (in the words of journalist Maureen Conlan). We Christians have been taught that the body is "the temple of the Holy Spirit," and the corporal works of mercy express a respect for the body. Think, for example, of all the hospitals founded by religious orders over the centuries.

Yet when it comes to women's reproductive capacities, Christian tradition too often looks the other way. A contempt for the body, especially the female body grows out of more than two thousand years of philosophical dualism. Greek philosophers promoted a belief that the soul's true home was the world of ideas. They saw the soul as being in opposition with matter, the mind in opposition with the body, culture in opposition to raw nature. People came to assume that the soul, the mind, and culture were not only at odds with *but far superior to* matter, body, and nature. Rather than seeking integration or connection between mind and body, they viewed them as polar opposites. Early Christian theology grew out of this Greek view. St. Paul wrote of "the spirit warring against the flesh." The flesh was seen as "fallen," infected, sinful, something to endure and transcend. Bodies came to be seen as the enemy, especially female bodies, despite the fact that they are created by God.

Johnson laments the denigration of women's bodies: "Within a system of dualism…both women and the natural world are separated from the men they bring forth and sustain. Both are assigned instrumental value, *with little or no intrinsic worth* apart from their potential to serve the needs and desires of men" (emphasis mine; Johnson, *Women, Earth, and Creator Spirit* 13). In other words, according to a dualistic worldview, women's bodies are not seen as dignified and valuable *in themselves*; rather they have value only to the degree that they can meet male needs. This pattern of dualism is evident nearly everywhere in our culture. For example, when I raise this subject with my students, most heterosexual males profess a love and appreciation for female bodies. Many have pin-up posters of slender young females in their dorm rooms, naked or nearly so. But when pressed, most admit they value only beautiful, slender bodies. They value women's bodies insofar as they can provide sexual pleasure or increased status *to them*. Pin-up posters promote fantasies of males' own sexual prowess, not of realistic love.

Of course, most of my students are young and have limited understanding of the opposite sex. But even mature men, men who truly love individual women, are often put off by inescapable aspects of the female body, such as the menstrual cycle, the changes of pregnancy, natural weight fluctuations, and the aging process. They have little understanding of the needs or the uniqueness of the female body. Mature women, in contrast, tend to be far more tolerant of the men's weight fluctuations and the aging process.[1]

Dualism also affects the way that women think of the female body. I've observed that most of my female students have little respect for their bodies unless they conform to cultural ideals of slender, young, and pretty. A teaching colleague assigned "Poem to My Uterus" to her class—a tender poem in which Lucille Clifton praises her uterus for "slippering" all her children into life. (Clifton is an African American poet whose work often expresses her delight in motherhood and children.) The students were "totally grossed out" by the poem, my colleague said. These students aren't squeamish about bodies or sex, but the results of sex—childbirth and its bloody aftermath—that's another story.

Made in God's Image

Dualism is especially damaging to pregnant women. Up until the point of pregnancy a woman may be able to accept the culture's view of her body as an object of male desire. But with pregnancy she jumps track. I recall during pregnancy feeling at once thrilled and betrayed—the same way I'd felt when I got my first menstrual period—as if my body had a life of its own. It felt like waking up on a fast-moving train. You can't quite remember boarding it, and now there's no getting off. The pregnant body has a momentum that follows its own track: gestation, delivery, lactation. This "track" has power, beauty, and a fulfillment all its own.

But our society has another track, one that veers sharply away from biology: Stay young, slender, bloodless, and sexy by the standards of young males. As for all the messes—bloody show, birth waters, lochia, breasts dripping milk, tears, droopy flesh—rid yourself of them as soon as possible. At least keep them discreetly hidden away and don't discuss them in public.

And yet here was Angela talking frankly, even showing bloody pictures! As she told how her views had changed, I found myself nodding in agreement.

"The experience of giving birth made me see myself differently. I developed a whole new level of respect for my own body," she said. "I'd never liked my body much before—I always thought I was too short, not slim enough. Pregnancy made me very aware of the limitations of my body. I was so sick with nausea the first three months that I had to be hospitalized. Even so, I was amazed by all its changes. And Jo's birth was such a powerful, thrilling experience!"

Like Angela, I found that motherhood caused me to change my sense of my body. I came to inhabit my body with a whole new level of comfort: respecting its wisdom, valuing its earthy accomplishments, reveling in its voluptuous pleasures. Pregnancy, birth, and infant care thrust a person into the life of the body. Those who come to motherhood through another route (such as adoption) are also thrust into the life of the body as they attend to the intimate physical needs of a baby and young child—then assist with those needs till age eighteen or even longer.

As a new mother, it came to me with the force of an epiphany: Women's bodies are the source of all human life; women's bodies comprise half the human race. Regardless of their size, age, or color, women's bodies are truly made in the image of God.

Breasts: Sustaining Life

Standing at the front of the classroom, Angela continued: "I decided to breastfeed Jo, and it has been the best experience—*the best!* It's nutrition, comfort, and pleasure for us both—so pure and simple. I see my breasts as external umbilical cords. They link us together, even as Jo develops into a separate person. And it's so affirming to see how Jo's face lights up when she sees my breasts! I feel pride in my body now, for the first time."

Listening to Angela made me remember my pregnancy with Gabe. All the body changes felt overwhelming: weight gain, rashes, lethargy. My body had taken on a life of its own that had little to do with what I wanted. I watched my diet, exercised, took vitamins—did everything right—yet still my body zoomed out of control. I gained fifty pounds—nearly 40 percent of my prior weight. How amazing that my body knew how to do all this without my conscious input—knew how to grow a whole new human being!

One afternoon in my late pregnancy my neighbor Chris Auer came over to coach me in breastfeeding. She's a registered nurse and professional lactation consultant. I sat in an armchair, my shirt unbuttoned, while Chris used a large doll to demonstrate the various baby-feeding "holds."

Then Chris observed, "Look, your colostrum has already started to come in. Squeeze your nipple—see that yellow crust? It looks a little like crystallized honey. The colostrum comes before the milk. It's called 'liquid gold' because it's so rich in nutrients."

When I looked down, my jaw dropped! What an amazing discovery—my body sneaking up on me and producing something precious without my even noticing. I felt both thrilled and betrayed—as if my body had changed overnight.

Chris's coaching laid the groundwork for a long and satisfying breastfeeding relationship with Gabe. Even more than pregnancy, breastfeeding let me see my own body as capable, trustworthy, and even wise! Breastfeeding was the first sustained period of knowing my body as *productive*—not just consuming—but actually churning out milk on a daily basis in order to continue the creation of a new human being. I watched with awe as Gabe's body doubled then tripled in size, nourished completely by my breasts! During pregnancy I couldn't see him growing in my womb, but this I could witness firsthand.

At the same time, I also discovered its limitations. A woman can't produce milk unless her body is well nourished, well rested, and not overworked. I'd always been a cerebral, hard-driving person who tuned out my body's needs for long periods, often skipping meals and continuing to work when sick. Breastfeeding quickly taught me that if a body doesn't rest, eat, and drink enough, her milk supply dwindles. I started paying attention to my body in ways that have endured ten years later.

By the time of my first birth, I'd already been coached by Sister Miriam in contemplative prayer. She'd taught me the value of surrendering to God, relaxing in God's presence, what she called "falling into God's arms." Such prayerful surrender made it easier to relax during childbirth and later during breastfeeding. I can't speak for all women, but for me breastfeeding often felt like the deep relaxation and sense of union that often accompanied prayer. Surrendering to the experience contributed to a rich sense of God's presence and to a deepening trust in my own body, even as I relished nourishing my baby.

Though Chris hinted at it, I didn't yet realize the intense ambivalence surrounding breastfeeding. Mothers' attitudes toward it run the whole gamut—they are even more varied and highly charged than the larger society's. Some view it as a disgusting reminder of our animal origins. At the opposite extreme are those who advocate infant-led weaning, even when it means babies nurse till age three or four. Medical experts like the American Academy of Pediatrics have strongly endorsed breastfeeding for at least the first year of a child's life, and lactation specialists insist that nearly every mother is biologically capable. Breastfeeding advocates argue that extended breastfeeding (a year or more) reduces allergies, strengthens an infant's immune system, increases IQ, and enhances a mother's health and confidence, with the result of huge savings in medical costs. Still only a small percentage of women do breastfeed beyond three months, and many do not at all.[2]

Heart to Heart

Tending to children's physical needs can foster a spiritual intimacy in which it's no longer possible to separate body and spirit. Canadian author Greta Nemiroff describes this well: "Children bring us a sense of intimacy which cannot be replicated in adult relationships. An adult discussing bowel movements, hunger, or discomfort will at least be considered a bore; at the most pathological. Yet such subjects are the very material from which all lives are made" (74). Nemiroff believes that caring for children leads to a "consciousness-rebuilding" on the part of caregivers that puts them in touch with human experience, and thus helps them become more adaptable and spiritually grounded. "If we lose touch with these matters, we risk becoming rigid and traumatized" in the face of illness or the aging process (Nemiroff 74). Caring for a child's body can give a person a deeper love and respect for her own body, and for *all other* human bodies.

This deepening love and respect for the life of the body seems to me an important value for us Christians who believe in the incarnation, in spirit fully entering the body. In my own experience, breastfeeding and physical caregiving forged a link between valuing my body and honoring God's presence in my life. As a result, I made up my mind to keep myself as strong and healthy as I could.

Still, many women turn away from this opportunity. According to a childbirth educator named Laurie Phenix, many women say, "The less I know about the birth process the better. I don't want to see any blood or feel any pain. I want to get it all over with as quickly as possible! And then I want to get back to *normal.*"

"Normal" is seen as discretion, distaste for and detachment from the life of the body. While it's natural for anyone to want normalcy, birth can help a person discover a new standard of normal. If a woman can learn to accept the pain, blood, and mess of birth as natural—indeed *normal*—she is far more likely to accept the ongoing embodiment of motherhood. In the long run, relaxing into the inevitable messiness of motherhood will result in *less danger and stress.* Running away from the mess—denying it—will likely cause more stress and discomfort.

Hands: Tending the Body

Angela went on to talk about other practical aspects of new motherhood. "Since Jo was born, I've come to see the connection between nurturing the body and nurturing the soul. Because I nurture her soul by nurturing her body—they are intricately connected. Tending to her physical needs lets her trust that the world is a safe place. I believe that this is some of the most important work I will ever do."

Watching Angela speak from behind the podium, I find myself paying special attention to her hands gesturing and turning over her pages of notes. Do the other students in this classroom have any idea, I wonder, of all that those hands have done in the last sixteen months? A baby immerses a person in the world of touch: holding, stroking, changing diapers, bathing, dressing, feeding, burping, rocking….Deliberate touch occupies many hours of the day, often imprinting intense memories on muscles and psyche: "The mere smell and texture of the baby's clothes and skin evoke yearning from anyone who's mothered….Bearing and caretaking a child tapped into feelings I did not know existed…manic highs, extravagant joy, monumental wonder, syrupy tenderness, exquisite love" (Thurer xvii).

All this touch can be overwhelming and exhausting, especially if done in isolation and on little sleep. Still, hands-on mothering is deeply instructive, creating body wisdom that endures and can influence a woman's subsequent endeavors. One mother writes, "[H]umans need caring physical contact throughout our lives—especially into old age. We desperately need to link to others by touch, by that bodily warmth which is repressed by our constricted cultural notions about private space….Children [keep] us in touch with our human needs. Being attentive to physical comfort, hurt feelings, the ability to play with total concentration and joy…the nakedness of childhood preoccupations helps us to keep in touch with ourselves, with the child imprisoned within each adult" (Nemiroff 74). Many women report that even decades after their children's infancy, the sound of a baby crying elicits a milk-letdown response, that flash of instinct to suckle a child, as spontaneous as sexual desire. Even though the breasts have long ago stopped producing milk, the body responds to a baby's cry.

When I visited a nursing home once, the director explained why the Alzheimer's wing was equipped with a rocking chair, life-sized dolls, and a changing table. "For some of our women residents, the time when their children were babies was the happiest time in their lives. Now it comforts them to hold dolls and baby things." Breasts, hands, and psyche all carry bodily memories of caring for a child.[3]

Church as Lover: A Disturbing Dream

During the time that I was sorting out the cognitive dissonance regarding motherhood, I recorded this vivid dream in my journal: *I'm traveling with a man who is rugged, adventurous, and handsome. He looks like actor Harrison Ford. We're visiting his friends in a desert area near the mountains. As long as I follow his lead, he's very attentive to me, and I'm falling in love with him. He says he loves me too—very seductive. But then I get my period unexpectedly and don't have any tampons with me. Embarrassed, I discreetly ask my "mountain man" for directions to a shower and a store. He tells me there are no showers or stores. It's the desert. He keeps stalling, and meanwhile I'm sitting on a bed, and my blood is seeping into the white bedspread. Finally I quietly say, "I have my period and I need a shower now and won't you please, please help me?" But he won't. The mountain man who first seemed so exciting and loving now seems dead-set on his own agenda. He doesn't want to hear about my problems. Can't I make my messy female needs just go away?*

Later when I reread that dream, it became clear to me that it was about my relationship with the Christian tradition, especially in regard to my female body. For as long as I could remember, I'd been in love with God and thus with the Christian tradition. Concepts like the family of God, all humans being made in the image of God, the reign of God were very meaningful to me; they guided my life. I believed that I was a valued part of the church.

Then big and important changes occurred in my life—notably becoming a mother. Like getting my period, this gave rise to messy and inescapable needs that simply would not go away. In order for me to continue to travel with the mountain man in my dream, I needed for him to pay attention to me, to take my needs seriously, my physical as well as my inner needs. I didn't ask for anything unreasonable—only for him to value and love me as I loved him. He tuned me out, just as the churches I visited seemed to "tune out" me and other troublesome women.

Looking to my Christian tradition, I saw rituals to mark other important life passages like marriage but nothing that celebrated a woman's other passages. The female body seemed associated with shame and temptation, not joy and creativity. If only others had helped Angela and me prepare for motherhood, like the midwife who sings this song in the novel *The Red Tent* (Anita Diamant):

> Fear not, the time is coming
> Fear not, your bones are strong
> Fear not, help is nearby
> Fear not, God is near
> Fear not, the earth is beneath you…
> Fear not, little mother
> Fear not, mother of us all

Making Love

In her presentation to my class, Angela also addressed the changes a baby causes in marriage. "As delightful as she is, Jo's been a big challenge to our relationship. Marriage has gotten much more complicated. The hardest thing is balancing my attention between the baby and Matthew. He really needs me, but it often seems Jo needs me more."

Angela hit upon a critical issue among parents of young children. If a woman has a partner, suddenly he's displaced by a legitimate rival. Her view of sexual love changes. Earlier, sex may have been a source of pleasure, a spontaneous expression of love, a comfort, a playful escape. Now it can become a conscious, strategic choice with long-term implications for herself and her child. Often a woman is overwhelmed and preoccupied by the needs of her new baby and may have little interest in sexual intercourse. Even so, it is important to stay connected to her mate. The months following childbirth are a time of great vulnerability for marriages. A woman's mate may already feel emotionally displaced by the baby. Avoiding intercourse may make him feel abandoned, which in turn may cause him to pull further away. Thus, more than ever, sex becomes a strategic choice, for her own well-being as well as the well-being of her mate and child. At this time a woman and her partner need to find a way to remain connected, even amidst the added stress of a new baby.

Authors of *A Man's Guide to Sex* describe this widespread phenomenon: "Articles [in women's magazines] are filled with new mothers' voices saying they've just totally lost interest in sex, and for a gamut of physical and emotional reasons. Coitus can be very painful for several months after the birth [due to cutting or tearing of the perineum], hormonal changes are brought on by breastfeeding, baby has replaced hubby as the center of her attention" (Bechtel and Stains 208). Even long after the actual birth, sex may prove elusive because "Children annihilate your leisure time and energy and whatever spontaneity was left in your romance" (208).

The authors go on to suggest ways to reignite the flame of love and romance: "Many sex therapists tell their clients to schedule time for sex. This is even being called the Bic Cure, because therapists know that the only way some clients will really stick to their agreements is to write down the time and day in their planners—*in ink*….[This] creates an opportunity for sex. The only opportunity some people get" (207).

I discussed this passage with a mixed-age group of students. I pointed out that the term "Bic Cure" sounds like a reference to a disease.

"What exactly do they hope to cure?" I asked. "Is lack of intercourse a disease?"

"It's not an illness, but it is a dis-ease, a lack of ease," a young man pointed out. "The equilibrium of the relationship has been thrown off, so there is a lack of ease. Somehow the ease and closeness needs to be restored."

I suggested that the postpartum period is a perfect time to redefine and deepen a couple's sex life. That with patience and skill the physical difficulties could be eased, though it might take different forms than in the past. "Sensuality needn't always lead to intercourse—there's always kissing, cuddling, sweet talk, massage, and other types of mutual fondling and intimacy. Intercourse is only one route to sexual satisfaction."

"But kissing and fondling aren't sex! For men, sex means intercourse!" the young man pointed out.

"For women, kissing and fondling *are sex,*" a female student countered. "Having babies and breastfeeding—it's all part of the same package!"

"How a person looks at sex changes over the course of a lifetime," another student observed. "My dad says that the way a guy thinks about sex at fifty is different than at twenty. When a guy is young, sex feels so urgent. When he's older, it's more about the relationship. He says that older guys think about sex more like women do."

"You're all partly right," I interjected. "What it means to be sexual does vary with the person and it changes over time. What it means to be sexual is probably going to be different for most couples once they've had a baby." I went on to suggest that couples have to find common ground that's acceptable to both partners. Tenderness toward a woman during this vulnerable time might in fact lead to a richer, more trusting sex life down the road, as the couple becomes more versatile and adept at "making love." By the same token, loving understanding of the displaced male is also important. Too many women become so swallowed up by motherhood that they forget that they are also wives.

A male graduate student named Dan, a father of three, spoke up. "When we had our first baby I felt completely bumped out of the picture.

We eventually recovered but not everyone does. When I talk to the other dads in my neighborhood, most say their marriages hit the skids after having kids. If not with the first kid, then with the second or third one. It's really important for couples to find a way to stay close, and most of us aren't warned about how vulnerable we'll be."

Dan's remark made me think about my interviews with mothers. Several women had confided that their husbands had been unfaithful following the birth of a child. One woman said her husband had an affair while she was in the hospital recovering from the birth of their second child. "He knew it was wrong, but he said he just couldn't deal with feeling so lonely and left out." Several said that their husbands checked out emotionally after the birth of the second or third child. Most said that their marriages eventually recovered but not without undue hurt and struggle.[4]

One woman reflected on the breakup of her marriage some twenty years earlier: "The third birth pushed us over the edge. With the first two births, Peter would get up in the night, change the baby, and bring her into bed to be nursed. But with the third child, he was more stressed in his work, and I was in a daze of nursing and sleep and child care." She went on to describe how her husband had walked out one night, leaving her to raise their three children alone.

Mom's Misunderstood Body

At the center of such misunderstandings is the mother's misunderstood body. Too often, women and men alike lack understanding of the female body and the demands placed upon it by pregnancy, birth, and child care. A woman with young children has people depending upon her for their very lives; she's vulnerable and dependent in a way she may never have experienced before. It is the time in her life she most needs support from loved ones, and yet many women receive little practical help.

One of the women I interviewed described a very different postpartum experience in her home in Sierra Leone, Africa:

"[Back home] when you become a new mother, you don't even cook for a long time. You just sit and take care of the baby—you don't even have to get up….Everyone is at your beck and call. You don't even have to ask. People just stream to your house and do everything for the baby. They send food. [An older woman] will take charge of your baby and come every morning and wash the baby's hair, bathe the baby, do everything for you. It's not just the women either. The older men of the neighborhood come too—whoever is free. It's a community event!"

In some parts of the world, such treatment is standard during "the fourth trimester" (the three-month postpartum period), as a woman's body heals and her breasts establish a stable milk supply. Such attention to the new mother might also enhance her marriage. Instead, today most women return home after a day or two in the hospital—with the full-time care of a newborn baby added to her other responsibilities.

The Sloppy Stuff

Angela was a big hit with my students. I encouraged them to write thank-you letters, which I sent in a bundle to her.

Later I found myself telling my friend Susan about their letters, as we sat at her dining-room table. "They thanked Angela for raising their awareness—they were clueless about what a big deal it is to have a baby. They had no idea, they said, about how disruptive and time-consuming and messy it is."

"Most first-time parents have this romanticized view—a sweet baby, true love, and happily ever after. They've seen too many magazine ads." Susan has been teaching first-time parents for twenty years. "New moms suddenly discover two things: one, with a baby, your body and your head get connected real fast, or else you're in *big trouble.* And two, motherhood is a one-way bridge. Once you've crossed over, there's no going back"

"You ought to expand those childbirth classes to cover all the body stuff they need to know," I suggested to Susan. "Breathing exercises are small stuff compared to all the poop and fevers and painful sex."

"Nobody wants to learn about the mess—all the earthy, sloppy stuff! Many women are so squeamish about their bodies that they won't actually touch their own breasts or nipples! Their own breasts!" Susan explained. "So they're clueless about the other body-things. Not till they're in the trenches and it's midnight and the baby's screaming and they call the Dial-a-Nurse-line…."

A Wholistic View of Health

Of course, those midnight phone calls are just the one stage of learning about the life of the body. Many of us don't realize our own ignorance of health until we become mothers.

And the early years are just the tip of the iceberg. My well-worn copy of *Take Charge of Your Child's Health* suggests a multitude of concerns: allergies, bee stings, choking, fractures, lice, poisoning, vomiting, and dozens more. Learning how to deal with all this would be hard during the best of circumstances.

And then there is the role overload that often is part of health concerns. At one point, to ease the angst of my son's stomach flu, I wrote a poem to lighten my stress. Called "Midnight Madness," it reflects the divided heart of many mothers:

> Deep in slumber, you get the midnight call.
> "Mommy, I'm sick" in the next room he squalls.
> You leap out of bed, stub your toe in the hall.
>
> Put hand to his forehead, your darling is hot!
> He was fine at bedtime, now what has he got?
> Wonder about work tomorrow, is it shot?
>
> Swing to action, wake up, your agenda is set:
> Find thermometer, check for rash, has he thrown up, is he wet?
> Is it virus, is it earache, measles—maybe strep?…

The rhyme continues for eight more stanzas. I needed humor to mitigate the intense stress of such times. When it was published in a local parents' magazine, many other working mothers remarked, "I can relate!"

For years, the questions echoed in my brain: How on earth did you get to this point knowing so little about basic health care, about the body's most basic needs? How could you be such a numskull?

But in time I realized that my alienation from the body wasn't just a personal quirk. Rather, it is typical of our whole American society, which views the body as a "rent-a-car" for the brain. Its purpose is to look good, have good sex, and work hard with minimal maintenance. Most Americans know little about how to care for the body well—not even the basics of good nutrition and regular exercise. In the long range, this ignorance has led to epidemics of heart disease, high blood pressure, obesity, and other so-called "lifestyle diseases." In the short range, a great many mothers race to the doctor or emergency room whenever anything goes wrong. Often they are completely dependent on their doctors, knowing very little about preventive treatment or home care.

And ignorance is not limited to ordinary people, the so-called "consumers." It extends to most medical providers, too. After I decided to wise up about health, I started asking doctors questions: How can I prevent this problem from happening again? Could nutrition play a part? Is there a home remedy that would help?

Most often doctors (the specialists, even more than "primary care providers") dismissed my questions. A doctor would look at one set of symptoms with very little context and prescribe a drug. It was the old rent-a-car approach—fix the most urgent problem in the quickest way, with the least exchange of understanding between the doctor and myself. There was no concern with lasting health and well-being. No one wanted to inform or *empower me* as a health-care provider to my own family. I developed a growing dislike for doctors' arrogance and for their fragmented, disease-oriented approach to health. Most practiced a mechanical, soulless medicine that lacked true respect for the body. Bodies might just as well have been computers or car engines in need of repair.

An interest in holistic health grew out of my frustration. I turned to books and started to imagine another approach to the life of the body. I was delighted to discover, for example, Christiane Northrup, a holistic MD who's written the immensely popular *Women's Bodies, Women's Wisdom.* She encourages her patients to imagine a new approach to health: "What would it be like if you reclaimed the wisdom of your body and learned how to trust its messages? How would your life be different if your body were your friend and ally?...if you learned how to love and respect your body as though it were your own precious creation, as valuable as a beloved friend or child? How would you treat yourself differently? What would it be like to know, in the deepest part of you, that every part of your anatomy and each process of your female body contained wisdom and power?" (771).

At first I applied this approach to Gabe's health—trying to view his little body as a source of wisdom. Instead of asking, "How can I make this symptom go away?" I'd ask, "What is this telling us?" For example, when I noticed him rubbing his ear (often a sign of an ear infection), I treated him with echinacea, garlic, and rest, rather than calling my doctor for a prescription for antibiotics. As he grew old enough to understand, I taught him that his body was full of healing powers—he could trust himself. "Did you notice how quickly that cut healed up? As a kid your body is especially strong—it knows how to heal itself....If you take care of it, it will take care of you!" Gradually I learned more about nutrition, made sure we exercised and rested enough, and discovered home remedies that helped ward off problems—all to build on a basic respect for his body's innate goodness instead of a resorting to a "quick-fix" mentality.

This new respect started to spill over to my attitudes toward the rest of my life. Back during pregnancy, I was shaken by the feeling of my body being out of control. Now I started to see that yes, it was out of my complete control, but the body was governed by an underlying wisdom. This was especially obvious in Gabe's body as I watched for developmental milestones: sit up around six months, use a pincer grasp a few months later, run by age two. Even language and intellectual growth followed predictable paths: a toddler is likely to know fifty words at age two—and almost a thousand by three. For most children, these all unfold according to a predictable pattern.

As with pregnancy, all this happened without conscious input from me—all I had to do was provide a safe, healthy environment and his body did the rest! Like a scientist amazed at the orderly unfolding of a tree or a solar system, I was fascinated and comforted by Gabe's steady growth. Who would have imagined that the lowly "flesh"—the maligned human body—could be the source of so much pleasure? The focus of so much loving attention?

As I began to trust myself more, situations that would have once alarmed me started to bring comfort. During Gabe's early childhood, I recall many middle-of-the night vigils that began with his fussy cries waking me. I'd take him in my arms and rock and tend to his needs. And as I grew more skilled in tending ailments (like an ear infection or an upset stomach), there came the pleasure of helping him feel better and even a great sense of intimacy as the two of us sat up in the silence of the night. Sometimes I thought of Sister Miriam rising at 4 a.m. to pray the Liturgy of the Hours (her "matins") in the big silent chapel even as I sat in my rocking chair with Gabe, praying my own early morning prayers. We soaked up the same sweet, intimate presence of God.

Such moments helped me to grow into a deeper religious faith—a faith that esteems the human body. Not just the "body of Christ"—but the bodies of ordinary men, women, and children too.

Notes

1. In the past decade it has become socially acceptable in popular culture to portray the nude pregnant body. Lisa Rinna and Demi Moore, for example, received much publicity when their nude photographs appeared in national magazines (*Playboy* and *Vanity Fair*). Yet these photos were airbrushed and idealized; they were clearly presented in erotic poses intended to cater to male fantasies. In the course of researching this

chapter, I discovered that there is a lively interest on the Internet in "lactating porn" and "preggo porn"; some sites feature women suckling men or squirting breast milk at men. The photos are more realistic than those of Rinna and Moore (e.g., varied body types, swollen breasts, dark areola) and suggest a greater acceptance of the pregnant or lactating body. Still, these could hardly be considered evidence of respect or understanding of the female body. Rather, they are presented without dignity or empathy, strictly as objects of male sexual desire, in much the same way that other pornographic Web sites portray "fatty porn" or "oldie porn."

2. Only 29 percent of American infants are still breastfeeding at six months of age. By twelve months, the number falls to 16 percent. The Ohio Lactation Consultant Association is in favor of eliminating barriers to breastfeeding and of mandating third-party payment for breastfeeding support and services to give women a genuine choice regarding breastfeeding. In other words, instead of paying for infant formula, for example, the government would subsidize lactation support for low-income women; similarly, medical insurance would cover lactation support for insured patients. This would substantially reduce government spending on formula and medical care for infants with avoidable illnesses ("1995 Breastfeeding Facts for Ohio" factsheet).

3. For more explanation of "body wisdom," see Northrup's book, *Women's Bodies, Women's Wisdom* (1998 ed.), especially chapter 2 ("Feminine Intelligence") and chapter 3 ("Inner Guidance").

4. One woman I interviewed said that now, *thirty years* after the birth of her child, her husband still feels hurt by the fact that she completely tuned out his needs, including sexual needs, in favor of the needs of her three young children's needs. The priorities a woman chooses postpartum can have long-term implications, even for those whose marriages survive the crisis of children.

5

Composing Your Life
Spiritual Hunger and the Workplace

"So, motherhood suits you?" Miriam asked. It was an October afternoon under a radiant blue dome of sky. I'd stolen away for a weekend with Sister Miriam and we were sitting on a park bench on the convent grounds, watching little Gabe play nearby.

"I'm crazy about my kid, but more than once I've wondered if I'm cut out for this. I never dreamed it would be so hard to juggle everything— baby, job, marriage, groceries. There's not enough of me to go around."

"But you're such a good planner, and you've managed your responsibilities as long as I've known you." Sister Miriam was almost ninety now. Beside me, her shoulders looked as sturdy as ever beneath her black habit, but I knew her strength was failing. She had to lean on me to walk to this bench, and the fair skin of her face had a looseness that made her seem softer.

"It's not just that I'm busy," I explained. "I can't be in two places at once." I searched for words. How can I explain motherhood in terms a sheltered nun will understand?

"Like once when I first went back to work, Bill agreed to bring the baby to campus just before my night class. The plan was I would nurse Gabe and then teach my 7 o'clock class. But Bill ran late and didn't get there till class had started. Thirty students waited while I slunk off to breastfeed Gabe."

"What did you tell them?"

"Nothing—I was too embarrassed! My breasts were hard as rocks. When he finally nursed, my milk leaked all over my yellow silk blouse. I usually walk around my classroom, but I hid behind the podium all evening so they couldn't see the milk stains. I was so stressed!"

"I don't like to see you looking so tired." Miriam's voice was full of motherly concern.

"Most weeks I feel so closed in. No matter how well I plan, something goes haywire. Last week, I was heading into an important meeting when I got a call from Gabe's preschool saying he was running a fever. I had to drop everything to pick him up." I sounded like a fretful child. Stop whining, I told myself.

"Another time I was on my way home from work when I got caught in traffic. I ended up being ten minutes late getting Gabe. His school charges two bucks for every minute after closing!"

"Honey, God doesn't want you to be miserable." Miriam took my hand. "Your life is difficult right now. It's a chance for you to find an underlying freedom—to sink your roots a little deeper into God."

"Mommy, look!" Miriam and I both turned our attention to Gabe, who was chasing a red ball through the fallen leaves. In the distance behind him was the time-worn stone chapel and beside it a two-hundred-year-old oak, its bare branches stretching toward the boundless sky. Beyond the playing fields, the horizon was lined with scarlet maples and oaks turning gold. I feasted my eyes on the vista before us, and savored the soft warmth of Miriam's hand.

"Oh my, Gabe's discovered the old merry-go-round!" Miriam's face lit up. "Our pupils used to love that thing!"

I jumped to my feet and seconds later was holding Gabe secure on the metal merry-go-round. He squealed with pleasure as I raced beside him, making it whirl. For a moment I felt light and carefree, and wished we could spin off to never-never land.

Later, when Gabe was tucked in for the night, Sister Miriam urged me to open up. "I'm trying to understand why you're so unhappy, when you wanted this child for so long."

"I'm being torn in two! Lately my supervisor has been on my case because I'm not productive enough. He's given me a heavier teaching load this year, and everyone knows I'm falling behind!" Tears welled up in my eyes.

"I want Gabe to have a happy childhood, but how can he when his mother's a nervous wreck? He fights me when I strap him into his car seat. I look into that precious face and I want to screech: 'Sweetheart, I know just how you feel—strapped in—we're both trapped by a society with no room for kids!'" I groped for words. "It's not the *responsibility* of the baby that's weighing on me; it's caring for him while navigating a world so at odds with children. I had no idea how little people valued child rearing."

"Yet you can find some peace in this." Miriam spoke gently.

"I don't even like church anymore!"

"You've got to think of spirituality in a more expansive way. Sometimes it may seem like adding more things to your to-do list: Go to church, read the Bible, pray on your knees. But those are not the essence of faith. The essence is to know that God is always with you, always loving you. God loves every person in a limitless and unique way."

"How does that translate into real life?" I asked.

"It means cultivating attitudes of reverence and gratitude. Reverence means remembering that every person is important in God's eyes, and therefore is worthy of your full attention. You can train yourself to be fully present, to live 100 percent in the present moment. *Engagée* should be your password. It's a wonderful French word that means to be fully present to the Lord and thus to all his children."

"And where does gratitude come in? I don't feel very grateful," I pressed.

"Gratitude is a fundamental form of prayer." Miriam leaned toward me, speaking with conviction. "Even when you're miserable, look for small graces—the baby's smile, a nice person you meet, a sunny sky. God is surrounding you with love even on the most ordinary days. Prayers of thanksgiving will help you to recognize him."

As I looked into Miriam's kindly blue eyes, I felt as if I were gazing into the eyes of God—a well of tenderness. She was the one person who allowed me to be my *whole self*—mother, worker, wife, whiner, girl-at-heart. I didn't have to choose.

"I feel so torn," I whimpered.

"Perhaps you feel torn because you're trying to please everyone. But you *already* please God—just by being who you are. You are loved without measure. Staying connected to God isn't just a duty but a source of energy. Sink your roots into God in whatever humble way you can—and *that is enough.* Whether you're teaching a class or bathing your son, turn your heart to your Creator, *in that moment.* Ask for guidance, and you'll discover God's pleasure."

Work of Her Own

Not long after our visit with Sister Miriam, a book appeared in my mailbox: *Work of Her Own: How Women Create Success and Fulfillment off the Traditional Career Path* (1992) by Susan Wittig Albert. Inside was a note from an acquaintance from my parish: "Thought you might like this book."

The book studies the growing trend of women who are trying to "create whole, balanced, challenging, successful lives outside the world of all-consuming careers, commuting, and fifteen-hour days" (xxii). Albert interviewed eighty women who had left lucrative professional careers in favor of other kinds of work, including full-time mothering. Most had left jobs in corporations and other institutions in order to be self-employed, to stay home with their children, or to work for smaller, more flexible companies.

Many women of the Baby Boom generation find it easy to identify with the dilemma that Albert describes: Since the 1970s "a large group of women received something totally new in the history of human work…the opportunity to establish our citizenship in a part of our culture—the career culture—that had previously been closed to us" (238). For such women, "citizenship in the career culture" brought opportunities to develop our talents, to be singled out for recognition, and to earn financial rewards. Such opportunities were out of reach for most women in previous generations. As a result, many of us felt an exhilarating sense of *manifest destiny*—as if we were part of a feminist revolution, blazing trails that other women would follow.

And indeed, many women have followed. The *next* generation of women, Gen X-ers coming of age in the 1990s, accept as a given the idea that they will take their place in the career culture.

But all this advancement comes with costs that are often overlooked. Early one winter morning, I sat in my rocking chair and read Albert's personal story. She married young and had three children by age twenty-one. After five years at home, she realized she needed to do something different and decided to attend college. College led to graduate school, then to a fast-track academic career. By age forty-two Albert had been appointed the first female vice president at one of the fastest-growing universities in the United States and was on track for becoming a college president. "I had climbed hard and fast and loved the feeling of being accepted," she writes, "of being *chosen,* that marked each promotion" (xiv). During those years, Albert was able to climb "hard and fast" by working sixty- to seventy-hour weeks.

As I turned the pages, I wondered: "Who took care of her three kids? Did *her* breast milk leak onto her power suits? What happened when her meetings were interrupted by calls from her kids' school with news of ear infections?"

By her forties, Albert reached a point where work was no longer meaningful. Her children were in their twenties and busy with their own lives. She'd been divorced twice. She developed an assortment of physical ailments, including headaches and chronic insomnia. Early in her career, Albert had hoped to make her workplace more balanced and humane. Instead, she herself had changed to conform to "entrenched male values" such as rigid bureaucracy, mindless competition, and black-and-white decision-making styles. She writes, "I was lonely, with a deep disturbing loneliness that I could not bury even in work. I was empty, with no inner life, no spark of meaning to vitalize my actions" (xv). Hoping to regain her equilibrium and sort out her life, Albert asked for a year of unpaid leave, a highly unusual request for a university vice president.

Albert's book gave few details, so I tried to imagine her personal struggles. I too had been a star in graduate school, and later was thrilled to be working alongside talented, ambitious colleagues. I'd logged countless sixty-hour weeks, dragging home at 7 or 8 p.m. weeknights, and then returning to the office on weekends for more.

But now that I had a young child, my ambition was wavering. I thought of my son and husband, still asleep upstairs. I didn't want to wait till Gabe was twenty and my marriage had crumbled to "sort out my life."

The university where I worked prided itself on personal attention to students, yet there was little personal attention to *faculty*. Rather, personnel policies were organized around the needs of celibate male faculty of an earlier era; the university offered no day care, no provision for sick days or maternity leave, and no flexibility in career paths.

During her year off, Albert moved to a different city, improved her health, and, with the help of a therapist, tried to figure out how to restructure her life so she wouldn't feel enslaved to work. She fully expected to return to the university recharged and ready to slug it out again.

Instead, her life took a new direction. At the end of the year, she resigned from her job as a university vice president. Instead, she moved to the country to try to make her living as a writer. Albert reached this decision only after a great anguish, because she had devoted so much of herself to her career. When she handed the university president her resignation letter, he said, "I knew we were going to lose you, but I thought it would be to a presidency—not to...*this*" (xvii). "*This*" meant being a quitter, a dropout, someone who had let herself be defeated by a trivial discomfort with politics. Albert at first felt a sense of failure, "like a little girl with all Fs on her report card, playing hooky from school" (xvi). Hard as it was, she felt she had to make this choice. Her life was at stake.

I set Albert's book aside. It stirred such mixed feelings. On the one hand it validated my feelings of discontent with my career. On the other, it frustrated me. I was in no position to quit my job or to risk a major change. My family needed my income and my health insurance. Still, the seeds of change were being planted.

Practical Guidance

As I worked my way through Albert's book, I felt more hopeful, encouraged by Albert's many stories of real women who had reconfigured their lives in order to live by their own values. They had found more balanced lives, most through being self-employed or working for small companies. Among the successful career leavers were writers, lactation consultants, small-business owners, teachers, and others. Of the eighty women Albert interviewed, not all had succeeded in finding a "work of her own," but all had gained a new perspective on the satisfactions of work. I appreciated Albert's view that women today are "part of a new and very exciting trend…the process of choosing your own future" (xxii). I took notes in my journal on her guiding principles so I could refer back to them.

The first principle is to find work where you have a degree of control and choice. For Albert this meant becoming self-employed. For others it meant working for a small company or working as a consultant. The key is to have some choice over your schedule and your future career path—so you won't be forced into grueling hours, travel, relocation, or added responsibilities. In other words, you need the freedom to say no— or yes.

A second equally important principle is to rein in your spending. A conservative approach to spending and credit was essential to success "off the career path." Albert herself, in her year of leave, stopped relying on outside entertainment and restaurant meals; she even quit smoking and drinking. All the successful career leavers she interviewed made hard choices about cars, housing, travel, and other spending decisions. Conversely, the women who later returned to their old careers all blamed their failure on their inability to curb spending. Thrift is a key virtue. As I read, it also struck me that career leaving was more feasible for a person whose spouse had job benefits. Some workers were able to pay expenses by freelancing but couldn't afford health insurance.

Other principles include choosing a place to live that permits a simpler life. Choosing a spouse and friends who share your values and spending patterns. Holding to a firm sense of *why* you're choosing to leave your career. Albert emphasized that one must develop the trait of adaptability—a fluid and grounded definition of success. A career leaver must be able to design her life on her own terms and not let others dictate measures for success nor force her into gender stereotypes. In simpler terms, she must be a maverick, willing to think outside the box and not care if peers view her as a loser at times because she lacks outward status symbols. "The question of whether we can downscale our work depends almost entirely on whether we can downscale our appetites for the so-called good life," writes Albert. "It is an enormous challenge to live modestly in a culture that barrages us moment by moment with the message that *the only good living is high living,* bought with big dollars....*But it can be done*" (Albert 151–52, emphasis mine).

Although Albert is writing about professional women, women of all walks of life benefit from her insistence on redefining success. I've met many women who are at home with children or in noncareer jobs who feel inadequate because they aren't more ambitious. "I feel bad because I don't have a fancy job or education," remarked one woman. "My mother never felt like she had to be Superwoman to be successful, but there's so much emphasis on careers today. I feel like a big loser!" The pain over being a "loser" by society's standards runs very deep.

Work as a Spiritual Issue

Reading stories of Albert and the other women in her book, I was struck by the many ways that work is a *spiritual* issue. Many career leavers said they wanted to get away from the dishonesty, loneliness, spiritual starvation, and fear that they'd encountered in their careers. They longed for spiritual values like honesty, caring, generosity, and hope, and they were willing to make great changes to preserve integrity and an inner life.

Many women were motivated by a sense that they couldn't be honest, be themselves, in their professional work. Albert refers to a famous book, *Writing a Woman's Life,* in which scholar Carolyn Heilbrun explains how women of the past misrepresented their lives so as not to displease others. Even in their own autobiographies, extraordinary women (like Florence Nightingale and Jane Addams) sugarcoated their lives, downplaying both successes and hardships. "Well into the twentieth century, it continued to be impossible for women to admit...the claim of achievement, the admission of ambition, the recognition that accomplishment was neither luck nor the result of the efforts or generosity of others" (Heilbrun 24).

They didn't want to admit to "unladylike" traits like determination, ambition, and grit. Instead, they pretended their achievements came easily—the result of divine intervention, good luck, or others' help.

Superwoman Lives Happily Ever After?

In an ironic twist of fate, since the 1970s, the taboo has been directed against women admitting to *anything other than* determination, ambition, and grit. Albert observes, "Rarely do we hear of the physical cost of high-stress, high-powered competition; of the sacrifice of relationships; of the loss of the inner life" (Albert 158). When I read that sentence a vivid memory came back to me.

When Gabe was just a month old, I was scheduled to meet with a university vice president to negotiate a leave of absence. Our earlier agreement had been jettisoned by my medical complications. By the time he was born, I'd used all my medical leave but wasn't able to return to full-time teaching. That winter morning, I pulled my best power suit out of the closet—a jacket with big shoulder pads, a trim skirt, and shiny pumps. I hoped they would disguise my still stretched-out belly and swollen breasts. My only hope of securing a leave lay in my coming across as a tough, loyal professional. After a month of cooing over a baby, I stood in front of my bathroom mirror and practiced speaking with assertive confidence.

Then I drove through the snow to campus, left Gabe with a colleague there, and marched into the VP's office. I was a poised, determined professional on the outside, a torn-up, still-bleeding mother on the inside. The "front" helped me persuade him to let me keep my benefits and work part time, provided I promised to return full time the following semester.

Albert found that many women disliked such dishonesty. A former saleswoman regretted her false front, "My identity was based solely on my professional persona *du jour*. But being artificial, manipulating, charming, and phony take a great deal of energy, and I finally ran out of gas" (Albert 28). Others complained that, to succeed, they had to pretend to be a superwoman with no life outside work. Albert observes that for American women, the old Cinderella story has been replaced by a superwoman story, just as false: "Use your wit and resourcefulness to earn a marriage to the corporation, and live happily ever after" (158).

Moreover, too often the career culture is at odds with spiritual values such as caring, compassion, and kindness. For many, this can lead to a deep loneliness and sense of alienation in the workplace. Many career leavers said they felt cut off from people around them, especially other women. Albert summarizes the insights of author Margery D. Rosen: "The loneliness of the successful woman…is the product of many things: the frantic busyness of women who are doing too much, the divergence of our professional and personal lives, the loss of neighborhoods…and [the way] the career culture isolates us from other women" (Albert 31).

The women in Albert's study disliked not being able to be friends with women of other ranks, like secretaries, junior colleagues, or supervisors. Even among peers, many were unwilling to let down their guard, for fear of betrayal. Rosen's comments resonated with me. As a single working woman, I'd learned to cope with loneliness. I also assumed that with a new baby my friends would rally around. I couldn't have been more mistaken. After the initial flurry of baby showers, my close friends all disappeared back into their own overextended lives. They all had jobs, aging parents, and work-related travel. A few had children too. At work, I felt more isolated than before because I was trying to hide my double life.

As a single person, I'd cherished deep friendships. As a new mother, I was lonelier for friends than I'd ever been in my life. I loved my husband, but he was working long hours and couldn't understand the raw feelings of motherhood. This loneliness lasted for five years. Not till my son started public school did I begin to feel a part of the human family again!

A Starved Spirit

Many career leavers spoke of a starvation of spirit caused by conflicting commitments and a shortage of time. They felt their work prevented them from being generous, even with their own families. The conflict is especially intense for women with young children or other pressing family responsibilities. Many careers (especially those in traditionally male fields) make it virtually impossible to succeed at work and still be emotionally and physically available to children and spouse. A typical comment: "My work took more and more time and responsibility and left no time for family relationships. When I was on the job, I felt a pull to be with my little boy. But when I was home, I had a guilty conscience because I was neglecting my work" (Albert 30).

Then there's the exhaustion factor. When a person spends most of the day working outside the home, by evening she's running on empty. Little energy remains to attend to needs of home and family. Career women in Albert's study reported little time for personal friends or neighbors. A woman with three children and a demanding job said that by the end of her day she was too exhausted even to make a phone call: "By nine o'clock I'm catatonic....I just don't have time for women friends any more. It's a very lonely feeling" (Albert 31). At our house, it's a running joke that Mom always falls asleep on the first page of the bedtime story, while Gabe's still wide awake!

Career leavers in Albert's book also commented on the failure of the career culture to meet other important spiritual needs: for a sense of pride and integrity in one's work, for creativity, for an inner life, and for rest. A time shortage prevented women from finding outlets for these needs outside of work.

Such spiritual starvation can constrict a person's life. Having little free time or attention, she may develop a tunnel vision that makes her blind to the needs of the poor and to other social concerns. Volunteering, political awareness, and justice concerns all take a backseat to the demands of simply surviving in the career culture. If tunnel vision lasts for too long, it will distort her sense of reality and cripple her spirit. In our lives, for example, both Bill and I were aware of needs in our community, but it took jumping off the career track for us to be able to do anything about them.

Thomas Moore comments on the lack of time to process the psychic overload: "A common symptom of modern life is that there is no time...for letting the impressions of the soul sink in. Yet it is only when the world enters the heart that it can be made into soul. The vessel in which soulmaking takes place is an inner container, scooped out by reflection and wonder" (Moore, *Care of the Soul,* quoted in Kenison 32).

By the time I finished *Work of Her Own,* I was beginning to develop a clearer vision of the kind of life I wanted. Albert emphasized that a person needed enough imagination to envision an alternative to her current life. She needed at least a seed of a vision of how she wanted to change. Very gradually, Bill and I began to imagine another way of working. Though it would be several years before we could implement it, we started formulating our own vision of "right livelihood"—work "chosen thoughtfully, mindfully, with a full understanding of our needs, the needs of those we care for, the needs of the earth....[work which allows us to be] caring, compassionate citizens" (Albert 136).

Juggling Tasks vs Composing a Life

I was leafing through magazines one day at the library and noticed how many talked about women's lives in terms of juggling multiple tasks:

"Juggling Career and Motherhood," "How I Juggled Two Jobs, Four Kids, and Still Earned a Four-Point GPA," "You Can Cook Dinner and Make Sales Calls at the Same Time." Just reading the covers made me tired! Everyone assumes that to be successful, women—mothers especially—will be agile jugglers, able to take on many roles, tasks, and relationships and keep them all sailing smoothly through the air. A good mother can add more and more balls, never missing a beat. Or so the fantasy goes.

I came to loathe the term *juggling*. It's a damaging metaphor, suggesting tense and unrelenting busyness—a "frivolous trifling with what is most precious, and constant anxiety about dropping something, perhaps a baby" (Bateson, *Full Circles* 29). Juggling makes it seem that all priorities are of equal weight, as if running the vacuum is as important as rocking the baby.

A juggler is always reacting to outside forces, speeding up so she can juggle more and more balls. Juggling is a clownish performing art, not a way of life. It connotes a circus entertainer showing off a bizarre talent. It offers too little room for creativity, too little variety.

In *Full Circles,* anthropologist Mary Catherine Bateson offers a more fruitful metaphor. Each of us is *composing a life*—improvising like a musician or a painter. "The metaphor of composing suggests a search for distinctive ways of fitting diverse elements into a unity, combining the familiar with the new as artists work within their traditions and blend in materials from other cultures in novel ways" (Bateson 29–30).

Composing suggests more imagination on the part of the individual woman, as well as more choice. Rather than accepting every ball thrown her way, she *chooses* ones that will allow her to compose a life that suits her as well as others. Control shifts from outside forces to the woman herself and her "continuing search for both harmony and dynamic dissonance…unfolding through time" (Bateson 29–30).

I thought back to my college painting classes, where we learned to compose a still life, creating an arrangement that was both varied and harmonious—a bowl of fruit for color, a silver candlestick for light. I relished the freedom of composing a still life, then deciding how to paint it. Similarly, each mother can seek a harmonious blend of home life and other activities. For a woman like me with a child and stepchildren, the mix would be different than for a woman with six children, or another whose own mother lives with her. Just as a painter must operate with a limited palette, each of us composes with limited choices, but there is still room for creativity, for choice.

In contrast to juggling, the metaphor of composing allows more forgiveness and fluidity. It allows for variety, mistakes, and change over time. I think of Barbara, who focused her energies on her three children, then entered the paid workforce when they finished high school. Or Ginny, who cut back her law practice to part time so she could have more time at home; or Marymal, who chose to live apart from her children for a time while she found a sense of direction and trained for a job.

Bateson observes, "The stories our children need most to hear are not the stories of daunting success…but the repeatable stories of composing and improvisation in which adaptation is more central than dazzling accomplishment" (31). Flexibility, creativity, and a sense of inner direction all help women to "improvise."

A composition needs an underlying unity, but it also needs dynamic dissonance. In painting classes, I learned how to balance colors. In a landscape dominated by cool grays and green, for balance I might add a red shutter for contrast. So a mother might mix the traditional with the new, the predictable with the offbeat. I think of Zelda, who took up bodybuilding; and Betsy, who earned money as a clown in her spare time; or Patty, who found Buddhist meditation to be a lifeline. In each case, these mothers learned to manage a challenging set of circumstances by incorporating a bit of "dynamic dissonance"—that touch of color.

As I began to think of my future in terms of composing or improvisation, I welcomed the sense of playfulness, the freedom to experiment, and the openness to learn. Perhaps I could reinvent my life as an elegant little watercolor, instead of a wall-sized mural.

Sophia and Work

During this time I turned to the Bible for guidance. As I read the Wisdom books of the Old Testament, I was struck by how often the Spirit of Wisdom was linked to delight and joy. In Proverbs 8, Wisdom is described:

When [the Lord] established the heavens, I was there…
then I was beside him like a master worker;
and I was daily his delight, rejoicing before him always,
rejoicing in his inhabited world and delighting in the
human race.

(Proverbs 8:27, 30–31)

Reading about Sophia helped me to put my finger on the qualities that would be part of "work of my own." A sense of *delight* was central. I checked my dictionary for a clearer definition: great pleasure, gratification, joy, satisfaction. The word is related to *delicious* and *delectable,* and rooted in the Latin word *delectare,* "to entice or allure away."[1] Wisdom was enticing me down the best path: "On the heights, beside the way, at the crossroads she takes her stand;…[calling out] 'I love those who love me, and those who seek me diligently find me….For whoever finds me finds life…'" (Proverbs 8:2, 17, 35).

Another quality I yearned for was intimacy or at least a greater sense of connection and trust with other people. I wanted to let down my guard, to drop my front, to stop trying to prove myself. I was coming to see that the Superwoman was a false self, not the real me. The path of wisdom for me meant letting go of a Superwoman mask.

And then there's serenity or peace. I checked the dictionary again. *Serenity* means tranquility, peace, stillness, calm, composure—literally, to be composed. Serenity for me meant acceptance, an "OK-ness" with what is, with my life in its rough, unfinished, far-from-ideal state. I knew from experience that I could only reach "OK-ness" by trusting in a larger good-ness, a Higher Power leading me along the path of life.

In addition to trust and serenity, Sophia also promised true nourish-ment. The author of Proverbs describes her in terms that anticipate the eucharistic imagery of Christ: "'Come, eat of my bread and drink of the wine I have mixed. Lay aside immaturity, and live, and walk in the way of insight'" (Proverbs 9:5–6). Miriam had spoken of "finding God's pleas-ure." Now I was slowly gaining a sense of how that might translate into my harried life. I prayed that Sophia herself would show me the path.

"Through a Lens of Women Flourishing": Oars for the Journey

In time I discovered the metaphor of oars as a way to be mindful of my own priorities. In her book, *Experiencing God with your Children,* writer Kathy Coffey compares the spiritual life—our "exploration into God"—to launching a boat. That boat is propelled by the choices we make, and the oars that guide the boat are two powerful words: *Yes* and *No.* These two "oars for the boat" must be in balance or we'll veer off course. While it's important to say no (as any mother knows), it's equally important to say yes.

These two oars guide both personal and political choices. It's essen-tial, writes Coffey, for a family to be able to say no to danger and self-indul-gence, and "to a culture so geared to productivity that it hangs a dollar value on everything....No to corporate policies which run roughshod over families, requiring overtime and constant moves....No to government policies that jeopardize the health and education of our children" (97).

Coffey also writes about her yes's: "For starters, yes to compassion and the importance of parenting, to creativity, celebration, and rest..." (91). Yes to a grateful spirit. "On a spiritual plane, our gratitude to people can be enlarged into gratitude toward God, the source of all gifts [which can lead us to] a sense of profound well-being" (95).

Inspired by Coffey, I made a colorful ten-by-twelve-inch sign for my desk. I used colored markers to list core values that guide my choices:

"Compassion, creativity, celebration, rest...." I also listed my priorities for that year. Each season I recopy the list and customize it (yes to visiting the in-laws more, no to compulsive house cleaning...). Then, when I sit down at my desk to make out my daily to-do list, compose a shopping list, or balance the household budget, the sign is there in plain sight. My "oar list" helps me to live by my own priorities, not by the priorities blaring at me from advertisers and TV shows, and it's there on my desk visible to Gabe or anyone else who walks by.

Explaining the "oars for the boat," Coffey writes, "Every family will want to contribute their own yes's and no's, personalizing this list of priorities." I could imagine a mother helping a child make his personalized "oar list" of yes's and no's. Imagine how different the world might be if all of us could live by our considered values!

Notes

1. Similar to delight is the word *exuberance,* with its connotation of fertility, fruitfulness, and abundance. Its root is the Latin *uber,* meaning breast or fertile (Old English *uder* for udder; see *eudh,* p. 1515, *American Heritage Dictionary*).

6

Which Way to Go?
Decision Making and Prayer

By the next time I visited Sister Miriam, the path was growing clearer. "Miriam, I'm facing an important decision."

The two of us were sitting in "the Temple," the warehouse that housed her emergency food bank. She sat at a counter with a checklist, while I unpacked boxes filled with donations.

"What is it, dear?"

"I got a letter from a big shot at the university last week. I've been invited to apply for an important administrative job at the university and I wanted to talk it over." I went on to explain that such positions seldom opened up. To be invited to apply was an honor in itself, though I'd have to compete against others, of course. It would bring higher visibility, more money, more long-term options.

"Have you talked this over with God? Of course you have, you always do. You'd have a larger scope of influence as an administrator. You could help determine the direction of the college. A male institution like that could really benefit from your perspective." I sometimes forget that Miriam spent many years as a dean at Chatfield College, the college she'd begun on the convent grounds. "Perhaps God's opening a door for you, especially since it's come without you seeking it. I've sensed a restlessness in you. You've outgrown your job. What's your heart telling you?"

"When I was praying about it, I remembered a dream about my grandmother from the end of my pregnancy."

"It's been three years. I recall how afraid your doctors were that you'd lose your baby—or your life."

I pulled a notebook out of my bag. "I found my pregnancy journal. Can I read it to you?"

"Of course, dear." Framed by her black veil and wisps of white hair, Sister Miriam's face was full of tenderness.

I opened my notebook and began to read: "'I dreamed I was with my sister and her kids in Grandma K's playroom in the old frame house my grandparents once lived in. It was the original kitchen with wainscoting, tall cabinets, and a ten-foot ceiling. When a more modern kitchen was added on, it became a perfect playroom for all the cousins. Grandma's parakeet was in there, and old toys, and so many good hiding places. In the dream I wasn't a child but a grown woman, eight months pregnant. The mood of the playroom in my dream was cozy and fun.'" I looked up. Miriam was listening intently.

"It's a lovely scene, very consoling."

"There's more. 'In the dream I walk from the playroom into the adjoining kitchen where Grandma and my aunts are all sitting around the table. Grandma must see the worry in my face because she says, "Trudy, don't you worry about that baby. Everything's going to be all right! We'll help you! We're used to having plenty of little tykes around here!" My worries melted away.'" I paused to see if Miriam was still interested, then continued. "'Gram has been sick with Alzheimer's for many years, but in the dream her voice is good-humored and strong.'"

"Perhaps God sent that dream when you were in danger to assure you that everything would be fine." Sister Miriam's tone was thoughtful.

"*My thinking exactly.* And it turned out that everything *was* fine—at least in the short run. My placenta previa was healed, the birth went smoothly, and Gabe was healthy. The adjustment was smooth for both of us. Then I went back to work...."

"And you see a connection between this dream and this new position?" she asked.

"The dream captured all the things I associate with happiness," I explained. "The warmth and playfulness of living with kids. Loved ones nearby. All the female energy that flows among mothers and children and aunts. The playroom captures a different side of God—a playful, relaxed, and practical side. It's Sophia, really. That dream has become a touchstone for the kind of life I want. Even though my whole family is three hundred miles away and I feel fragmented so often, this dream gives me a vision of what I want." Sister Miriam understood that after a lifetime of calling God "he," I needed to name God "Sophia."

"And would this new position contribute to such a life?" Miriam's eyes searched mine.

"No, I don't think so. At least not now. If I want to be playful while Gabe is young, I can't be an administrator. With him just three and me a full-time teacher I don't have a lot of spare energy. The new position would mean being on campus every day, with lots of meetings. Part of me feels I should apply for this because it's a once-in-a-lifetime opportunity, but my heart wants to be with Gabe as much as I can."

Miriam was quick to reply, "Honey, as I've told you so many times, *no opportunity is once in a lifetime*. If God is inviting you to be an administrator, more chances will come. I thought you might be ready to be a dean. But perhaps your call is to give yourself more generously to your family and let the promotions wait. Perhaps your new path is the path to your grandmother's playroom."

"That's the way I was leaning, but I wanted to run it by you. I'm telling them I'm not interested in the job."

When I returned home from the visit I felt a sense of lightness and clarity. Without saying much, Miriam always seemed to hand my life back to me a little better than I'd imagined.

Two Competing Urgency Systems

Later I discovered a helpful line of thought in a book called *The Second Shift,* in which sociologist Arlie Hochschild explains that the pace of the workplace is inherently at odds with family life. For millennia, humans lived according to the sun and to the rhythms of the human body with its need for both rest and busyness. Only with the rise of industrialization did great masses of people begin to live by the clock, as more and more men took jobs in factories and offices.

Even so, until recently most women and children still toiled at home, at a more natural and flexible pace. Women have always worked, Hochschild points out, but at home women had some control over their schedules. Only in the last thirty years has working at a distance from home become the norm for the majority of middle-class American women. The result is that home is no longer protected from the values of the industrial workplace. "[I]n taking paid work outside the home, masses of women live in two competing urgency systems, two clashing rhythms of living, that of the family and that of the workplace" (239). It's not just that women are busier, Hochschild says, but that they navigate on a daily basis two different cultures that are fundamentally at odds, trying to reconcile personally two separate spheres that two hundred years of industrialization have torn apart.

In the career culture, time is measured and standardized and seems to move at a faster beat. The career culture is ruled by the clock, with time demarcated into schedules meant to measure productivity and commitment. Productivity, efficiency, status, material goods, and standardization are prized values.

The home culture, like preindustrial societies, is by necessity based on seasonal and biological cycles. That doesn't mean schedules are always leisurely, but they are more in touch with real human needs—rather than the needs of industry. The norm at home is "process time" in which tasks and human needs resist standardization. Throughout history, most humans have lived by process time, pacing their lives according to natural rhythms. They planted by the sun and moon; when their bodies grew weary or ill, they rested. In earlier centuries, humans had little need for precise clocks and calendars.

A problem arises because the career culture has come to seem more exciting and valuable than the home culture. That is, after all, where status, money, and opportunity seem to reside. So in recent decades, many have avoided the home and then have tried to impose the values of the career culture on family life. Parents feel pressured to have children on a fixed schedule, and some regard offspring as products to be judged by the larger world. As a result, there's pressure toward earlier schooling for children, for more lessons and organized sports. It sometimes seems that children are expected to begin working on their resumés in preschool, so that they will be ready to take their places in a competitive global marketplace.

And yet the career culture serves the needs of industry, not human beings. Not enough attention is paid to enduring human needs: needs for friendship, community life, leisure, creativity, comfort, rest, even delight. The career culture makes few allowances for inescapable realities like children's needs, illness, and love. As I reflected Hochschild's ideas, I saw a connection between the dominance of industrial values and the rise of social and psychological problems. Mental illness, addictions, divorce, and domestic violence are the scourges of our time.

Hochschild's book strengthened my resolve that the clock would not govern my home life. I grew determined that all of us would have time to enjoy one another as well as time to daydream and gaze at the clouds.

Sleeping with Bread

At a local rummage sale, I discovered a helpful book: *Sleeping with Bread: Holding What Gives You Life.* Written by Dennis and Sheila Linn, and Matthew Linn, SJ, it describes the time-honored tradition of daily *examen of conscience,* a practice established centuries ago by St. Ignatius of Loyola, now adapted by the Linns for families. The title is drawn from a story about World War II.

The authors explain that during the bombing raids in Europe, many children were without homes or food. Many refugee children were taken in by relief workers. But still, children could not sleep at night for fear of waking up hungry and alone. They could not be comforted, till someone came up with the idea of giving each child a piece of bread to hold at bedtime. It worked: they fell asleep knowing, "I ate today—I will eat tomorrow."

The authors use the metaphor of "sleeping with bread" to explain the *examen* in terms both adults and children can appreciate.[1] Used by Christians for over four centuries, it's a daily practice of spiritual reflection intended to help a person become more aware of the presence of God in her life. Before falling asleep, a person asks herself, "For what am I most grateful? For what am I least grateful?" The questions can take other forms such as:

- When did I give and receive the most love today?

- When did I give and receive the least love today?

- When did I feel the most alive today?

- When did I feel the most life draining out of me?

- When did I have the greatest sense of belonging to God, the universe, and myself?

- When did I have the least sense of belonging?

One may do this as part of evening prayers, speak this aloud to another person, or even list the impressions in a journal. I formed my own questions in Sophia terms: Where did I find delight, intimacy, and peace? Where were they most lacking? Where did I sense lightness and freedom? Heaviness and bondage?

According to the Linns, over time this practice becomes a powerful tool for creating a more satisfying life. Generally, God leads us to do more of those things that bring delight and peace, fewer of those that bring heaviness and dis-ease. "Sleeping with bread" can lead a person to a much fuller self-knowledge, which in turn can lead to a deeper sense of what many call "God's will for my life." By tuning out the noise (advertising, the media, others' expectations), a person can better hear her authentic self. From that deeper self, she can make big life choices (Should I marry this person? Switch jobs? Have another baby?) and smaller daily choices about priorities (Should I be on this committee? Take piano lessons? Sign my child up for this sport?).

"Sleeping with Bread" can be especially valuable for women. The only female of the three authors, Sheila Fabricant Linn observes, "The *examen* helps me to be who I am and not who others think I should be. As a child I was not encouraged to trust myself. I learned to feel ashamed of my needs and desires and to deny them in an effort to accommodate what others seemed to expect of me. The *examen* has helped me to learn to trust my needs and desires, as I watch the pattern of what brings me consolation and desolation" (13).

A girl is much more likely than a boy to grow up distrusting herself. Even if she reaches adulthood unscathed, motherhood will be a huge challenge to her sense of self. She will be bombarded with versions of motherhood that seek to force her into a mold. The Linns' approach offers an elegantly practical alternative. As a tired mother, I couldn't always summon the energy to read the Bible or pray at length at bedtime, but I *did* have time to ask myself, "Where did I feel most peace today? Where did I feel the least peace?" Over the course of weeks and months, I grew more aware of the Spirit of Wisdom in my life, noticing many moments that I might once have regarded as insignificant.

When Gabe started kindergarten, I found my favorite time of day was our walk to school. Most parents drove their kids, but I relished the chance to walk three blocks with my son, greeting other parents and kids. I might wave to fifth grader Alex cruising along on her roller blades, or compliment fourth grader Lyneisha on her elaborate new hairstyle, or stop to chat with my neighbor Sue, pushing plump baby Duncan in the stroller. This simple routine brought me so much pleasure that for several years I planned my daily schedule around our morning walk.

The daily *examen* also helped me make practical decisions. For example, I felt it was important to volunteer on behalf of my son's school, yet I dreaded making phone calls to request baked goods or chaperones. When I paid attention to how draining this was, I also noticed how much

I looked forward to volunteering in the classroom as a reading tutor. I decided to leave the phone calls to someone else and concentrate on what I really enjoyed.

"Sleeping with bread" *seems* too simple—of course anyone would want to do more of what she likes, less of what she loathes. Yet how many of us *live* that way? Our Puritan heritage pushes us to believe God prefers that we do those things we least desire, that suffering is better than delight, "no pain, no gain." Why else would we agree to the schedules we keep?

Used over many years, the *examen* helped me create space for simple but energizing habits like getting up early to relax over a cup of coffee with my spouse, watching the sun set from my kitchen window, or playing tetherball with my son.

"Sleeping with bread" for me has evolved into this form: "Today, did I enjoy the gifts God has given me? Did I love the people God has put in my life? Where did I miss out on loving or enjoying?"

Money, Time, and Laundry: Practical Changes

Women's magazines offer many articles on how to simplify your life or realign your priorities. For our family, the challenge wasn't figuring what to change so much as having the patience to make the changes very gradually. It's been a slow process.

We followed the advice from *Work of Her Own* (by Susan Wittig Albert) and chose, from the outset, to keep our expenses down and seek flexibility in our schedules. For the first seven years of our marriage, Bill paid child support for his older children. As they reached independence, we made a conscious effort to continue to live modestly. We were happy enough to drive older cars, live in a small house, and avoid the use of credit—all those old-fashioned practices advocated by earlier generations. We also made a deliberate choice to preserve flexibility in our schedules. I reduced my work travel to two weekends a year and limited my outside commitments on evenings and weekends so that we could share a nightly meal around a table. Bill limited the growth of his business so he could have more free time. We were also vigilant about how many outside activities Gabe took on. We wanted to provide him some enrichment but we didn't want every weekend tied up with soccer games and play dates.

These choices meant a lower income, which we were willing to accept, because the benefits were so valuable. These choices permitted Bill to become a more involved parent and citizen. Gradually, we began to approximate the coparenting ideal that I'd dreamed of since the beginning of our marriage.

The changes required creativity and patience. Bill had worked all his adult life (over thirty years) and was happy to work a more relaxed schedule. For me the biggest adjustment was facing the hard truth that I couldn't be the kind of person I wanted to be and still stay on the academic fast track. I'd entered my career out of a love for teaching and research, but somewhere along the line those motives were pushed aside by a desire for *recognition*. I wanted to be at *the front* of the pack, the best, the most productive—and be applauded.

But I'm not Superwoman. I often recall the words of Trisha, one of the women I interviewed: "Our identity isn't in what we accomplish or in how many degrees we can list after our name. Our identity is in God." For me that translates into: My true identity—my peace of mind—lies in staying connected to God, my own spirit, and my loved ones. Those connections are the keys to living a meaningful, satisfying life. It was a false pride that made me so driven to excel, to be so insatiable. Accepting my limitations has led to a growing sense of freedom.

At last I can echo the words of Susan Wittig Albert: "I have found right livelihood: work that is an expression of my truest, deepest self; work that not only affirms me but also confirms my care for others....As artisans, [we] take pride in our work, deriving our status from our competence [not outward accolades]....We also make time for other work that we feel good about....We love what we do and that love reveals itself in our healthier, happier lives" (xix–xx).

Notes

1. The term *examen* comes from a spiritual discipline articulated by St. Ignatius of Loyola in the sixteenth century, whereby a Christian took stock of daily consolation and desolation. This became a way of "discerning" the guidance of the Holy Spirit. St. Ignatius founded the Society of Jesus (the Jesuits), which has preserved the tradition of the daily examen. For a more thorough treatment of the *examen,* see *The Spiritual Exercises Reclaimed: Uncovering Liberating Possibilities for Women* by Katherine Dyckman et al. (Paulist Press, 2001). A secular version of the *examen* is available in *A Life of One's Own* by Marianne Milnor (Tarcher Press, 1981; originally published in 1934 under the pen name Joanna Field).

7

Sister Miriam Dies
Losing a Mentor

(Born Virginia Justine Thompson)
Born March 3, 1906. Died November 22, 1996
Seventy Years in Religion

The beginning of wisdom is this: Get wisdom, and whatever else you get, get insight.
Prize her highly, and…she will place on your head a fair garland;
she will bestow on you a beautiful crown. (Proverbs 4:7–9)

One June evening, while strolling downtown, I ran into a sister from Miriam's community.

"Have you heard from Sister Miriam? She's been failing," she explained. "Just this past week, she took a turn for the worse." Though Miriam regularly wrote to me, she never mentioned her health. I made a mental note to call her soon.

A few days later, Miriam's framed photo fell from my study wall. I hung it back up. The next day it fell again—a signal that Miriam wanted my attention.

I caught her by phone just after her dinner. After years of friendship, I knew her schedule as well as my own.

"Can I come tomorrow to visit? To spend the night? I think I can get away by myself."

"Yes, come. I'll reserve a room. I want to see you."

On the drive out I remembered a visit with Miriam a dozen years earlier. For Mother's Day, I'd brought her a prism, like one that hung in my window at home, scattering bits of rainbow across my study. It symbolized for me the many facets of God and the way the world was steeped in bright Mystery that we could only sometimes glimpse. Opening the gift, Miriam understood my thinking without me explaining. "I'll use it with retreatants! It's like the St. Teresa's diamond—an icon of God!" she said.

Since that long-ago May so much had happened to us both. My career as a professor had taken off, and I'd mailed her postcards from a dozen distant cities where I'd been invited to give talks. Miriam was proud of me—the daughter whose orbit reached far beyond her rural convent.

But she was ninety and failing now—what to expect? Would she be well enough to sit up? Even talk? I'd packed a Bible and a book of poetry. If she was too weak to talk, at least I could read to her.

Once again Miriam surprised me, opening the door of Brescia as soon as I rang the bell, her face alight. "Darling, I'm so glad you came! Sit down—you look tired. There's so much I've wanted to tell you."

After dinner we relaxed on the terrace and talked and laughed as the sun settled over the fields. The sunset was reflected in shades of peach and lavender on the glassy convent lake.

As usual, Miriam wanted to hear all about Gabe, my family, and friends—about what I'd been teaching and learning. She described an anthology of three biographies she'd just finished reading, the lives of three women mystics. I noticed she'd lost weight and her skin had taken on a pallor. Miriam's eyes were still alive with intelligence, and I noticed how sharp her hearing was as we quietly talked. Framed by soft white hair and her black veil, her face was animated and lovely.

She told me how happy she'd been lately, reading psalms of praise, and feeling so exhilarated, so aware of God's presence in her life, so grateful for the way God had used her.

"Sometimes you see old nuns whose faces look much younger than their years," she commented. "They've lived hard lives, and yet they've formed the habit of casting their cares on God. Every day they put all their concerns in God's hands, and their faces don't age the way you'd expect." This was the message she'd always given me: Faith in God was the bedrock. God would be faithful, no matter how trying the circumstances of life.

Cancer and Cats

All evening we kept returning to the subject of death. My forty-year-old brother-in-law had died recently from a heart attack. Many of the sisters in Miriam's community had passed on in the last few years; she told me about the deaths of Sisters Dorothy and Imelda, who both died at home, at Brescia. "They both went so bravely," she said, "as if they knew their work was done, and they were eager to return to God's arms."

"What about *your* health? You look like you're failing, Miriam. Do you know what the problem is?"

"The doctor thinks it might be cancer, or my heart. He wants to do exploratory surgery, but I'm too old for that! The surgery would be worse than what I have now. I've lived a full life. If God's calling me home, I don't want to prolong it."

Sensing that this might be our last time together, I told her once again how much I loved her, what a difference she'd made in my life: "Your love has made me who I am. I could never have gotten my PhD without you, never have persevered in trying to have a baby. No one has had as big an impact on my life as you have, Miriam."

"It was meant to happen this way," she responded. "You've been a daughter to me. This was how God meant to work."

As a crescent moon climbed the sky, Miriam told me a funny story about Father's pet cats. The local parish priest lived nearby and sometimes dined with the sisters. He had two pet cats, sweet white Autumn, his favorite, and a mischievous orange tabby named Pumpkinhead. Sister Miriam wrote notes to Father on behalf of Pumpkinhead, scolding him for pampering "that spoiled Autumn" and neglecting him; they were signed with a paw print. At ninety Miriam was still playful. We enjoyed the dusk settling over the convent grounds, even stayed up well past her nine o'clock bedtime to listen to the crickets. Like so many times before, beside Miriam, I sensed we were on holy ground.

Over the next months, I called to check on her. Cindy, who worked at Brescia, said she was continuing to fail. "I think she's going to die soon, and she'll go in some way that's very private, very quiet, maybe in her sleep. Sister's a tough lady. She's going to work right up to the very end—and go out with her boots on."

When I called in September, Cindy said Miriam was no longer strong enough to be up or to receive visitors. Only her Ursuline sisters were permitted in her room. I was disappointed, but I'd accepted long ago Miriam's strong need for privacy.

After I mailed a box of cookies, another sister wrote back, "I think Miriam will be slipping away to heaven soon." In November, I learned she'd finally been diagnosed with pancreatic cancer. But even in her final months, Miriam found meaning. Cindy quoted her: "I'm surprised at how much I feel God's presence. The terminally ill who end their own lives don't realize how much God can use their suffering, right to the end."

Mass of Resurrection:
We Return in Love What Is Given in Love

The final call came in late November—Miriam had died in her room at Brescia. The next week her mass of resurrection was celebrated in the big chapel on the convent grounds—the same chapel that had given her daily refuge since girlhood, the chapel where she had taught so many people to sing or to pray.

On the day of the mass, the elegant chapel was filled to overflowing. Rich and poor filled even the balcony, their faces soft with grief. Most of the crowd was somber, clad in black, but several people wore red; Miriam would have been delighted by those festive reminders that Christmas was approaching. There were farmers in denim jackets as well as civic leaders in black cashmere. Taking my place in the pew, I wondered if others felt as I did—privileged to celebrate the culmination of a life so fulfilled and rich, so improbable.

The gospel reading was Matthew 25:31–46, the perfect reading for the occasion: "'I was a stranger and you welcomed me, I was naked and you gave me clothing, I was sick and you took care of me, I was in prison and you visited me'" (Matthew 25:35b–37). I remembered that winter day many years ago when I first came to Miriam as a broken-hearted stranger and she welcomed me. How many other people here had been taken into Miriam's big heart?

After communion, Sister Joan took the pulpit, a nun in her sixties who'd been a protégé of Miriam's. She invited us to close our eyes for a moment. Then Joan said, "Now open your eyes and look around, at this beautiful chapel, the flowers, the stained-glass windows, the magnificent variety of people here. This was Miriam's greatest gift to us—the ability to see light, color, people, the variety of life—as all part of the Lord's love for us. She had a vast delight in music, literature, drama, cats....Sister Miriam splashed our lives with color. She taught us to see, to really *see*."

Joan went on to recount highlights of Miriam's seventy years as a nun. I could have listened all night as Joan described Miriam's belief in God's immense compassion, her great interest in the world around her right up to her last months, her whimsical sense of humor, her unstinting advocacy for women and the poor—"all woven together with a deep and pervasive sense of prayer."

Joan ended by saying, "Miriam's greatest gift was her re-creating love for all who came to her....She challenged us to develop our own gifts fully so that we can better spread God's joy and compassion to all people. She'll continue to help us until we join her."

"Pray for us now and at the hour of our death...."

After the mass, I walked across the grounds to the reception at Brescia. The November afternoon was clear and crisp, with a frosting of snow on the ground. The setting sun cast clear yellow light across the lake, lighting up the evergreens and the statue of Saint Ursula. The colors grew richer—the green of the old trees, the lavender and gray of the western sky, the red brick of Miriam's girlhood home in the distance.

What an improbable life she'd lived: Born in 1906, the oldest of eight, raised by a widowed mother, living her whole life in this obscure corner of rural Ohio. Who could have guessed Miriam would have made so many things happen, touched so many lives?

After the reception, I caught a ride with several sisters driving back to the city. During the hour's drive, we traded Miriam stories. How she'd taught one sister Gregorian chant, given someone else an outfit from her free store, tutored another in French, encouraged me to go to college. One sister told about Miriam's actual death.

That last morning, Cindy noticed how labored Miriam's breathing had grown, so she called in several of the sisters. Throughout the community's long history, most nuns had died in their own beds, surrounded by their sisters singing. Even though the sisters no longer lived monastically, Miriam had hoped to remain at her beloved Brescia.

By 8:15 several nuns and others gathered around Miriam. They sang song after song during the next half-hour, songs that she had taught them years ago when they were young nuns. After one less than perfect Ave Maria, someone joked, "We can do better than that! We can't send Miriam to heaven on a flat Hail Mary!"

Though not conscious, Miriam seemed to sense their presence, as one held her hand, and another stroked her hair. She died peacefully. "We prayed and sang and talked and laughed," she recalled, "all the things a person should do when a saint passes out of the world."

In the days that followed, I expected the weight of grief, but instead felt buoyant, as if a pair of hands were lifting me up, and would be lifting me for the rest of my life. For years afterward I savored Sister Joan's eulogy: "She splashed our lives with color....She'll continue to help us until we join her."

CLASHES

8

Betrayed by a School
Talk Back When Your Child Is Hurt

Women Are Awakening

According to Elizabeth Johnson, women today are experiencing an important spiritual awakening. It is as if we've been asleep for a very long time but are now waking up to our own "strength, giftedness, and responsibility." She sees this awakening as a true conversion, a turning, "a deeply religious event which is already bringing about new articulations of divine mystery" (65). For me, waking up to my mother-self was every bit as exhilarating as discovering a buried talent. My first year as a mother was a time of many discoveries. Gabe was a sunny and lively baby—getting to know him was a healing pleasure; his first several months, I felt we were both waking up to the world together. Little did I know but that year was only the first of many new awakenings.

Early on, a friend from church brought me a stack of *Mothering* magazines ("*The natural family living magazine,*" says the cover). As I read them, I discovered a vibrant American subculture dedicated to "attachment parenting." This approach embraced a range of appealing practices: extended breastfeeding, natural childbirth, holistic health, the family bed, and more. Already I'd begun to practice some of these. *Mothering* pointed me to books and companies that supported such "natural mothering." It validated a new me—the earth mother who had come to life when Gabe was born.

I enjoyed being at home so much that I stretched my leave of absence for nine months by teaching part time. I was happy to be at home, but the university needed me full time and my family needed my health insurance and income. So when fall semester rolled around, I returned to full-time teaching.

During the next few years I often felt as if I were a tightrope artist working without a net. Bill worked long hours, and much of free time was spent with his older children and elderly parents. This left me to shoulder responsibility for Gabe. I found a wonderful "home day care" with Pipin, and later with another mother. Yet I often felt as if we were living in a house of cards. If Gabe or his caregiver or his caregiver's kids fell sick, I scrambled to take time off from work. My in-laws were in their eighties and too old to help in an emergency. We had no other family nearby who could help, and all our friends worked full time. The world seemed a hostile, uncaring place. Like most "working mothers," I learned to live with anxiety always lurking at the door.

When Gabe turned three, I breathed a huge sigh of relief. He was old enough to start nursery school—ready for a bigger world than home. School offered more stimulation and friends for my only child, and it would also be more reliable than home day care. As for me, I was starved for female companionship. Surely, a good school would help us meet other caring parents!

The Flower School

Of the different nursery schools I visited, one promised to be perfect for Gabe. At the open house, I fell in love with it. The classrooms were painted in shades of pink and filled with objects from nature and with toys made from natural materials like wood and wool.

The "Flower School" endorsed a philosophy of education based on reverence for the individual child. They believed school should be as homelike and nurturing as possible, hence the cozy pastel classrooms and "natural" toys. Children learned to play the recorder and they designed their own textbooks. The school endorsed attachment parenting, holistic health, and the importance of family life. The school's philosophy was expressed in a book called *You Are Your Child's First Teacher* (by Rahima Baldwin), which emphasized that an attentive parent was the key to a child's well-being. The mother was the child's "first teacher" and the school built on that foundation. If the mother was nurturing, the child would be gentle and happy. This reasoning made sense.

I was also impressed by the small class sizes, the dedicated teachers, and the emphasis on art, nature, and story telling. Bill jokingly called it the "Flower-Child School" because many of the teachers wore the long hair, no make-up, and the ankle-length skirts he remembered from the 1960s counterculture.

We had to apply to the school almost a year in advance—proof that this was a selective school, and we were lucky to get Gabe in. For many months we all anticipated the day Gabe could start.

Indeed, his first year was full of happy surprises. Not only was it a loving environment for children, the Flower School also offered workshops for parents in story telling and holistic health, and it sponsored seasonal festivals such as Mayfaire, at which children actually danced around a Maypole! The parents were kindred spirits—La Leche League members, artists, massage therapists, and more. Many of the mothers had given up high-powered careers to stay home with their children. At long last we'd found a place that truly valued children and family life!

Something Is Wrong with Your Child

Naturally there were some difficulties. For weeks Gabe cried when I dropped him off in the morning, and all year he resisted naptime. Yet at the end of the year his teacher felt he had grown a great deal. She encouraged us to re-enroll him for a second year.

The second year, naptime became a source of conflict. Gabe refused to sleep. He defied Annie, the young attendant who supervised naps. On several occasions that second fall Annie called me at work to retrieve Gabe because she couldn't handle him. I tried to discuss the problem with Annie but she was never around when I picked Gabe up and she didn't return my calls. Another parent explained that Annie was new to the school—she was only twenty-four and had been a bartender in her previous job.

Later I learned that the school had a reputation for inflexibility. Midyear, the director of the school would call the parents of rambunctious boys and invite them to remove their children. One couple at a time, parents were told that their child was too restless or "lacked a peaceful spirit"—could they *please make other arrangements?* The mother cried, the father fumed, and the family slunk away quietly, embarrassed and alarmed. The child simply never returned to school after the holiday break.

All this was handled so quietly that only seasoned parents saw a pattern. One woman with two children in the school told me that her first grader was asked to leave midyear because he annoyed the other children. With just two weeks' notice, she transferred her son to a city school she would never have considered under normal circumstances. It struck me as ironic that pupils had to apply to the school a year in advance but could be summarily dismissed.

I knew none of this when Gabe's "nap trouble" began. I *did* know that the school had changed the staffing for its after-care program. Nursery school was held all morning, and during the afternoon a smaller group of children stayed on in after-care until parents got off work. The program was small and had faced constant staffing problems. The school endorsed "full-time parenting" and provided the after-care program reluctantly. Only a fraction of the parents used it.

One day in December I was chairing an important meeting at the university when an emergency message reached me. I needed to come right away.

Driving to the school I fumed. Why couldn't an adult control a four-year-old? Gabe weighed less than *forty pounds!* True, he was a high-energy child who didn't like naps but *Annie was the adult.* The school was run by early childhood professionals. If I could get Gabe to behave at home, *why couldn't they?*

By the time I arrived, I'd calmed down and so had Gabe. Annie had left for the day, so another attendant delivered Gabe to me.

The next day I called the school's director. We needed to talk, I said. It was impossible to keep leaving my work in the middle of the day—I had other responsibilities. I understood that Annie was new to her job, but surely the school could provide backup. The director set a time to meet with Bill and me the following week. She said she'd invite Gabe's teachers to join us.

The Team Meeting

It was an overcast winter afternoon when Bill and I reached the school at the appointed time. In the meeting room we found a large "team" that included Annie; his teacher, Miss Vicki; and two other teachers, as well as the director.

"Great," I thought. "With all these smart, caring people, we're sure to get to the bottom of this!"

The director began the meeting. "Before we can address Gabe's adjustment problems, we thought it would help to hear everyone's perspective. The school really wants to help Gabe, so we've all talked this over. Now if we could just go around the room and *share*."

Bill squeezed my hand. We were going to get Gabe on track!

Annie spoke first. "Gabe just won't settle down for his nap. He's having a negative effect on the other children. *He's bitten other children.*"

"He won't sit still during circle time. He moves around and interrupts."

"Other parents are complaining—they say their children are afraid to come to school. He's disruptive."

"Gabe is preoccupied with the dark side of life. He talks about monsters and aliens and killing bad guys. It's *very disturbing* to the other children."

"We think he needs more time at home. More one-on-one nurturing will make him feel more secure."

I probed. "Do you think he has a learning disability? Or maybe allergies, or ADD [attention deficit disorder]—some of his cousins have that. Do you have any suggestions?"

"We aren't psychologists," said one of the teachers. "But *something* is wrong. Gabe needs to be in a special place that's appropriate *for children like him....*"

By this time, I was numb with shock. The meeting was intended to find a solution, not to trash Gabe, but so far no one had offered any positive suggestions except to keep Gabe home. The child they were describing sounded like a hell raiser, not the lovable child we knew. A menace. A future delinquent.

I looked over at Annie, dumbfounded that she could paint such a violent portrait of Gabe. For a moment I imagined myself leaping across the room, yanking her long frizzy hair. How dare she gang up on us?

Instead I *composed* myself. "This is a lot to take in. We need time to think this over." I pointed out to them that Gabe was only away from home thirty hours a week—he was not a neglected child!

"It sounds as if you've already decided you don't want Gabe in the school," interjected Bill.

"We only want what's best for Gabe," the director insisted. "The children's well-being is *all that matters*. We're willing to give him a few more weeks and see if things improve. He can stay in the morning nursery school but not the after-care program."

"We've never encountered a child like Gabe before," Miss Vicki added. "We really think he needs more time at home."

Our "team meeting" took place on the last day before winter break. We had a few weeks to figure out our next step. I was a vat of emotions. Gabe seemed normal enough to me. He'd always been "a handful"— wasn't that natural for active little boys? Yet the teachers thought he was deeply troubled. Had we missed the signs of some deeper disturbance? I made phone calls and arranged a psychological evaluation of him in January, the soonest opening. I read a book about attention deficits, another about developmental delays. I called other parents from the Flower School and learned about other children who had been "asked to leave" in earlier years, but no success stories. My dreams were invaded by thoughts of *special education, institutions,* and *disruptive children.*

Meanwhile, we still needed child care during work hours. Even if Gabe remained in the school, someone would have to pick him up at lunchtime and care for him till one of us got off work.

With more forewarning, I might have made arrangements for another professor to take over my classes, but I was already in the thick of a busy school year. We couldn't afford a private nanny, and other preschools and day-care centers all had waiting lists. Even if they'd had openings, would they be willing to admit a *disruptive child*?

Stepford Moms

One night over the holidays, we watched a video of *The Stepford Wives*. First released in 1975 during the early women's movement, this classic thriller portrays a woman named Joanna (played by Katherine Ross) who moves with her family from New York City to a suburb named Stepford. Soon after they arrive, she notices something wrong with the other women in the town. All mothers, their only interest in life seems to be caring for their husbands and homes. They seem stilted and vacuous—with no personalities or minds of their own.

Meanwhile, Joanna's husband is invited to join the thriving Stepford Men's Association. He soon learns why the women of Stepford are so strange. The Men's Association is dedicated to improving their wives. One member has expertise in robotics and can make robots that so closely resemble their wives that not even their own children can tell the difference.

One by one, each wife is lured away to a mansion on the edge of town where she is killed, and then her body is discreetly disposed of. The person who returns home resembles the wife who left, except that she's become "perfect" according to her husband's specifications. She cooks what he wants, finds him fascinating, performs sexually, and never disagrees. The needs of children take a backseat to those of the husbands. The men all congratulate one another. No one in Stepford sees a problem except for Joanna and her scrappy friend Bobbie, another newcomer.

Then Bobbie goes away with her husband and a robot "Stepford wife" returns home enhanced by an uplift bra and eager to talk about spot removers. Now Joanna is frightened and alone.

One rainy evening, Joanna comes home and her husband says their children are gone for the night. Sick with worry, she searches the town and ends up in the mansion that houses the Stepford Men's Association. At first it seems empty except that inside she hears a child crying for her mother—her daughter's voice.

With mounting terror, Joanna follows the voice to a remote room. Too late she sees a large tape player and realizes that the voice is not coming from a living child at all—it's just a tape recording of her daughter. Just then a door locks behind her and Joanna realizes she's trapped. Soon afterward, viewers see an exact replica of Joanna—programmed to kill her.

As I watched the movie, a lightbulb lit up in my head. I too felt trapped. Gabe's teachers were convinced he was troubled because he didn't have enough time at home. As his mother, I was all-important *but I had no say in the matter.* I felt as though they were trying to manipulate me in order to make their own lives easier.

By now I'd spent four years as a working mother in the "mother zone." So far I'd managed to keep my family and myself more or less intact, despite many pressures. Bill and Gabe were my first priorities. My boss and colleagues wanted me to be the hardworking professional I'd always been. My in-laws and stepkids wanted me to put their needs first. The Flower School required baked goods and volunteer hours. So far I'd managed to keep my balance on the increasingly unsteady tightrope. I'd expended so much energy, and instead of getting better, things were getting worse.

Now the jig was up. I was falling. As I listened for my son's cries of frustration, guilt pushed me off balance. Fear followed on its heels. I could resist other pressures but not my hurting child.

Yet I strained to hear. *Was that Gabe's voice I heard crying out for me? Or was it the school's distorted version?*

Is There Anyone We Can Trust?

Over Christmas dinner I told Bob, my eighty-six-year-old father-in-law, about our problem. He was gruff, "There's nothing wrong with Gabriel. He has more push than most kids. The world needs push!"

Yet the school authorities had more experience, and they believed something was terribly wrong. Biting, disruptive behavior, and monster talk all pointed to a serious problem.

In January Gabe returned to the school but only lasted a week. When Miss Vicki phoned, we both agreed things just weren't working out.

Once he left, Gabe started acting out at home. He'd bite his forearm and say, "I hate myself—I wish I was dead" or "I wish I could burn down that school." He said he hated me. He drew pictures of space monsters with guns. He had tantrums in public places, alienating our friends and humiliating me.

Up till now, Gabe's behavior at home had been manageable—never alarming. But now I was alarmed—besieged by doubt and guilt. *I* was the one who'd chosen the school. I'd missed the signs of trouble. It was crazy to think I could nurture Gabe and hold down a job. I was an earth-mother-mold imposter and it was *my fault* that Gabe was such a misfit at school. Self-doubts multiplied.

The procedure for assessing attention problems requires teachers and parents to complete behavioral checklists, so Bill and I spent many hours filling out checklists, providing a thorough history, and ourselves taking standardized tests.[1] Annie and Miss Vicki also completed checklists. The psychologist spent only fifteen minutes with Gabe, basing her diagnosis on the paperwork. Her diagnosis: Gabe was definitely troubled and we were "in denial." His behavior was certifiably "atypical" and could be caused by a neurological defect, possibly ADD, Pervasive Developmental Delay, or Bipolar Disorder. My anger might be spreading to Gabe, she suggested. He was too young for medication or talk therapy, so the only recommendation was to "wait and see."

Another verdict—*and no help.* Now I wasn't even allowed to be angry, lest my anger "spread" to Gabe. I didn't *enjoy being angry,* but under the circumstances it was natural. I'd scrambled to piece together child care on short notice, I was neglecting my students, others were judging my mothering, and my child said he wanted to die! Now not just *my well-being* hung in the balance—*Gabe's future was at stake.*

I recalled a story in the local news. The mother of a first grader came into his classroom and slugged the teacher in full view of all the children. The TV newscasters were appalled—what kind of mother would do such a thing?

Now I knew the answer: a mother who's been pushed over the edge by an unresponsive school. Better to slug the teacher than the child. I started noticing stories in the newspaper about children who were beaten after a call home from the principal. School children had even been *killed* over such things. I wasn't in danger of hurting Gabe, but had nightmares about torching the school.

But I couldn't dwell on my anger; there was work to do. Over the next few months I maintained an outward calm, teaching my classes, coaching Gabe in the alphabet, visiting local kindergartens in hopes that he could attend the next fall. But I was aware of terror growling at the door. My confidence as a mother had been shattered. Was there anyone we could trust? What did the future hold for Gabe? We'd had such high hopes for the Flower School. If he couldn't handle a small, nurturing place, how would he ever fit in at a big mainstream school?

Sophia Speaks

One Sunday in late March a breakthrough came. It was a gray afternoon when I took Gabe to a meadow near our house for a hike. For weeks now I'd been praying for wisdom. What should we do to help Gabe?

As I hiked along the path I reviewed the ways God had been with me in the past. I'd survived a hurtful divorce when I was twenty-four, hard times in graduate school, a brother's mental illness. Each time I'd felt overwhelmed but somehow reached deep inside myself and found a center, a core of strength. Jesus—the Holy Spirit, Sophia—and I had pulled together. Together we'd always found a way through.

Nearby, five-year-old Gabe raced across the meadow. The weather was raw but he sang as as he ran, his blond head bobbing above the weeds. I'd never seen a child with so much energy, so much zest for life. He *was* a high-maintenance child. But his goodness far outweighed any flaws. I remembered how Sister Miriam used to say, "Comparisons are odious....Each life is a unique work of grace." Gabe wasn't like most children, but he was still a child of God. Sophia seemed to whisper, "Trust yourself. Trust Gabe. *I will help you.*" I returned from our hike with a lighter heart, with a new hope that a path would open up for us. Sophie would help Gabe heal.

For a long time, we searched for understanding. For over a year after the team meeting, Bill and I had grave doubts that Gabe could attend a normal school—ever have a normal life. During that bleak year, I often thought back to Kathleen, a spiritual director I'd met with for a time. Once she'd explained the idea of false guilt to me, "It's important to make a distinction between the voice of your upbringing and the voice of God. To hear the Spirit, you need to tune out other voices that may not be from God, like the voice of your parents, or of society. Guilt is appropriate when you've done something truly wrong, but often people feel guilty because they accept other people's rules."

Kathleen's comment helped me to see why the Flower School's pronouncements held so much power. My own mother had stayed home and placed great faith in the authority of teachers. From the cradle I'd been taught not to make waves or to challenge people "in charge." My mother had raised five children, and for all her mothering years she held to the belief that if she did her part by creating a loving home life, teachers would do theirs.

Now I could see that Mom's approach to schooling wouldn't work for us. I couldn't assume that teachers would look out for Gabe's best interests. I had to listen harder to hear the voice of God. Though her voice was quiet, Sophia seemed to be saying, "Trust yourself, don't guilt-trip yourself, trust me to guide you."

A younger me would have caved into guilt and depression, accepting the teachers' judgments. In my twenties, I thought "imitating Christ" meant deferring to others, even when it meant dismissing my own perceptions. Now I realized it meant listening harder—trying to hear the voice of Wisdom guiding me, helping me discern the best path. Sometimes I recalled Miriam's and my conversation about my "grandmother's playroom"—the image that had become a template for the kind of life I wanted.

Several weeks after that March hike, another Sophia moment occurred. Our house sits on a residential street that runs perpendicular to a major thoroughfare. At the junction of the two streets is the public elementary school. The school was one of several we were considering for fall.

As we drove down the street I could see the school two blocks ahead through the rain. As we approached, a bright rainbow suddenly appeared, arching over the building. The colors glowed so richly that we parked in the school lot. Both Gabe and I laughed aloud as we scrambled across the wet playing field behind the school, in search of the end of the rainbow.

Again I returned home with a lighter heart. I thought about the Old Testament account the rainbow sent to Noah as a sign that the flood was over and God would bless his family. It was a sign of hope. Surely our rainbow was a reminder that Sophia was looking after us. This school would be a good place for Gabe—his time there would be blessed.

From that day on, I made up my mind that the most important thing I could do was to regain my faith in Gabe and in myself. I needed to pay less attention to the outside authorities—more attention to the voice of God inside me.

"Though a Lens of Women Flourishing"

During the year of dread, one thing that kept me from falling apart was repeating affirmations. On several index cards, I printed phrases that I often recited. I offer them here to readers who may need coaching:

- The world needs all kind of mothers and kids, not just those who fit the mold.

- My son is a child of God and he will find his way. We are all children of God!

- Every mother is a working mother. Our work is vital to society's well-being.

- I am a caring, creative mom who is looking out for her child. Sophia helps me.

- My child has many talents that are still to be revealed.

- God, help me to be patient with my imperfect, "in process" life.

Notes

1. There is no actual medical test for ADD, which we suspected was Gabe's problem. Children are "diagnosed" strictly based on others' observations and by a psychologist interviewing parents. Once diagnosed with ADD, a child is usually treated through a combination of stimulant drugs like Ritalin (methylphenidate) and behavior-modification plans that involve tokens or behavior charts. Though these ways of treating ADD are often quite effective, they seem "unnatural" to those who favor a more intuitive approach. As we went through the evaluation process, it dawned on me that all these approaches were at odds with the holistic philosophy of the school; perhaps one reason they were eager to dismiss Gabe was to avoid compromising their purist philosophy.

9

The Illusion of the
All-Nurturing Mother

Countercultural Parenting

Writing about our experience several years later has provided me enough perspective to see ways that what happened to our family at the Flower School is a sort of microcosm of trends in our whole American society. In earlier eras, the larger society shared the responsibility of safely raising children to become stable, contributing adults. In contrast, our society sentimentalizes motherhood but often allows mothers no voice. It pays lip service to the needs of children and families but offers little practical support. The result is often "hothouse mothering," whereby most mothers function at home alone, lacking contacts with helpful or wise adults during their children's early, formative years. This isolates mothers and allows the larger society to abdicate their responsibilities to the next generation. As a result, a great many adults have virtually no exposure to or understanding of young children.

These mixed messages contribute to a vast number of misunderstandings and power plays between parents and various institutions. Dramas like our Flower School fiasco are played out in schools and day-care centers across the nation. When I interviewed women, many told stories about humiliating encounters with school authorities. Children with ADD, learning disabilities, or behavioral problems are most likely to run into trouble; rambunctious boys are also at risk. But I also heard "awful school" stories from parents of gifted children, hearing-impaired children, and other children with so-called special needs. Many mothers told of demoralizing team meetings that left them feeling castigated and helpless. Children get caught in the crossfire between parents and school authorities.

At the same time, over the past fifteen years, there has been a backlash against women, which has had an especially corrosive impact on mothers. Women who work outside the home are sometimes seen as negligent of their children, women who work at home are seen as nonproductive, and neither is accorded much respect for the demanding work of child rearing. Large, influential groups promote unrealistic ideals for American mothers, and many mothers hold one another to impossible standards. All the while, the media has focused on the "mommy wars" that pit so-called working mothers against stay-at-home moms.

Many women have responded by aligning themselves with several growing countercultures that have reacted against these trends, each in its own way. The natural childbirth movement, the "Moral Majority," the home-schooling movement, the advocates of attachment parenting, and others all reject the dominant culture and press for more "family-centered" values, though not always the *same* values.

The Flower School and other "natural" schools like it are part of this reaction against the larger culture. Because of its professed commitment to children and family life, the school enchanted me. Its commitment was genuine. The school was deeply committed to being "countercultural"— rejecting what they saw as a materialistic, soulless society. The passion of this commitment led to a "siege mentality," which caused them to react against anything that smacked of mainstream education. The school leaders were purists who believed in only a certain "natural" approach to parenting and education. With hindsight I see that when I began mentioning ADD, the school workers and leaders closed rank against me. ADD meant Ritalin and behavior modification, which fell far outside the school's value system. The Flower School embraced high ideals regarding natural childhood and wanted no part in *drugging a child* or *treating him like an animal in a Skinnerian lab!*

Later a social-worker friend told me that if I'd been *less* capable at home, or had been low-income, our pediatrician or a social worker would likely have referred our family to a social service agency for assessment of Gabe and "early intervention," which would have provided me with resources. It struck me as ironic that because I worked so hard to cope, we fell through the cracks.

Glimmers of Wisdom

In the meantime, we had to move forward and make decisions about Gabe's future. As we muddled through, several glimmers of wisdom led the way.

The first glimmer of wisdom was the realization that we as parents had to take the lead in our son's education. We couldn't assume that teachers or principals or anyone else could know what was best for our child. As his parents, we needed to know him best and to find ways to collaborate with others in his life, even to lead the way by educating teachers about his unique needs.

Deciding to be proactive led to a whole series of practical decisions: I immersed myself in publications about children with "special needs," and over the next years educated myself about learning styles, attention problems, child development, and "giftedness." I joined an advocacy group (the local ADD Council), where others coached me in how to make sure a school honors Gabe's legal right to an appropriate education. In time, Bill and I became avid classroom volunteers, willing to do whatever we could to help the teachers do their best (something we both came to enjoy greatly!). We used the phrases "We appreciate you!" and "How can we help?" as often as we could.

Within a year after leaving the Flower School Gabe was diagnosed with ADHD (attention deficit/hyperactivity disorder) and began to take medication during school hours, and his new teachers worked with us to set behavior and education goals. In first grade I pressed for him to be given a "504 Plan,"[1] a tailored education plan that allowed him to have special classroom accommodations (like added time for certain tasks, or a desk near his teacher).

The second glimmer of wisdom was my steady evolution into a different way of thinking about my mothering. Kathleen, my spiritual director, had helped me to trust my own instincts—to listen more to my own intuition and inner leadings and less to the voices of authorities. Prayer was an essential part of the process as I poured out my anger and fear to God and listened for the Spirit's "still small voice." I couldn't find wisdom by looking to a God "out there" somewhere. I needed to believe that God was alive within me, within Gabe, within our family life. This faith in an "inside god" helped me to pay close attention to Gabe's needs, and it empowered me to collaborate with the teachers in Gabe's new school. Eventually, this faith helped me to forgive those at the Flower School.

A third glimmer of wisdom involved naming our son. We insisted that Gabe have opportunities to do well and to be seen in light of his strengths, not just his shortcomings. American society has grown so impersonal and bureaucratic over recent decades that there's tremendous pressure to pigeonhole people, including children. Because of legislation meant to protect children with "special needs," such students must be labeled to receive services. Ironically, there is no similar movement in schools to identify students' special talents.[2] Parents must attune themselves to the whole child, and be alert to their child's talents and potential, not just his flaws. This requires *attentive and particular love*—viewing the child as a person, not a label. Just as parents name a child at birth, they continue to name him as he matures. Such naming should reflect the multifaceted, always gifted individual.

When Gabe was in first grade and I was still wondering if he could survive in school, he was identified as "gifted" in several areas and thus became eligible for enrichment at school. He benefited enormously from small "pull-out" classes with other bright children. Then when it came time for his first IQ tests in third grade, his scores weren't high enough for him to remain in the gifted program. Aware of how much he'd benefited, I assembled a portfolio of anecdotal evidence about Gabe's various strengths. At our yearly "504" meeting with the principal and teachers, I presented this information, insisting that the test had failed to assess the whole child. All present agreed that Gabe was indeed gifted and would remain in the program.

At home we tried to create a "judgment-free zone" where Gabe and other children were seen in terms of their strengths. This requires a level of awareness and restraint as we make a conscious effort to understand and appreciate all different kinds of people. We emphasize the importance of compassion toward others as well as toward ourselves.

As a result of these efforts, our son has steadily grown more confident and capable. By the end of third grade, Gabe tested well above the ninetieth percentile for a wide range of academic skills. Gabe's success was due in part to a principal with an open, "can-do" philosophy and to able teachers. I find great satisfaction in knowing that my attentive love has helped name his talents.

Over time, these three glimmers guided our path: being proactive, trusting an inner authority, and naming our child's gifts. These glimmers also changed many of my own assumptions about motherhood. I had to cast off some of the cultural baggage I'd unwittingly accepted. Although I reveled in being a natural "earth mother," I had to learn to let other parts of my personality take root as well.

The Many-Breasted Mother: A Treacherous Ideal

During what I regard as the "year of dread" that followed the Flower School fiasco, I came across a book by a Jungian counselor named Melissa West. Its title caught my eye—*If Only I Were a Better Mother.* The book describes her own spiritual journey of coming to terms with our cultural construct of the Perfect Mother, the ideal of the selfless person who is always loving, cheerful, and giving. West believes that this ideal is really a false self that we construct in order to "squeeze ourselves into the life-denying mold of motherhood we are given by our culture" (26).

For years feminist writers have written about the destructive potential of this ideal. They sketch her: She enjoys being around children—all children—all the time. Her love knows no bounds. Mothering comes naturally for her—it's instinctive. She can feed others without feeding herself. If she is good enough, her children will be good also and will never have to suffer. She never loses her temper, never collapses from exhaustion. In some incarnations, the Perfect Mother is also young, pretty, and slim. She's assumed to be heterosexual—or better yet, asexual. And she can do this all by herself—no one needs to help her!

Popular culture reinforces this ideal at every turn—in parenting books, on television, in novels and bad poetry, in movies, in greeting cards, in advertisements. The icon of the selfless Perfect Mother permeates our society so much that she's impossible to consciously *see* and yet impossible to miss.

A writer named Sue Monk Kidd calls the Perfect Mother by another name: "The Many-Breasted Mother." Kidd believes she shapes *all* women, not just mothers: "Women have been encouraged to embrace the all-nurturing (many-breasted) role of womanhood as the crown jewel in the female crown. And while mothering can be a deeply beautiful role, it can also become distorted by self-negation. The Many-Breasted Mother ends up caring for an array of children, including projects, needs, groups, and persons, that may not even belong at her breast" (*Dance* 54, parentheses hers).

In real life the Many-Breasted Mother can end up sucked dry, taken for granted, without a center. Kidd describes an image that illustrates these dangers: "An overwhelmed mother dog was nursing a small litter of newborn kittens along with her own brood of pups....The mother dog laid sprawled on her side overrun with mouths, some that naturally belonged to her and some that didn't" (54).

Kidd believes that the Many-Breasted role can cause us women to "forfeit our souls as food for others" (54). A human female who tries to live out the Many-Breasted ideal is in grave danger on many fronts. She is *all breast*—with no mouth, no hands, and no feet. She can't do anything but nurture. She's easily exploited by others who want her to give and give and give with no thought of reciprocation. She doesn't speak up or talk back. She is in danger of being sucked dry because she isn't fed herself.

The Great Mother

To grow into true personhood, a woman must see the limitations of this ideal. According to Melissa West, the first step is to realize that the Many-Breasted Mother is not a real person (not even a role model) but a manifestation of an archetype. She is a part of the image of the Great Mother that appears in many cultures and times around the world. According to West, cultures that embrace the Great Mother understand at a deep level that birth and death must always exist together. The Great Mother has many aspects, including an angry, even destructive, side. She represents both birth and death, both creation and destruction

As I read West's words, it seemed to me that the Many-Breasted Mother was in fact an aspect of God—a god who creates out of nothing, the burning bush that burns without being consumed, the bountiful breast that is never depleted. This image appeals to our infant selves who once yearned for the ever present, all-giving mother. She is the omniscient, godlike creature we may have imagined our own mothers to be when we were infants.

The problem, according to West, is that American culture (and Western culture generally) has split this image, embracing the Many-Breasted Mother and rejecting as evil other aspects of the Great Mother. We then impose a one-dimensional template of the Many-Breasted Mother on real women. The parts of ourselves that don't fit this template are relegated to our unconscious where they remain powerful despite the rejection. Thus mothers try to bury their anger, their sadness, their frustration, their sexuality, their restlessness, their fire. Even basic human needs—like the needs for self-determination or self-expression or sleep—are buried. They are often viewed as luxuries for mothers, something we should forfeit for the good of our families.

Even in a society like ours, which prizes materialism, superficial appearance, and violence, women (especially mothers) are expected to be Many-Breasted nurturers. Often this leads to a rigid perfectionism that causes mothers to hold themselves and one another to impossible standards. Many mothers set such high standards for themselves that they feel they're never good enough. They also can become harshly judgmental toward one another.

In a book about contemporary gender roles, journalist Peggy Orenstein describes a mother named Carrie who spends a great deal of time with her two preschool children yet feels guilty because she sometimes drifts off, feels exhausted, or loses patience. Carrie's impossible standards call to mind the teenage girls who, no matter what their weight, see themselves as fat. Orenstein observes, "I don't know whether there's a Perfect Mother equivalent to an eating disorder, but I wondered: How good does a mother have to be before she feels good enough?" (178).

An Alternative Is Possible

One of the main tasks that modern women face, in order to grow spiritually or to become whole, is to "differentiate ourselves from the powerful cultural expectations to be this Good [Many-Breasted] Mother and learn to reincorporate their darker side" (West 41). Orenstein puts it a little differently: Women must roll up their sleeves and "wrestle with their deepest convictions about motherly self-denial and identity" (287). Giving up this ideal "requires the courage to stand up to society's censure and a great deal of faith that an alternative is possible" (Orenstein 287). Yet to find this alternative, we need a great deal of imagination, the ability to step back and think critically, and practical help.

With time I came to see that Gabe had received plenty of nurturing from me. By the time he was forced out of the Flower School, he needed a more well-rounded mother: a scrappy, in-your-face mother who could go to bat with teachers and others too willing to pigeonhole him. As much as I had loved the Flower School (or at least what it pretended to be), there was more to education than their narrow "natural" philosophy. By temperament I was a nurturer, but there was more to me than breasts. I had fire in me too—a voice, a point of view, and a "darker" side.

For my part, I had to come to terms with my anger—the snarling, crouching tiger that the Flower School had unleashed.

Gabe also needed other adults in his life, better teachers—and his dad.

Notes

1. A "504 Plan" is a tailored educational plan for children with learning problems less serious than those that warrant an "IEP" (Individualized Education Plan). The title refers to legislation that made such plans available.

2. Except in the area of sports, in most schools it's easy for children's gifts to go unrecognized. For example, in many states there is no consistent funding to provide services for unusually gifted children. Yet there is a national mandate (and funding) to identify and provide services for children with "special needs." In this regard, schools operate somewhat like medical insurance companies that demand a documented diagnosis in order to provide coverage. It's a deficit, "fix-it" mentality, rather than a wellness mentality.

10

Taming the Tiger
Coming to Terms with Anger

Tyger! Tyger! Burning bright
In the forests of the night
What immortal hand or eye
Dare frame thy fearful symmetry?

"The Tyger," WILLIAM BLAKE, 1794

Recently PBS aired a special about a woman named Sally becoming a foster mother to a five-year-old girl named Logan. Sally had two biological sons but she'd always wanted a daughter. She was approved as a foster mother, Logan was placed in her home, and Sally soon began the process to adopt her. The special included film clips of Sally speaking with utter confidence about her mothering abilities. When asked by a social worker how she would handle a child who threw a temper tantrum, Sally replied, "I can't imagine any child of mine having an out-of-control tantrum! It would just never happen!"

Sally was proud of her sons and certain that she and her husband could successfully raise *any child*. After all, she was an experienced social worker with a long history of teaching other parents how to rear difficult children. On the screen, Sally came across as strong and competent, even smug. As I watched, she reminded me of other know-it-all mothers I knew.

Sally's attitude changed after several months with Logan. The little girl was charming but suffered from what psychologists call "attachment disorder." She had been torn from her biological mother and bounced from one foster home to another. As a result, she wasn't able to form a secure attachment to Sally. She'd be sweet one moment then whirl into an out-of-control tantrum the next. Without warning, she'd thrash and scream "I hate you!" at Sally.

"It's one thing to study books about defiant children, but another to live with one day in and day out," Sally observed ruefully. Still, she was sure she could handle Logan.

Even though years had passed since our demoralizing experience with the Flower School, Sally's comments stirred bitter memories. One time that year, we stopped to visit a new neighbor that I really wanted as a friend. When the visit was over, Gabe didn't want to leave and threw a tantrum right there in her basement. My neighbor was appalled that a five-year-old would behave so badly, and I was completely mortified. Gabe shouted, "No! I hate you! I won't leave!" while I wrestled him out to the car. I was so angry I could barely drive home.

Later I told Bill, "I can't take this any more! I've been knocking myself out and he's getting worse. Other people treat me like I'm total loser! I'm just not cut out for this!" He suggested that I take the week-end off. After a day away I began to calm down and even miss Gabe. Over time we figured out how to redirect his energy so that the tantrums subsided, but I never forgot the furious side of myself I saw that year.

Sally's story ended differently. One winter afternoon Logan flew into a rage. Sally later told the reporters that she put Logan in the basement and encouraged her to "scream it out" while she went upstairs to make dinner. When she checked on Logan later, she said Logan had hit her head hard enough to become unconscious. She was rushed to the hospital.

Afterward, when police investigated, the evidence suggested another story. It looked as if Sally had duct-taped Logan into a high chair and taped her mouth shut to silence her screams. Adhering to the yards of duct tape that police had found, there were thick strands of Logan's hair and pieces of her clothes. It was asphyxiation that caused her to fall unconscious, not a blow to the head. In any case, five-year-old Logan died.

Logan's death was a tragedy for *all* involved. Sally was given a long prison sentence for manslaughter and lost custody of her two sons. The whole community mourned the senseless death of a young child. How could this happen in the home of well-respected, upright citizens?

I was horrified by the story—but I could understand it. The ingredients for tragedy were there: A child who was acting out, a proud mother who'd tried everything she could and was frustrated and angry at the lack of progress, a snowstorm that had kept everyone inside too long, and the time of day—it was early evening, "arsenic hour," when dinner was being prepared and tempers were short. Logan threw a tantrum. Something in Sally snapped, and by the time she regained her composure it was too late. Sally never *intended* to hurt the child she truly loved, but her emotions had raged out of control.

Sally isn't alone in her anger with her child. Raising children is demanding. It requires hard physical work: the daily routines of feeding, bathing, clothing, and tending to hurts and illnesses. These tasks are relentless and tedious. Cleaning house, washing clothes, and keeping food on hand often go hand in hand with child care. And of course there are constant interruptions and chronic lack of sleep.

Just as taxing are the psychological demands. Children's emotions run toward extremes, and often the mother serves as a shock absorber. Think of the colicky baby who will not be comforted, the bickering siblings, the fourteen-year-old who constantly finds fault with Mom, the high schooler who stays out all night, and the trusted son who winds up stealing money for drugs. Dealing with all this requires stamina—physical, emotional, mental, and spiritual strength.

In an chapter 3, I outlined "the dangerous Ds"—disrespect, dependency, distractibility, and so forth—that make child rearing especially demanding in our culture. The physical and psychological demands of child rearing, combined with the dangerous Ds, make all mothers prone to anger. And yet our society teaches that *good mothers* don't get angry. The disconnect between mothers' natural emotions and society's expectations can make a woman even more vulnerable to anger, especially since she's likely to be ashamed of it.

Anger at its worst may drive mothers to child abuse or suicide. More often it goes underground and surfaces in the forms of depression, overeating, fatigue, and free-floating irritability.

Surely there must be another way. We must *create* other ways for mothers to respond to anger.

Wave Theory: Anger Flows from Love

As I thought about anger and other frightening emotions, I began to see that they were inescapable aspects of motherhood. Who could disagree that becoming a mother can unleash powerful emotions? Some we acknowledge readily—protectiveness, attentiveness, exhilaration, love, joy. But the so-called "positive" emotions are often matched in intensity by feelings that seem negative: rivalry with other mothers, exhaustion, fear, frustration, remorse, self-doubt, guilt, and, of course, anger.

Among women like me, raised in the Christian tradition, anger is especially scary. It can lead to broken relationships, fighting, and violence—even war. The Bible admonishes us to "Be angry but do not sin; do not let the sun go down on your anger, and do not make room for the devil" (Ephesians 4:26–27), and historically wrath is considered one of the seven deadly sins.

Yet I wanted to believe that anger didn't have to be a damaging force. Perhaps there was some *gift* in my anger, some potential for good—if only I could *harness* it. I needed to "reframe" my anger, find an interpretive framework that didn't see it as a poisonous sin.

I began to think of motherly emotions in terms of a wave. Basic laws of physics dictate that when a wave occurs, a peak will be matched by an equal trough. The greater the peak, the lower the trough. The distance between peak and trough is referred to as amplitude. I liked the dictionary definition of amplitude as "greatness of size, magnitude; fullness; breadth or range." But it would be a mistake to think of the peak as the opposite of the trough. Rather, both are expressions of the same force or energy moving through matter. A trough will inevitably give way to a peak, and the peak will give way to a trough, and so on as the wave runs its course. Rather than being opposites, they are different faces of the same energy.

Considering the wave metaphor, I realized that if a person reveled in the joys of motherhood, she also had to be ready for the more complicated emotions like anger. I wanted to be an *ample* mother, fully human, with a big heart and a supple spirit. It made sense, then, to expect amplitude in *all* directions. Anger wasn't the *opposite* of love; rather it was a different *manifestation* of love. I imagined my love for my family as a vast sea that was sometimes calm, sometimes stormy. Even though I preferred calm waters, I wanted to be able to ride the waves like an agile surfer— a surfer who didn't shy away from the big breakers, who could keep her balance without capsizing, no matter how large the wave or how deep the trough.

Dancing in the Dark: The "Dark Mother"

I discovered a fresh perspective on maternal anger in Melissa West's book, *If Only I Were a Better Mother.*[1] She uses the term "the Dark Mother" to describe the parts of herself that she represses and hides from the outside world: anger, grief, pain, fear, jealousy, loneliness, and more. The Dark Mother may embody our wounded-child self and the fears that haunt us as adults—fears of losing control, failure, embarrassment, the future. She may embody our sexuality and yearnings, too. All those traits we consider unworthy are funneled into the Dark Mother.

Most mothers stifle the presence of the Dark Mother in themselves, pretending she doesn't exist. By driving her underground, we turn her into a beast that threatens to bring devastation. According to West, the Dark Mother is dangerous precisely *because* we reject her. Inescapable parts of our humanity—emotions or drives that are inherently neither good nor bad—become monstrous because we deny their existence. Even if we manage to keep "the beast" under wraps, such repression may lead to numbness, depression, and resentment.

And we may project the Dark Mother onto other people—mothers of other races or cultures, or even the mother next door who mothers differently than we do. Too often we label them "bad mothers" and distance ourselves from them, or find ways to punish them. In Jungian terms, West explains, the Dark Mother is a manifestation of the shadow-self, all that we repress, reject, deny, dislike about ourselves.[2]

West connects the Dark Mother archetype with the dark-skinned mother-goddesses that exist in various world religions: The Black Madonna, Pele, Black Tara, and Kali. Describing her own spiritual journey, West focuses on Kali, a goddess in the Hindu pantheon who is both creator and destroyer. In Hindu art, Kali is portrayed with fierce eyes, four arms, and an undulating body. She represents "the vital principles of the visible universe—the active energy at the heart of the world…gracious, cruel, loving indifferent" (West 168).

Stories of Kali resonated with me, but the image that still held the most power was a tiger, a stalking, crouching tiger with fierce claws and fire in her eyes. It was easy to imagine my anger as a wild and dangerous beast, so great was her fierce passion. My first response was the desire to kill the tiger. In the aftermath of the Flower School, I couldn't simply destroy the tiger. The feelings were too powerful.

West explains that the shadow-self (the Dark Mother) need not be an enemy. When integrated in a conscious way, she can bring vitality, strength, and depth. The shadow can help a person "throw off the straitjacket of over-socialization" (Aron 217, 219).

I kept returning to my tiger. It was true that she was fierce and dangerous, but a tiger was also agile, beautiful, and purposeful. A tiger is a powerful hunter—not easy to kill.

At church one Sunday, I was surprised to hear the homilist say that ancient priests or shamans clothed themselves in the skins of animals as a way of asserting their connection to divine power.

I began to imagine that my anger might be an ally.

A New View of Holiness

During this time, a friend urged me to read an article by Mary Daly, "After the Death of God the Father: Women's Liberation and the Transformation of Christian Consciousness." First published in 1971, the article has become a theological classic.

Daly believes the traditional theory of Christian virtue is an effort to curb the behavioral excesses of men. Historically, Christianity has placed a great emphasis on the "passive virtues"—charity, meekness, obedience, humility, self-abnegation, sacrifice, and service. Men (at least privileged men) are prone to arrogance, self-centeredness, and pride, Daly says. For this reason, men need to consciously cultivate such virtues in order to grow spiritually. However, women have different spiritual needs. She says that passive virtues contribute to the exploitation of women under patriarchy. Women who try to be meek and obedient are likely to know their "place." A "bear-your-cross" spirituality keeps women stuck and quiet when they'd be better off active and outspoken.

Daly challenges women to articulate for ourselves a spirituality grounded in personal wholeness. Instead of accepting traditional views of holiness, she urges women (and men as well) to strive for wholeness: "By becoming whole persons, women can challenge the artificial polarization of human characteristics" into male and female traits. We can "develop a wider range of qualities and skills in [our] selves and thereby encourage men to engage in a comparably liberating procedure...and thus bring about a change in the fabric of human consciousness" (264).

I wasn't ready to discard the "passive virtues," but I began to see that they weren't enough. Women like me who have embraced the Christian tradition are, for example, too quick to embrace gentleness, service, and forgiveness. Those traits needed to be rounded out by virtues like confidence and courage. In my mind I began to develop a list of other virtues: compassion in action, holy boldness, a vision of justice, healthy pride, tenacity, generosity, and servant-leadership. It seemed to me that to thrive, women needed these—and humor and adaptability, as well.

During this time, I was teaching Gabe about the life of Jesus. As we read the gospel stories aloud, I noticed what a live wire Jesus was. At every turn, he was asking questions, challenging the status quo, pressing for justice. Rather than being selfless, Jesus exhibited a strong sense of self. He stole away to be alone at times, he said no, he held his ground in the face of religious leaders. We read about the young Jesus conversing with the elders in the temple, Jesus angrily overturning the tables of the temple moneylenders, Jesus befriending the reviled Samaritan woman, Jesus delivering the radical Sermon on the Mount. Far from being a passive sufferer, Jesus was what many call him: "a peasant with attitude." He questioned laws and attitudes; he put people first. He was so passionately committed to goodness and justice that he made trouble, lots of trouble.

How was it that through all the years of religious training I'd come to imagine Jesus as mild? The pictures in my childhood Bible all showed him as pale and sweet. On the crucifix he appears so broken. A strong emphasis on the death of Jesus had given me a distorted view. I needed to pay more attention to the *life* of Jesus. Sometimes imitating Christ might mean bearing my cross, but it could also mean standing up, having confidence in my own perceptions and values, and challenging the status quo.

Grappling with a Disability

A few years later, I secured a small grant to study memoirs by several different women who had raised children with disabilities, so-called "special needs" children. I found books by women who had successfully reared children with Down's syndrome, autism, ADD, and other brain-based disabilities. Every one of these mothers went through a period of intense anger. For most, this anger surfaced early on, and it took time for them to learn effective ways to channel it constructively.

There was Clara Claiborne Park, for example, whose daughter Jessy was autistic in the 1960s, when few medical experts had any idea of how to deal with such a condition.[3] When Park realized her toddler was not developing normally, she sought help from several doctors. They diagnosed Jessy with "childhood psychosis." They didn't listen to Park's concerns or insights. Instead, doctors suggested that *she* was responsible for her daughter's autism, since she'd had mixed feelings about her pregnancy with Jessy, her fourth child, an unplanned pregnancy. Doctors labeled Park, a quiet, reserved woman, as a "refrigerator mother." (Psychologists in the 1960s believed that parents who were undemonstrative, intellectual, or ambivalent caused autism, hence their term, "refrigerator parents.") Park pointed out that she had three older, well-adjusted children, but the doctors didn't listen to her. Instead of offering help, they encouraged Park to institutionalize Jessy for the rest of her life. They held no hope for her.

Park recoiled at the idea of Jessy spending her life "wailing in a back ward" of a state mental hospital, so she kept her at home. I was struck by the way that Park channeled her anger into determination and creativity. For years she and her husband searched out professionals who took their insights seriously and could offer true help. In the meantime, she and the rest of the family (her husband and three older children) found ways to help Jessy communicate and eventually learn to converse, read, and calculate—all things that the doctors felt were beyond her reach. By the time Jessy was school age, she displayed remarkable talents in math, so Park sought to enroll her in the local elementary school. The principal insisted that Jessy's supposed math talent was nothing but the fantasy of an over-ambitious mother who was blinded by love. He turned her away.

Again, Park was hurt and frustrated, but she persevered, finding many creative ways to help Jessy learn. For example, the family hired a succession of students from the university where Park taught. These "Jessy girls" were paid companions and tutors; they were able to help Jessy in ways that her family members couldn't.

Jessy, today in her forties, still suffers from her autism, but she has been able to live a remarkably productive and independent life. She's a talented painter whose income from her paintings augments her work in a post office. As she was teaching and coaching her daughter, Park kept careful observation notes that she eventually published in the form of articles and books. These have helped other parents and professionals find effective ways to work with autistic children and adults.[3]

In my study project, I discovered that most mothers of children with special needs went through periods of extreme grief and anger. Anger surfaced as they dealt with the initial diagnoses and continued to surface for years following as they encountered obstacles with neighbors, professionals, schools, and others who harshly judged both them and their children. Yet Park and others eventually found ways to channel their anger into effective action. Park searched till she found genuine helpers: a sensitive therapist, an insightful tutor, and a flexible job for Jessy. These mothers educated themselves, searched, networked, advocated, and, most of all, kept alive a rock-solid faith in their children *and themselves.* Even amidst great fear, anger, and mistreatment, they were able to ride the waves through hard times.

Through my study project, I also learned that over the centuries, mothers have been members of an important chorus of voices calling attention to issues of human rights. Activist mothers have led the way to better and more just treatment of people with disabilities, promoting, for example, more inclusive public education, better workplace policies, the "community living movement" for adults with mental illness or mental retardation, and more. They've formed powerful organizations such as ARC (formerly the Association for Retarded Citizens) and the National Alliance for the Mentally Ill (NAMI). Militant mothers have also fought for reforms in the fields of criminal justice, medicine, and social work.

Park describes how her love for Jessy forced her to grow. She refers to the mystic poet William Blake: "Parents can accomplish much through intelligent love. Despite what doctors believe, intelligence and love are not natural enemies. Nothing sharpens one's wits for the hints and shadows of another's thinking as…love that 'seeketh not itself to please, / Nor for itself hath any care, / But for another gives its ease, / And builds a Heaven in Hell's despair.' There are millions of parents who practice this love daily and know that love is a technique as well as an emotion" (*The Siege,* quoting Blake's "The Clod and the Pebble").

Although not overtly religious, many of the mothers with "special needs" children draw upon spiritual imagery. One writes, for example, "Until I had Jeremy, I didn't understand the expression 'child of God.' But now I do. I understand that God's alive in him....He has completed me—wrenched me in and out of myself...and elevated me so that I can stand up and see who he is and who I must somehow be, to be his mother" (Kephart 167).

What struck me most about these mothers was that they had met the tiger. Rather than running away, *they had embraced this beautiful beast.* They had gone through periods of intense grief, anguish, frustration, and anger. In the midst of despair they had found ways to press forward. Fueled by anger and love, they had learned ways to help their children and themselves live full, joyous lives. This was a very slow process, unfolding over months and years. Such mothers suffered self-doubts and setbacks, but they refused to give up faith in themselves and their children. They were not victims or martyrs; they actively insisted on help from others. In time their efforts paved the way for other parents.

I began to consider Park and other role models for the kind of mother I wanted to be—one who didn't shrink from infuriating circumstances, an *adult* who learned to befriend the tiger in herself—to let the tiger teach her.

Love's Wild Sister

Seeing how other mothers turned their anger to good made my own anger less frightening. Mary Daly observes, "Rage is not a stage. It is not something to be gotten over. It is a transformative, focusing force" (quoted in Johnson, *She Who Is,* 258). Jesus cleansing the temple is an example of righteous anger that is a healthy and positive response to injustice.

When a woman consciously acknowledges and learns to express anger productively, it becomes "a sharp, fresh power, a cleansing and renewing energy that opens new channels of commitment." Far from being a terrible sin, such anger can be an "excellent image of God's indignant power of wrath kindled by injustice" (*She Who Is* 258). She offers the image of God as furious as a mother bear deprived of her cubs: "I will fall upon them like a bear robbed of her cubs, and will tear open the covering of their heart; there I will devour them like a lion, as a wild animal would mangle them" (Hosea 13:8).

Sue Monk Kidd examines the connection between *rage* and *outrage:* Rage is an internalized emotion, an inner tempest that can turn to bitterness; outrage is rage that's been transfigured into a "creative force or energy that changes the conditions that created it." In other words, *rage* can be changed into *out-rage.* Kidd explains, "Outrage is love's wild and unacknowledged sister." Outrage jumps into the fray, and "grappl[es] with her life, reconfiguring it, struggling to find liberating ways of relating" (Kidd, *Dance* 187).

Just as rage can become outrage, it can also become courage, literally cour-rage. The words are linked. The root *cour* means "heart," so that courage actually means "rage of the heart." I thought of Richard-the-Lionhearted. Why not Trudelle-the-Tiger-Hearted?

Transfiguring Anger

As I sorted through all these ideas, I wrote in my journal, "One of the things I most want to give Gabe is access to his anger as a creative force. Instead of letting anger be wild and undirected, I want him to learn to use it well. Not to fear it but to use it—to protect himself and others from violation, to resolve conflict and not suppress it, to address injustice. How can I help him unless I learn to do this myself?"

I began to look around for religious symbols that made room for anger. In her best-selling novel, *The Secret Life of Bees,* Sue Monk Kidd writes about a family of three African American sisters who display a life-sized carving of Mary, "Our Lady of Chains," in their living room. Mary stands with a fist upraised and a red heart painted on her bosom.

One sister explains that they first found the carving washed up on a beach. "She's really just the figurehead off an old ship, but the people needed comfort and rescue, so when they looked at it, they saw Mary, so Mary took it over. Really, her spirit is everywhere…but sometimes it just will get concentrated in certain places and just beam out at you in a special way" (141). Mary has an upraised fist as well as a heart, suggesting both anger and tenderness existing together. Friends gather regularly to pray and "touch her heart, and find a little strength to go on," explains the sister.

The Process of Transfiguring Anger

For rage to become cour-rage and out-rage, it must be "transfigured" (Kidd's term). Sometimes this process happens spontaneously, but often it requires deliberate effort.

Physician Christiane Northrup suggests the following steps for learning from negative emotions: First, acknowledge what I am feeling without making any judgment about it; feel it *fully*. Next, acknowledge that there is a *reason* I am feeling this way, then spend time *identifying* what is causing the energy to flow negatively. Then (this is key) "ask myself what I do want….Asking myself what *I do* want shifts my focus back to positive thoughts and thus moves my energy toward my wants." Naming what I want leads to affirming that I have the power to pursue what I want (Northrup 64).

During the Flower School aftermath, many times I turned to my stained and earmarked copy of the classic book *The Dance of Anger* (1985). The author, psychologist Harriet Goldher Lerner, goes into much greater depth than Northrup. She believes that for a woman to change the way she processes anger, she must first change the way she thinks. As her thinking changes, her ways of behaving and her relationships also change.

I've coined my own mnemonic to practice her approach: FOIL— Feel, Observe, Improvise, Learn.

The first step is to fully feel and recognize the anger and accept that it has a legitimate cause. Not just "I feel bad" but "*I feel angry.*" Then try to figure out the best way to work with the feeling—take a time out, take a walk, punch a punching bag, or say something to the person who's causing the anger. Sometimes just getting away from the situation is the best response. It's best to have several strategies to choose from.

When I applied this step to my anger over the Flower School, I was better able to find a path through it. I was feeling angry, the most intense anger I'd felt in years. I also felt ashamed and publicly humiliated because all the other parents and teachers knew Gabe was being asked to leave the school.

The next step is to observe—to step back and *with a cool head* look at what is actually occurring. Instead of responding impulsively or out of habit, give yourself time to think about it. What's the source of the negative energy? Where is the energy flowing or being blocked? Lerner suggests asking questions like: What am I really angry about? What is the problem and whose problem is it? How can I sort out who is responsible for what? Is someone benefiting from this situation?

In my case, there were real reasons for these feelings: the harsh, mixed messages we received from the teachers, even as they insisted they had Gabe's best interests in mind. They seemed to be blaming me for Gabe's troubles and completely disregarding the fact that I had a job that was necessary for our survival, and thus needed child care.

The next step is to improvise. A part of this step is to figure out what you really want and what your choices are. Then look at the way you usually respond to anger. If that response isn't helpful, try something else. You might write a tactful note or try to talk directly. Another possibility is to change the situation causing your anger or to get away from it.

In the case of the Flower School, I wanted Gabe to learn and be happy in school. I wanted the peace of mind that he was in a safe place while I worked. I wanted good partnerships with his teachers. I wanted my own perceptions about Gabe to be respected. What choices did I have? I was unable to effectively channel my anger with the Flower School but in the coming years I was able to make choices about how to interact with subsequent teachers.

These questions continued to help in the long haul: What do I want? *What can I do to pursue my wants?* Find another school, find people I could trust to help us, hold on to faith in my child, myself, and God.

In the years that followed, I attended team meetings with the principal and teachers in Gabe's new school in the course of making accommodations for his special learning needs. I had learned my lesson. I never attended a meeting without a clear idea of what I wanted the outcome to be (subject to compromise, of course). I also always came prepared for the worst: aware of Gabe's legal rights, ready to stand up for him and myself, supplied with documentation of his needs. Prayer and meditation in advance helped me to keep a cool head. Subsequent meetings were effective.

Over the years this approach has become more natural for me, and I've found ways to use it with more far-reaching problems. For example, my university was notoriously lacking in family-friendly personnel policies. This lack made me so miserable that I made a pledge to press for better policies even after I no longer needed them. Because I was outspoken on this issue, my dean invited me to chair a committee to research the "work climate" in my college. This led to recommendations, including ones meant to improve the work environment for parents. For example, we suggested a "stop-the-clock" provision that would allow parents of young children to extend their probationary period (during which they are under pressure to "publish or perish" to earn tenure). Because most professors are in their thirties by the time they complete their education, many are in the position of earning tenure at the same time they are starting their families; this provision gives them the option of postponing tenure rather than postponing childbearing for another six years. This provision was eventually passed, so that it's now an option for all parents, male and female.

In the face of social problems, the FOIL approach can be helpful: Feel the anger; Observe the situation and your response; Improvise (by trying several different responses); and Learn (through reading, researching, working with others, experimenting with the institution). Even very entrenched institutions can change, but it takes pressure from thoughtful people to bring about structural change.

Practiced over years, this new approach to anger has changed my life both at home and at work. Before I spent a huge amount of energy trying to avoid conflict and keep the peace. Now I bring conflict out in the open where it's more likely to be resolved. My supervisor told a mutual acquaintance, "You can trust what Trudelle says. She puts things on the table!" Another colleague said, "You're tough!" For someone like me who's been a "people pleaser" all my life—I consider that highest praise! It's brought a huge sense of freedom!

Growing a New Backbone

As a result of all this wrestling with anger, I'm becoming a more complete version of myself. My anger is no longer frightening. Far from bringing devastation, it's grown into an inner ally—a huge Siberian tiger that can be brave, strong, steady, and wise. In C. S. Lewis's *Chronicles of Narnia,* Christ is portrayed as a powerful, gentle lion who promises to protect the four children who are the main characters. Riding Aslan's back as he soars over Narnia, the children feel free and safe. My tiger offers safety, too.

Unlike the old naïve me, she views the world with greater emotional intelligence: My tiger warily questions people's motives, she's vigilant where her kit is concerned, and she can pounce when necessary. This inner tiger has given me freedom and strength, as if I've grown a second backbone. She's always ready to protect and pursue.

Going Public

This courage was put to the test one day when a reporter approached me about a feature story she was doing on ADD for our city newspaper. Someone from a local advocacy group, the ADD Council, had given her my name as an informed parent. Could she interview me?

I agreed, assured that I would be one of several parents and doctors interviewed.

A few days after the interview, my phone rang. It was Sue, the reporter.

"Can I set a time for our photographer to come to your house? I got such good material in the interview that I want to focus the story on your family. Hopefully it'll run on the front page of the 'Tempo' section. When can our guy come by to take pictures of you and Gabe?"

I was caught off guard. It was one thing to be quoted along with others, another to be in the local limelight. The city paper had a circulation of over 500,000.

"Can I call you back with a time? I have to check with my family."

I hung up the phone. Sitting at my desk, I thought it over. Bill and I were still coming to terms with Gabe's diagnosis. I was keenly aware of all the judgment and controversy surrounding it. Many mothers and teachers use the term "ADD kid" interchangeably with "wild, rotten kid." Others dismiss ADD as a way of making excuses for troublemakers or of getting special treatment at school. Many parents view treatment with medications like Ritalin as a cop-out. Though medication had really helped Gabe, I was sheepish about admitting it.

Already we'd talked the news story over with Gabe. He liked the idea of his name being in the paper, but he was just a second grader and had no idea of the stigma attached to ADD. I was the one afraid of being judged. I could just imagine people at Gabe's former school saying, "She's drugging her child! Typical working mom!" Would everyone reading the paper label Gabe a bad kid and me a bad mother?

Then a paperweight on my desk caught my eye: a five-inch ceramic tiger that Gabe had made in school. It was lumpy and out of proportion but unmistakably a tiger. He'd painted it with swirling black stripes, and his art teacher had fired it with a yellow glaze. Gabe had given it to me for Mother's Day saying, "You and I really love tigers, Mom!"

We'd taught Gabe to speak up for what he believed in, to be true to himself and not worry about peer pressure. Should I hold back when I'd taught him to speak up? The fact was the ADD diagnosis had really *helped* Gabe. Because we'd intervened early, he was avoiding most of the school and social problems that plague children with ADD. I'd noticed other children in his school who were having problems most likely related to ADD or other Learning Disabilities, but no one had identified them. If parents didn't know the signals, the school wouldn't catch the problems till fourth grade or later. By then many children would be pigeonholed as troublemakers or dummies.

I thought, too, of Clara Claiborne Park. She'd hesitated to "go public" with her daughter's autism. Yet she had, and her books had helped thousands of families. Here was a chance to educate other parents who might help their kids avoid years of misery. Was I brave enough to step forward?

I picked up the phone and called the reporter back. "Tomorrow after school will be fine. How about four o'clock?"

The story ran a week later with the headline: "Addressing ADD at Home." It was accompanied by great close-up of Gabe reading on my lap in a rocker, and by sidebars on "Defining Attention Deficit Disorder" and "Focus on Practical Ideas." The reporter had pulled together a wealth of information. I valued her slant: "Supportive practices at home are just as important as therapy, counseling, and medicines...."

After the story appeared, I felt a great sense of relief. ADD didn't seem so terrible once it was out in the open. We certainly weren't alone in our struggles. A coworker commented to me, "It really took guts for you to be so open. That article will help a lot of kids!" People approached me to say that their children were struggling in school and that the article had shed light. "I loved the practical slant," said one. "There were so many concrete ideas that only a parent could give."

The Tiger Shirt

One evening a year later, Bill and Gabe came home from a shopping trip and Gabe proudly modeled his new purchase: A bright orange polyester sport shirt with a border of kelly-green palm trees. The shirt itself was covered with a dozen crouching tigers—an oriental design. My first thought was, "No child of mine is setting foot in public wearing that lurid shirt."

Instead I held my tongue. "He picked it out himself?"

Gabe strutted around the house. "I love this shirt, Mom. You know how I love tigers! This shirt gives me power!"

The orange "tiger shirt" became his favorite piece of clothing. He wore it as often as he could. Gabe was beside me at church the day the homilist spoke about ancient shamans clothing themselves in animal skins to claim divine power. Gabe whispered to me, "Just like my tiger shirt!"

Then one day I was sitting in on Gabe's classroom. I'd taken a day off work to visit and arrived before the third graders did. In walked Gabe, and for a minute I saw him through a stranger's eyes: a nine-year-old badly in need of a haircut, wearing a shabby orange-polyester shirt covered with grotesque tigers. My first thought was, What kind of mother would let a child dress like that? That poor neglected child!

A wave of embarrassment washed over me. The old me would have seized the first chance to burn that hideous shirt and haul Gabe to a barber.

But the impulse only lasted a minute. Instead I recognized that voice as coming from a false self, the wannabe Many-Breasted Mother who created her son in her own image. I mentally took a step back and looked at Gabe with soft eyes. Here was a youngster marching to a different drummer, obviously sure of himself. The children were working on a special project that day, a puppet show that involved an elaborate backdrop of a volcano and a brilliant red sky. Gabe worked easily with the other children, making many creative suggestions. His teacher winked at me across the room, impressed by Gabe's contributions. Perhaps Gabe was right in saying that his "tiger shirt" gave him power.

It was then I realized it wasn't just myself who had become a freer person. Gabe had become freer, too. My inner tiger had taught me to see more clearly. I was better able to pick my battles, to separate essence from appearance, to shun peer pressure from adults. I was more able to truly be myself—and in turn, *to let Gabe be himself.*

"Through a Lens of Women Flourishing"

The following is a summary of how a person can experiment with turning rage into outrage:

Feel: What am I feeling? What's causing this feeling? What desire is beneath the feeling?

Observe: What is the larger pattern that contributes to this feeling? What's the problem? Whose problem is it? Is someone benefiting from the situation? How do power relationships contribute to the problem?

Improvise: What do I want? Is my response to this emotion helping me get what I want? If not, what else can I try? What choices do I have? What are the costs and consequences of these various options? Should I act, wait, or try a different tack?

Learn: How do I normally handle anger (or other emotions)? How does my family handle it? How do other people around me respond to anger? Which responses are effective? What makes certain people become bullies or "bully magnets"? How can the cycle be broken? Are there resources that can help me learn about new options (books, articles, counselors)?

Notes

1. An excellent resource for learning more about the connection between unrealistic ideals and anger is the work of Polly Young-Eisendrath, *Women and Desire.* She sees a connection between the idealization of mothers and the tendency to turn a child into a little god or a demon.

2. I want to emphasize that this is a projection based in ignorance. Caucasians attribute traits that they dislike to dark-skinned persons. According to Andrew Hacker's *Two Nations: Separate, Unequal, and*

Hostile, blacks also unfairly attribute disliked traits to whites. Jung's view is different. He says that a person projects her own undesired, unconscious drives onto another. These drives are natural human *drives* (rather than traits) that in themselves are neither bad nor good. Such projection may lead to a false self that is a limiting version of the true self. For a provocative discussion of how false selves and projections can play out in the mother-child relationship, see Polly Eisendrath's work.

3. Another example is Beth Kephart, whose son Jeremy was diagnosed with "pervasive developmental delay," a catch-all diagnosis with no clear treatment. Kephart's memoir, *A Slant of Sun: One Child's Courage,* chronicles the steps she took to help her son overcome this condition. It also offers a frank account of her anger and determination.

11

"I Hate
The Giving Tree!"

"I don't like Mrs. Henderson. She read *The Giving Tree* to all the second graders and everyone loved it but me! It's a stupid book!"

Coming in the door from school, at age seven, Gabe was having a minor crisis of conscience, voicing an unpopular stand.

The next day I saw several children's themes posted in the school hallway. "I loved *The Giving Tree* because the tree gave everything for the boy," read one. On another, a second grader's scrawl declared, "My Mom is like the tree in the story." Gabe was the sole dissident. His paper read, "I hate *The Giving Tree* because she gives everything, then the boy chops her down."

Gabe's position didn't surprise me.

We had read Shel Silverstein's *The Giving Tree* aloud just a few months earlier. It's an immensely popular picture book that has stayed in print since 1960—even our small neighborhood library has *fourteen* well-worn copies! It's the story of a relationship between a little boy and a beloved apple tree. In the beginning, the tree and the boy have an intimate and joyful relationship. "And every day the boy would come and he would gather her leaves and make them into crowns and play king of the forest. He would climb up her trunk and swing from her branches and eat apples….And the boy loved the tree very much."

As the boy grows up his needs change. The tree gives him her apples to sell, later her branches to build a house, and eventually her trunk to make into a boat so he can sail away. In time, the boy returns as a tired old man when the tree has nothing left to give. She invites him to sit on her stump and rest, and "the tree was happy." Happiness comes to the tree long after she's given everything with no thought of return. Though the book portrays a relationship between a tree and a child, it's easy to see the parallel with a mother and child, or between God and humans. It's a book that makes most mothers' eyes get misty.

"That Stupid Giving Tree"

Even when we first read the book a few months earlier, Gabe was angered by the tree. "How could she do that to herself? She killed herself—she told him to chop her down! A stump can't live!"

"People like this book because it's about sharing," I explained. "The tree is so loving to the boy."

"But it's not about sharing—it's about the boy *using* the tree. He's disgusting!" retorted Gabe. "How could he be so mean? She was nice to him, and he chopped off her branches and then he went away for a long time. If he loved her, why did he use her up?"

Gabe's anger made me think further about a tension at the heart of raising children. Most of us mothers want to do what is best for our children, and at the same time we need to take reasonable care of ourselves. These seem like modest goals, yet we get little help from our society in combining them. Instead, much of our popular culture emphasizes the importance of parents, especially mothers, making sacrifices for their children. For Mother's Day, a local newspaper ran a set of stories by readers entitled "Why I Admire My Mother." A neighbor wrote, "My mother was always there for us when her six children were growing up—for every game, every school program, every late night. She never gave a thought to her own needs till she was in her fifties and all her children were grown with families of their own. Now that I'm a mom, I want to be just like her!"

Why would any woman *voluntarily* model that kind of behavior for her children? It sounded like a recipe for misery and resentment.

Love as Self-Sacrifice: The Dangers

One day, browsing in a Christian bookstore, I discovered a book called *Through the Eyes of Women: Insights for Pastoral Care,* a collection of theological essays edited by Jeanne Stevenson Moessner. I was intrigued by the heading across the book's bright red cover: *The Handbook of Womencare.* I'd read several books on child care but "women care"—was a whole new concept for me!

The essay I found most challenging—most provocative—was called "Love Understood as Self-Sacrifice and Self-Denial: What Does It Do to Women?" Written by a woman named Brita Gill-Austern, a former pastor now a professor of "pastoral care and practical theology," the book provides an alternative to the Giving Tree model for love.

Reverend Gill-Austern writes that "self-sacrifice can be an essential element of authentic, faithful love—the self-fulfilling self-transcendence to which Jesus calls us" (315). Yet she makes a distinction between conscious, *freely chosen* self-giving and the enforced self-sacrifice that Western society imposes on most women, especially mothers. She argues that the equation of love with self-sacrifice is contrary to the aim of true Christian love and is "dangerous to women's psychological, spiritual, and physical health" (304).

Gill-Austern lays out a long list of ways that an overemphasis on self-sacrifice can damage women. First, self-sacrifice can damage a woman's sense of self. By focusing wholly on the needs of other people, she can lose touch with her own needs and desires. Especially if she hasn't yet achieved a strong sense of identity as a mature adult, it's easy to damage her sense of self and to lose her own voice. She may mistrust her perceptions and fail to stick up for herself or even speak up for others (like her children). The loss of self and voice makes a woman vulnerable to exploitation and domination by other people, be it her spouse, her employer, her children—anyone!

When I talked this essay over with Jenn, my research assistant, she was quick to make the connection between self-sacrifice and domestic violence. She interned at a women's crisis center. "Lots of the women who come in to the center truly believe they deserve to suffer, especially the religious ones. They figure 'Jesus suffered for love, so should I'—even when it means a guy's slapping them around or hurting their kids. They just don't have the backbone to stick up for themselves."

Gill-Austern further notes that not only can self-sacrifice damage a woman's soul and psyche, it can actually damage the very relationships she wants to nurture. Self-sacrifice frequently causes a woman to overfunction on behalf of others and underfunction on behalf of herself (what psychologists call *codependency*). "The underlying purpose of such [self-sacrificing] behavior is to do, to care, to be for others, but for the purpose of winning approval, affection, and help," she explains (312). Such overfunctioning can cause the other person to feel incompetent and dependent, leading to resentment and guilt. The woman herself may end up feeling cheated if her self-sacrifice fails to achieve the desired result. Rather than fostering deep mutual relationships, self-sacrifice can undermine them. I think, for example of a man whose doting mother is now elderly and lives in a distant city. "I can't stand to be around my mother anymore," Stan remarked. "She's always guilt-tripping me—wants me to come home more often and look after her. She has no sense of how important my work is!"

Self-sacrifice can also contribute to unnecessary stress and strain within the woman herself. Gill-Austern observes that many women today are trying to be superwomen who seek to play conflicting roles as caretakers and breadwinners, without the systemic supports that could make it possible. One needn't look far to find women who are holding down jobs while tending to children, husbands, aging parents, and sometimes even grandchildren. Women at home with children are also prone to take on more than they can manage; I know, for example, one mother of three children under five who ferries them to frequent play dates, volunteers for her church, orchestrates elaborate birthday parties, and wonders why she's perpetually frazzled.

Many women today exhaust themselves doing as much as they can for their kids, extended families, bosses, and communities, and *still* feel they aren't giving enough. It's as if they lack a sense of their human limitations; they are often out of touch with their own needs and capabilities.

Such overfunctioning can undermine a woman and her family because it prevents her from practicing wise discernment. Instead of sorting out what is essential from what is secondary, she tries to "do it all." Overfunctioning also shortchanges the larger society. Until a woman is able to step back and acknowledge that she's attempting an impossible task, she cannot think critically about her own circumstances, and thus she's hobbled in her ability to improve her life. She keeps asking, "Am I giving enough? Trying hard enough?" when more appropriate questions might be "What's most important?" or "How can I get the help I need?" or "How does society (or my family or my workplace) need to change?"

In an earlier chapter, I wrote about Clara Claiborne Park, whose daughter Jessy developed autism in early childhood. In the 1960s when Park sought to enroll Jessy in elementary school, she was told that public schools had nothing to offer Jessy; indeed, such children "could not be educated."

Instead of accepting no for an answer, Park learned to be an advocate for Jessy. She worked with her a great deal at home and also found creative ways to enlist the help of others. Eventually Jessy was able to enroll in school and as a result learned and developed more than anyone ever expected. Park is an example of a mother who loved her daughter deeply but was able to see the limits of self-sacrifice. She was able to step back from her situation, think critically and creatively, and enlist the help of others.

In addition to shortchanging children, misguided self-sacrifice can harm a woman physically. Gill-Austern sees a connection between stress and strain and a myriad of physical ills including "digestive problems, allergies, high blood pressure, strokes, nervous tics, insomnia, and sheer exhaustion" (313). (I add to this list: depression, overeating, obesity, anxiety, loss of physical stamina due to lack of exercise, smoking, substance abuse.)

Buried Talents

To me, the most disturbing concern on Gill-Austern's list is her observation, "Love understood as self-sacrifice can lead women to abdicate their public responsibility to use their God-given gifts on behalf of the greater community and for the common good" (313). A self-sacrificing woman may fail to acknowledge or develop her own talents. In trying to care for others, in always putting her family first, a woman may sabotage the much-needed talents that would make her a better person not just for her family but also for the whole of society.

Sometimes self-sacrifice is inescapable; think for example, of the mother who works a second job to pay for a child's eyeglasses. But other times such self-sacrifice becomes a way of relating that is no longer beneficial to the giver or the receiver; for example, there's the mother who works overtime (or skimps on her own medical care) to pay for a teenager's new car or tropical vacation. Or the divorced mom who fails to set aside money for her own retirement in order to buy expensive gifts for her children and grandchildren. Then there's the "soccer mom" who spends all her time chauffeuring her children to lessons and sports events, but would never think of taking a lesson or participating in a sport herself. She wants to give her children every opportunity so she overlooks her own God-given talents and needs. Yet a mother who attends to her own health and talents sends a powerful message to her children: Adulthood is something to look forward to because learning and growth never stop. She communicates a strong respect for the personhood of all people.

Barbara Kerr has written a classic book, *Smart Girls, Gifted Women,* which documents the chronic underachievement of women once considered "gifted girls." Kerr reports on long-term studies that tracked gifted children from high school through adult life. Boys identified in high school as exceptionally gifted were found to be likely to complete advanced degrees, become leaders in their career fields, and achieve superior earning power. Gifted young women, on the other hand, went on to become adults who set aside career ambitions, failed to complete their education, and achieved only modest earning power.

In most cases, underachievement was directly linked to motherhood; women were unable to find ways to combine motherhood and professional accomplishment, *even when they had small families and worked for twenty or more years after the children left home.* Kerr's study is flawed, I believe, because she limited her definition of success to things that could be easily measured (degrees, earning power) and didn't consider the contributions women made through "gifted" mothering and volunteer work. Still, Kerr's book makes a compelling case against society's tendency to waste women's gifts. "It's a national tragedy that a mere handful of gifted women have attained eminence while the remainder accept obscurity," writes Kerr. "How long can society continue to squander the brilliance of gifted women?…[T]hey owe the world more than their cheerfulness, compliance, and children" (Kerr 119).

Trees Planted by Streams of Water

One day, reading my Bible, I noticed a passage in Psalm 1 that I had highlighted long ago. It's describing "the blessed man" but it could apply to a woman as well:

> [The blessed ones'] delight is in the law of the Lord,
> And on his law they meditate day and night.
> They are like trees planted by streams of water
> Which yield their fruit in its season, and their leaves do not
>   wither.
> In all that they do, they prosper.
>
> (Psalm 1:2–3)

I loved the metaphor of the "trees planted by streams of water"—there was
~ntion of chopping off branches. The blessed person is the one who
law of God and thus "yields fruit in due season" and *prospers.*

As I reflect on this passage, three things stand out. First, it is essential that I sink my roots into God—whether prayer, meditation, Bible study, or other spiritual practices. An inner life is not a luxury than can be put off till after the kids are grown; it is a necessity *now*. Second, I need to take personal responsibility for my own growth. I can't assume it will happen automatically, or that someone else (priest, pastor, mate?) will look out for my well-being. I have to choose to "meditate on God," to sink my roots, to make sure I am planted near "streams of water." Third, I must intelligently reflect on spiritual teaching. Like the persons who "meditate day and night" on God's law, I have to think and act. I can't delegate my thinking, questions, and intentions to someone else.

This might involve questions like: How does a text or teaching apply to my life? What is God saying to me through *my life circumstances,* as well as through Scripture and tradition? Am I listening to the Spirit with an open mind? Where is the lack of freedom? More specifically, in regard to self-giving, I can ask: What does it mean for *me personally* to be planted by streams of water? How much can I give *without losing myself?* How might our family life be different if we looked for ways that *all of us* could prosper? Are we considering *all* the possibilities?

Such questions will lead to different ways of thinking about resources and decision making in the home. In the midst of all this, I need to be patient, realizing that individuals, like trees, live through seasons: I will "yield [my] fruit *in its season*" (emphasis mine). But it's not enough to simply be patient—to be blessed, I also have to sink my roots, take responsibility, and think with intention to act.

A woman I know well embodies the prospering spirit described in Psalm 1. Sunny married at eighteen and birthed three children. Always conscientious and hardworking, as a young mother Sunny made up her mind to be a Giving Tree who did all she could for her husband and children. As the years passed, her husband grew more and more self-centered and Sunny became chronically depressed. When her oldest son was fifteen, he developed an alcohol problem that led to delinquent behavior and contributed to a series of crises with the younger children as well. These forced Sunny to rethink her priorities.

In the midst of crises, Sunny eventually discovered Al Anon, a support group founded to help families of alcoholics. The group fostered a spiritual rebirth in Sunny: "My new friends in Al Anon taught and lived the Golden Rule and real inner spiritual truths. I learned not to be afraid and that *I was a valuable individual* and that *God truly loved me and didn't want me to be unhappy.* I learned that other people's mistakes weren't my fault!"

Fifteen years have passed since Sunny joined Al Anon, and in that time her life has undergone a stunning transformation. She has come to terms with her son's alcoholism. As she recounted to me the changes of fifteen years, I was struck by how much she resembled the "prospering tree" in Psalm 1. She sank her roots into God by "working the Al Anon program"—today she still takes time for daily spiritual reading and meditation. She takes personal responsibility for her own well-being and has come to see the limitation of her influence on her children (although she remains close to them). She makes it a priority to reflect intelligently on spiritual teachings and on her own life circumstances. In her younger years, she uncritically accepted the teachings of pastors or others, but now she thinks things through and respects her own questions and doubts, whether in regard to Al Anon or her religious beliefs.

Today Sunny's "prospering spirit" of self-care causes a vital energy to flow out from her to others, including her three children and seven grandchildren. A recent letter captures this vitality: "My emphasis is always on health when talking about my regimen of exercise and healthy eating—not on improving my looks. I want to be around for my grandchildren as a vibrant and active part of their lives. To indulge in an American diet and not exercise is, to me, a form of being selfish. Because someone then has to take care of you when you get old and sick and debilitated due to ill health that could have been avoided....I'm planning a fiftieth birthday bash and telling everyone how excited I am about being alive!"

It's hard to believe that this letter is from the same person who was a depressed young mother for so many years!

12

In Search of Mutuality
A New Pattern for Relating

A Falling Out with Sister Miriam

As I was pondering the difference between *The Giving Tree* and the tree in Psalm 1, I found myself recalling a conversation with Sister Miriam that took place years earlier. One chilly autumn evening I called her in desperation.

"Sister Miriam, I need your help." I'd already written her about my first tenure track teaching job, and about a thrilling new love—how smart and funny and sexy he was.

"What's wrong?" Miriam's kind voice helped me picture her in the bright kitchen at Brescia. Surely Miriam held the key to serenity.

"I feel like I'm sinking in quicksand. I just started this job six weeks ago, and it's a *huge challenge*. Then two weeks in, Tom told me he's not sure about our relationship....I feel I'm going under. I can't sleep at night and..." As I sat on the edge of my bed in my chilly city apartment, the words tumbled out.

"But Tom sounded like a solid man," Miriam replied.

"I've let myself fall hard for him. He felt the same way till he started having second thoughts. Now his old girlfriend's flying in for the weekend."

"Let me make sure I understand," Miriam said evenly. "Tom wants you to sit by and wait to see what happens between the two of them?" I held my breath, waiting for her soothing words. "And he delivered this news just after you started your new job?"

"He says he cares for me but—"

"He has no business treating you this way," she cut in. "He's making the two of you compete for his precious affection. Tell him not to darken your door."

"But I love him!"

"Trudy, you're placing too much importance on Tom, and his behavior is totally self-centered. The world is much bigger than what you see now."

"You don't understand!" I began to blurt out all the reasons I loved Tom. Miriam would hear nothing of it.

"I've got to go now." I slammed the receiver and sobbed. How could Miriam let me down?

She didn't know what the hell she was talking about, I fumed. She'd never been in a soul-shaking, flutter-in-your belly, can't-see-straight relationship with a man. *What did she know about love?*

In the weeks that followed I fumed at myself for expecting an old nun to understand my yearning for Tom. But she was more than a mentor, she was a second mother who'd coached me through many ups and downs. I decided that if Miriam wouldn't console me, I'd console myself. As the months went by, I gradually dug out of my depression and rallied on my job. An older friend remarked, "The fear of loneliness brings more damage than loneliness itself"—an insight I pondered for a long time.

Not until the following summer could I imagine a future without Tom, perhaps without any man. It felt like a tremendous relief to stop struggling to mold myself to another's needs, like casting off a too-tight swimsuit.

From time to time I found myself wanting to tell Miriam about my vacation trip to Montreal or an interesting new student, but I didn't make time to call. We'd never gone so long without contact. Perhaps our friendship had simply run its course—we lived in two different worlds, after all.

Then came the news that Sister Miriam's best friend had died. It frightened me to realize that my mentor herself might die, estranged from me.

I called Brescia to arrange a visit, hoping that we could pick up the threads of our friendship. During the hour's drive out, I reviewed the past year. I'd made a clean break from Tom. Miriam had a point—the further I'd gotten from Tom the better I'd felt. Yet there was much she did *not* understand. I needed to stand up to her, speak my mind. But what if I couldn't find the right words? What if she scolded me or turned away?

Sister Miriam greeted me at the door with her usual hospitality. Once we settled into two chairs, I summoned my courage. "In the past year I've come to some new insights." I shifted uneasily in my seat. "You shouldn't have been so hard on me last fall. There was a lot at stake with Tom. You and I are two different people and sometimes you just can't understand." I paused, waiting for Miriam to defend herself.

"Yes, dear, go on."

"I need to find my own way, even when it means not following in your footsteps." I glanced up at her. "My desire for a partner and children is just as valuable as my dream to be a great teacher. That's how God made me."

"Honey, I've always known that. I have far too much respect for your integrity to question a decision that comes from your heart."

"There's more to say," I continued. "You've had a huge influence on my life. *Enormous!* I've admired you so much that a part of me has always believed I didn't deserve to be friends with such a saint. I wanted to be like you—you've done so much! But we are different."

"Heavens, Trudy, I'm not a saint. You've been a joy in my old age."

"I need you to accept my dreams even when they aren't yours," I insisted.

Miriam chose her words carefully. "It's hard for me to see you hurting. But I will hold back on advice unless you ask for it." She took my hands in hers. "Now tell me about your classes—."

I'd expected more resistance, but Sister Miriam was ready to try this new footing. Soon we fell into our familiar habit of conversation and laughter, as we brought each other up to date.

A few years later Sister Agatha greeted me: "Miriam looks forward to seeing you because she can let her guard down. Everyone else puts her on a pedestal." Agatha's remark made me realize how much the balance of power had changed. The conversation when I stood up to her had ushered in the most satisfying stage of our friendship yet.

I pictured my bond with Miriam like a teeter-totter that had reached a balancing point. For so long she'd been my cherished mother figure. That bond had reached completion, and then given way to something new—when the adult child is ready at last for friendship with the parent. It was like waking up to realize I was a *grownup,* no longer a child, as if I stood up tall. I would never be Miriam's peer—she was nearly fifty years older. But I could be a mature younger sister—a comfort, a source of stimulation and fun—*a friend.*

This change brought a new depth to our friendship for our remaining seven years together, till she died. I came to regard standing up to Sister Miriam as a turning point. Miriam began to confide in me her private thoughts, the struggles of her younger years, and her feelings about approaching death. I grew more at ease in speaking frankly, even about thorny topics. I could disagree with her, challenge her to see things from another perspective. I could tease her, ask more personal questions, and help her step down from her "high horse." The relationship deepened, with more trust and laughter, a freer give and take. I sometimes even called her by her nickname, Mims, and made up my mind that I would name my daughter—if I had one—after her!

Mutuality: A Greater Excellence

One day I sat at my dining-room table sorting out all the letters I'd received from Sister Miriam over the years. Among them was a snapshot of the two of us on the convent terrace, me youthful in blue jeans and sweater, Miriam ancient in her long black habit. To a stranger, we might appear to be an alumna dutifully visiting a former teacher. But in fact, though we'd started out as mentor-student, over the years we'd created something much richer, a bond that helped create a new template for other relationships. Arranging Miriam's old letters, I thought about the ways my life had changed.

Since that turning-point conversation, a new sense of equality had begun to flow into other arenas. As I learned to speak up to the venerable Sister Miriam, I grew more forthright with my boss and others. In my first marriage, my husband had been the "head of the family" and I was the support person, an arrangement our church and families endorsed. When I married Bill, I wanted a different kind of marriage, yet still had to work against my old programming. Again, I savored the image of a teeter-totter that sought a balancing point. The values of reciprocity and mutual respect had grown dear to my heart. Then in Elizabeth Johnson's book I found the perfect word: *mutuality.*

Mutuality occurs when two people regard each other as equals, explains Johnson, with both partners giving and receiving. As I reflected on my friendship with Miriam, several aspects of mutuality seemed worth pondering. First, instead of scripted roles, mutuality is grounded in the realities of the individuals involved. Second, its foundation is equality and mutual respect, rather than one person being dominant and the other subordinate. Third, mutuality is characterized by freedom for both partners. And finally, it leads to interdependence and intimacy, creating a kind of fullness that does not occur in many relationships.

First, mutuality is firmly grounded in reality. Both partners have a strong "reality quotient." Instead of accepting socially prescribed roles (like teacher-student, husband-wife, mother-child), the partners grow beyond them. This requires self-knowledge, acceptance of the other person, and a willingness to assume personal responsibility for oneself and for the health of the relationship. It is important that partners accept each other even with their flaws and shortcomings. I thought about Miriam's long life in the convent—over sixty years of hard work, living by the Ursuline Rule, mostly in roles of responsibility that she felt unprepared for. I understood better why she was bossy at times, had little understanding of sexual love, and was sometimes impatient when others seemed frivolous or timid. Yet there was so much to love about her, not because of her role, but because of the kind, encouraging person she'd become. At the same time I needed to respect myself, even when it meant challenging her.

Second, mutuality takes as the norm equality and mutual respect, rather than one person being dominant and the other subordinate. Jean Baker Miller, a psychologist, writes about this dynamic as "temporary inequality" in which two people start out unequal but deliberately move toward equality as the stronger member fosters the growth of the lesser one, in the same ways a mother fosters the growth of a child or a teacher supports the learning of a student.[1] Baker Miller sees this as a movement from asymmetry toward symmetry. The purpose of "temporary inequality" is to become obsolete. Miriam and I had certainly started out unequal—me, a floundering twenty-four-year-old, and her, the experienced sage. But with time and openness, we had grown into an equality that deepened our respect and love. For this to happen, it was necessary for me to challenge her, but it was also necessary for her to release me.[2]

When attending Al Anon groups with friends, I've been struck by the fact that most of those present are the *mothers or wives* of alcoholics. They speak of working very hard to *detach,* to be aware of their own contribution to the addiction. It strikes me that detachment is a woman's issue; it is another side of love. Just as we form very strong attachments early in a relationship with a child or a spouse, we eventually have to balance that *attachment* with *detachment.* This detachment involves releasing the loved one, firming up boundaries, and acknowledging differences, even while continuing to love. It seems important to recognize that detachment is not the opposite of attachment—it's merely the other side. I think of the "wave theory" mentioned in my earlier chapter on anger.

Third, mutuality is also marked by freedom. Instead of being locked into an asymmetrical bond, partners are able to experiment, challenge each other, and change. Earlier I mentioned the stress, physical problems, and buried talents that come with unhealthy self-sacrifice. In contrast, mutuality is a more authentic way of relating, one that is more expansive and free. It is flexible enough for partners to grow and change, even when those changes are uncomfortable. There may be friction, arguments, and painful conversations along the way, but with love these can lead to growth, not alienation.

Finally, mutuality can lead to a deep level of interdependence and intimacy between partners, as something deep within one person connects profoundly with something deep inside the other. There is giving and sacrifice, certainly, but unlike *The Giving Tree,* it is not one-sided. Rather, there is give and take that leads to a new level of interdependence and understanding. Johnson speaks of the bond between a parent and adult child as an example of fulfilled mutuality. In infancy there is great intimacy between mother and child but little equality. The parent/child relationship "reaches its most interpersonally successful stage when the two negotiate the changes of the years and become related as adult friends, mutually giving and receiving across the generational line" (*She Who Is* 217). So it is when friends learn to negotiate conflict and change.

What had first made me love Sister Miriam was her extraordinary talent for listening. I felt she saw and understood me in ways no one else ever had—she seemed to know and love the deepest part of my soul. But I didn't know *her.* She was, after all, an old-fashioned nun who'd been schooled to avoid "particular friendship"—the term religious communities used for centuries to describe playing favorites (which might lead to jealousy and even sexual immorality). After I stood up to Miriam, she gradually began to let her guard down. Perhaps she sensed a greater strength in me, or maybe she found me more interesting once I became more honest. Our growing trust led, in turn, to a greater interdependence and closeness that sweetened her late years and prepared me for other relationships. In time, for example, I was able to grow close to—actually to *befriend*—my aging parents and difficult in-laws.

On the Road with Jesus

As I came to prize mutuality in my dealings with other people, my relationship with God also began to change. Theologian Marcus Borg helped me to better understand this change. Borg explains that there are a few "macro stories" that run throughout the Bible, overarching metaphors that appear in both the Hebrew Bible and the New Testament. These macro stories shape our views of the spiritual life in different ways.[3] One macro story is "the priestly story," which centers on the priesthood, the temple, and the ritual sacrifices of the Israelites. This story is expressed in the New Testament view of Christ as the new High Priest, a human sacrifice for the sins of not just the Israelites but of all humanity.

The priestly story views humans primarily as sinners who have broken God's laws and therefore stand guilty. Sin, guilt, sacrifice, and forgiveness are central components of the spiritual life, according to this view. The priestly story fosters a "Giving Tree" mentality because it encourages us to imitate Christ's ultimate sacrifice, the gift of his total self. Borg argues that the priestly story can lead to a static, uncritical view of the Christian life, making it into a repeated cycle of sin, guilt, and forgiveness. The priestly story focuses on what Christ has done in the past (died for our sins) and defines salvation primarily in terms of the future. Get right with God now, the message goes, so that you'll find salvation after death and avoid hell.

A different macro story is much more in sync with the idea of mutuality. Borg explains that "the journey story" imagines the spiritual life as a journey toward a deepening and transforming relationship with God. Old Testament stories of the exodus of the Jews from slavery, their travels in the wilderness, and return from exile all view spirituality in terms of a journey. Similarly, in the New Testament references to Jesus as *the way* or *the path* point to an understanding of the Christian life as *being on the road* with Jesus—traveling, listening to his teaching, being in his presence, feasting with him. Instead of being static, the journey story emphasizes movement and growth. Exodus from slavery leads to greater freedom; surviving the wilderness and returning from exile suggests homecoming, not just in the afterlife, but in our present mortal life as well. Not only does the journey story foster change in the individual, it opens the door to change in the church and society as well.

As a woman seeking to be faithful to God in a time of great social change, this journey story makes more sense for me. An overemphasis on self-sacrifice pushes women (especially mothers) into outdated roles and makes us distrust ourselves; in the words of Gill-Austern, it leads to the "unholy trinity of self-abnegation, self-doubt, and false guilt" (307). In contrast, the journey story helps us to move forward. Imagining ourselves "on the road with Jesus" motivates us to stand tall, speak up, have courage. The journey story can strengthen our hope in the future even as it strengthens our confidence that we are indeed made in the image of God. In our interactions with others, we can stop seeing ourselves as "Giving Trees." Rather, we are sister travelers on the path toward homecoming, toward freedom.

Notes

1. In the classic *Toward a New Psychology of Women,* psychologist Jean Baker Miller contrasts temporary inequality with "permanent inequality," in which partners are locked into roles of dominant/subordinate, with no intention of changing them, as in a master/servant relationship. Riane Eisler also explores the value of mutuality in *The Partnership Way.*

2. Those who study the adult life cycle observe that a mentor is an important but *transitional* person in a young person's life. Like a parent, the mentor's goal is to render herself obsolete; as a young person matures, the mentor becomes less necessary. In most cases this means that the relationship ends, often painfully. See Daniel Levinson's classic *The Season's of a Man's Life.*

3. For a more complete discussion of these macro stories, see *Meeting Jesus Again for the First Time* by Marcus Borg, 1995.

IMAGINING A
DIFFERENT FUTURE

13

A Home
That Cherishes

My Evening with Julia

Once I spent a summer evening with Julia, mother to one of my students. Although we'd both brought our husbands along, it was the two women who carried the conversation as we talked about our sons. Sitting on our porch, we traded stories about Michael, the firstborn she'd raised to be a charming, articulate college senior. I told her what a pleasure it had been to get to know him—how I admired his expansive vocabulary, his gracious manners, even his dapper wardrobe. We laughed at the ways Michael was mature beyond his years—how his rowing teammates teased him about sophisticated tastes. He listened to Frank Sinatra music and took pride in his all-cotton dress shirts and Brooks Brothers ties, while most of them listened to the Dave Matthews Band and wore droopy blue jeans and backward baseball caps.

As we relaxed, I shared a bit about Gabe. We soon discovered we'd both faced similar challenges as mothers of sons with ADD. She told me how hard she'd worked to help Michael improve his handwriting, to concentrate in school, to make lists and stay organized. We commiserated about insensitive teachers and about how satisfying it was to see our sons overcome difficulties. Julia also spoke of her two younger children.

At the end of the evening, Julia thanked me profusely, "He was such a special boy, and I don't get to talk about him enough."

A bystander would think we were two old friends boasting about our growing sons. But the fact was I'd never met Julia before that night.

I knew of her only through Michael, who had been a student in my writing class two years earlier.

He was a star in my class that spring semester. One April day he turned his writing journal in to me. That evening, Michael went out with his girlfriend and, at the end of the night, shot himself in the head. According to the story I heard, there had been drinking, an argument, a waving of the gun his father had bought him for protection. Michael died a few days later, leaving all of us grieving and dumbfounded over why a promising young man would take his own life. Was it suicide or an accident?

I combed Michael's journal for hints of depression or suicide plans. There was nothing. Over decades of teaching I've learned the danger signals. Michael's journal held none.

His death was even more poignant because it happened during Holy Week. He died on Good Friday, and the funeral took place a few days after Easter. Our big university chapel was packed, and I only saw Julia across the crowd. Photos of Michael at different ages were on display—a First Communion picture, a teenager, a young man. It was almost unbearable to look at the pictures and realize Michael's physical life on earth had ended.

During that Holy Week I recall sitting in our front yard watching six-year-old Gabe play in the sunlight. The big oak tree in our front yard was just breaking into leaf, and we studied the tiny emerging leaves—oak leaves no longer than an inch—a shimmery, translucent green. They were exactly the same shape as mature oak leaves yet so tiny. Who could say which ones would live to maturity? I played with Gabe and savored every single moment.

I was haunted by thoughts of Michael and his family—imagining how devastated they must be. In shock. Bulldozed. Heartbroken. I kept thinking of the image of the Pietà—Mary holding her son, lifeless after a wretched, ugly death.

A Loving Son

Michael's journal sat in my office closet for two years. I was afraid to add to his parents' grief, yet surely they'd want his notebook, the last thing their son had written. I bided my time.

Finally, after two years, the time seemed right. I penned a note to Julia, telling her how much I'd enjoyed her son, offering the journal, and describing its contents. Right away she called and said Yes!—she'd like the journal and she and her husband wanted to meet me as well.

The evening was one of those rare encounters that even as it unfolded we realized was an extraordinary time of grace.

"Michael was a remarkable young man. I could tell how well loved he was," I said to Julia. I gave her a form he'd filled out for my class. Under "Family Responsibilities," Michael had written, "To be a loving son and brother."

"I seldom see that. Most college guys write 'None!'" As I handed Julia the journal, I mentioned a few sections I thought were especially good.

The evening was far from heavyhearted. I felt as if a current of love flowed among us all, honoring Michael's memory, cherishing the children still in our care.

Bill remarked later, "You've given her a great gift—talking so openly about him. Most people would be afraid of a mother's grief." But I knew I had an important gift for Julia—the journal and my own happy memories of Michael. Once again, I had that sense of "God's presence"—Sophia hovering near us in the twilight.

Cherishment Culture

Julia had given *me* a gift too, a realization: Life is *never* guaranteed, and we must treasure it. She helped see that we cannot love our children too much; there will always be difficulties in child rearing, but we must not lose our perspective. Experts in child development say that every child needs to have at least one person in his life who is crazy about him, who sees him as precious. There's no guarantee that they will outlive us, and when their time comes they need to know they have been cherished. Our children are on loan from God, and our time with them is often too short.

Kathy Coffey writes about the woman who anointed Jesus' head with oil, not long before his death (described in Mark 14:3–9). She ignored the grumbling of the men who thought the oil was being wasted; instead she listened to her own heart. Coffey draws a parallel between this unnamed woman and our work as mothers. "We do not know what paths our children may take, or how much suffering waits along the way. We do know that for a few times during a few years, we have the chance to give them what she gave Jesus: beauty, relaxation, caressing care" (118).

The Japanese have a noun, *amae* (pronounced "ah-MAH-ay") that means "the expectation to be sweetly and indulgently loved." As babies, we are born with this expectation and seek it throughout our lives. This word speaks to humans' inborn need to feel cherished—our yearning for easy, loving reciprocity that, in the best of all possible worlds, mothers and babies share. In cherishing a child, perhaps the child can teach us to cherish others as well—to love spontaneously, playfully, and generously. How different the world might be if we all let ourselves love in this way.

My evening with Julia gave me a new perspective on my hopes as a mother. So much of our society is fixated on external appearances and extrinsic rewards: Adults urge children to get good grades, excel in sports, and look their best so that they will be able to *get ahead* in the future. In reaction, a youth culture has evolved that fosters a different kind of competition: Look good, be popular, buy a lot, and live intensely because, after all, "you're only young once." Too often this leads to drinking, drugs, and promiscuity. It seems to me that young people who develop addictions are reacting against society's hollow emphasis on externals.

Yet it is possible to set a different tone at home. There at least, we can try to create a "cherishment culture." We can teach our children a "creator mindset": They are not merely *consumers,* they are cocreators with God. Experts in creativity tell us children thrive when parents emphasize *achievement* over grades, provide lots of free time to regroup and daydream, and limit daily exposure to TV and computer screens. Parents can prize education and yet not let competition overshadow the greater importance of *enjoying* learning, of discovering one's own talents and likes, of viewing oneself as a creative problem solver with important talents. In our family, this has meant making sure our home is more than a pit stop. We keep on hand an ample supply of art materials, tools, and books; we assume that adults as well as children have opportunities to cook, sew, draw, make, and repair things.

Respect for a child's individuality is at the heart of the creator mindset, and as parents we can extend this respect to other children besides our own. My university sponsors students to study in Nepal for a year. From returning students I've learned a lovely Nepalese greeting: They place palms together in front of the chest and bow to each other saying "Namaste" (pronounced "NAHM-a-stay"). The saying translates into "The god in me greets the god in you." So we can teach our children that God abides in every individual. The core of our faith is believing that every person is a child of God and thus merits respect and love, regardless of background, appearance, achievement, or religious affiliation.

This attitude is much easier in theory than practice, of course. It means watching our attitudes and tone of voice as we speak of annoying people, including neighbors, coworkers, and relatives. In a society that places so much emphasis on ranking, categorizing, and pigeonholing, it is all the more important that our homes become judgment-free zones where people can just *be themselves* and feel accepted. How easy it is to judge people by externals like cars, degrees, clothing, and language; our challenge as parents is to help children see beyond surfaces.

We learned about respect one day when Gabe got into a fight with Roosevelt at school. When my son described how the other child had bullied him, my first impulse was to rush to Gabe's defense. Instead, his father and I met with the principal to get the whole story. Later, we explained to Gabe that Roosevelt's father had recently gone to jail. That didn't justify the bullying, but it did explain why Roosevelt was acting out. Helping children to understand others fosters respect and empathy.

Parents can also promote "cherishment culture" by helping children develop an authentic love of beauty, the arts, and learning *for their own sakes*. It has been important for me, for example, to instill the view that art isn't just a subject in school; rather it's a way of *viewing the world* with an ever growing appreciation of color, form, and composition. Sometimes I get Gabe up early to see the sun come up and listen to the birds singing. One of my students fondly remembers her father always playing Joni Mitchell as the children dressed for school. In the United States, literature, art books, and all sorts of music are available for free through the public library. They can often be purchased for modest prices at rummage sales or markdown tables at bookstores. Mozart never dreamed that a modern American could listen to a sonata while driving down the interstate!

Cherishment culture can also be fostered by reading for pleasure. When our son was in second grade, Bill and he stumbled into the habit of reading aloud before bed. They started with the Animorph series by K. A. Applegate, then moved on to Harry Potter and a wide assortment of science fiction, fantasy, and adventure books. They both enjoyed reading so much that they've read aloud almost every night for the past *four years*—thousands of pages in all! I confess that sometimes we've used reading as a "carrot" to inspire Gabe to finish his homework or chores: "No reading tonight unless you finish those math problems!" Although we didn't realize it at the time, in fact, reading aloud to children is *the single most important thing* that adults can do to help them become literate, according to researcher Jim Trelease *(The Read-Aloud Handbook)*. Such reading can be a great pleasure for adults as well as children.

Another way to foster cherishment culture is to help children to appreciate the majesty of nature. Scientist Rachel Carson has written a classic essay on the importance of exposing children to nature from an early age. In *The Sense of Wonder,* she describes walking along a bay late at night: "My companion and I were alone with the stars...the misty river of the Milky Way flowing across the sky, the patterns of the constellations standing out bright and clear, a blazing planet low on the horizon....It occurred to me that if this were a sight that could be seen only once in a human generation, this little headland would be thronged with spectators....[Yet because humans nearby] can see it almost any night, *perhaps they never will*" (68–69, emphasis mine).

Carson goes on to offer many practical suggestions for helping children, even very young children, appreciate nature in all her guises: night hikes, hikes in the rain, visits to the seashore, using a magnifying glass to study lichens and tree bark, and other ventures into the elements. She guides parents to explore nature with their children, using eyes, ears, nostrils, and fingertips. "Those who contemplate the beauty of the earth can find reserves of strength that will endure as long as life lasts" (100).

Home as Sacred Space

An author named Katrina Kenison has also given a great deal of thought on how to create a home environment that promotes "cherishment." *Mitten Strings for God* recounts her quest to clear a space in her hectic life for home life—"for silence, contemplation, wonder and spiritual renewal." She drew her title from a time when she and her young son curled up to crochet mitten strings. Quietly absorbed in his crocheting, Jack remarked, "This is peace, isn't it? I love this peace." At the end of his crocheting, Jack held up a very long blue "mitten string for God."

Though she grew up without a strong spiritual tradition, her two young sons awakened Kenison's spirituality. This desire led to a whole series of practical choices to create sacred space in their lives. For example, she and her spouse decided to limit the boys' involvement in structured activities—even to keep them out of competitive sports till age eight or nine. This gave them time for creative play, reading, and family.

In time her family declared Sunday a day of rest—a day to attend church, relax with the newspaper, and enjoy one another's company *with no set schedule*. "In Hebrew, the word *shabbat* means "rest."...For me

[Sabbath] means time out for the soul, time to lay aside my daily cares in favor of spiritual refreshment" (Kenison 179).

Meals and food are important themes in the book. For example, three weeknights a week, Kenison and two neighbors take turns tripling their dinner preparations, making enough for three families. The other two families show up with their own containers at 6 p.m. to fetch dinner. This dinner co-op assures an effortless dinner two nights a week for all three families. It also makes it easier for her family to gather nightly around a shared meal.

Part of creating the sacred is respecting children's need for whimsy, humor, laughter, and fun. Kenison describes the "brownie" who lives at their house. He visits while they sleep, tidying up the house and finding missing puzzle pieces. Her sons put their toys away so the brownie won't have so much work to do, and sometimes they leave treats for him. In our home we had a family of "Borrowers" (named after the children's book series by Mary Norton) who lived under the floorboards and continually "borrowed" marker caps, keys, and Lego pieces. People don't usually think of fantasy creatures like brownies and Easter bunnies as having spiritual value, but I believe that children who start out believing in fairies and magic have an easier time believing in God as adults. They intuitively know that the world holds beings that cannot be readily seen.

Kenison writes about grace before meals, bedtime prayers, teaching her children breathing meditation, a family getaway in a cabin, and treating one another with reverence. She's forthright about the difficulties involved in reducing income, changing gender roles, and in general going against the grain of a society that measures success in terms of busyness, conspicuous consumption, and income. "Most of us can make choices about our lives....[Despite the pressures of our times] we have the freedom to define our lives, to live according to our own values, to set our own boundaries" (231).

Interspersed in her book are many moments of grace, like this one: "Rubbing sesame oil on my children as they step, scrubbed and glistening, from their bath, I am awestruck by the purity of their shining faces, the perfection of young arms and legs, the ease they feel in their own bodies. And then another day ends and I am turning down beds....The sweetest moments are *right here in the moments we create and share*" (190, emphasis mine).

My own efforts to create "cherishment culture" make me feel I'm carrying out the legacy of Sister Miriam: "She splashed our lives with color. She taught us to see, to really *see*."

14

Fresh Images of God
Mother, Guide, Friend

Mothers perform essential, enduring work as we help form our children's souls. Elaine Aron, a psychologist, explains that every person's life is filled with "containers" that shape our lives. Some of these containers are concrete, such as certain clothing, a home, a neighborhood, a favorite building, or a place in nature. Relationships with other people can be healthy containers—such as a trusted parent, confessor, friend, teacher, or spouse. Then there are the inward, intangible containers: a person's deepest beliefs and values, philosophy of life, memories, attitudes, and inner worlds of prayer, images, and meditation.

Aron goes on to explain that the *tangible* containers *seem* the most real, but it is the *intangible* ones that are really the most reliable. People can endure horrible experiences if they have inner resources because "no one [can] take from them their private love, faith, creative thinking, mental practice, or spiritual exercise" (Aron 60). Victor Frankl writes about people who endured Nazi concentration camps but remained spiritually intact because they had inner resources. A strong spirit will help a person endure other hardships like war, imprisonment, and serious illness.

Though Aron is not focusing on children, the relevance is clear. It is in the early years that we must lay the solid groundwork for children's spirituality by providing language, images, and practices to give shape to their natural spirituality. Mothers are in a position to provide physical containers (home, food, clothing, routines) as well as relational containers. These can be the foundation for the spiritual containers that will last long after early childhood is forgotten. We want our children to be spiritually strong and resilient, like the clown punching bag that stands upright, weighted with sand; a child can knock the clown over but, because of its weighted base, it can right itself again and again, no matter how many times it's knocked down.

To foster such strength, we need to weight our young children with "sand," so to speak—to give them a strong grounding. We do this by providing relevant, authentic spiritual language, images, and practices. Aron goes on to explain that "Part of maturing into spiritual wisdom is transferring more and more of your sense of security from the tangible to the intangible containers," so that ultimately we can "conceive of the whole universe as our container" (Aron 61). A spiritual life that begins in childhood can equip a child with resources that can last throughout life.

One of the most important ways to ground our children with "sand" is to equip them with helpful images of God. Of course, ultimately, the human mind cannot understand God. But we can at least *begin to understand* God through language, image, and story. Scripture and tradition offer many metaphors for God: Shepherd, Vine, Lamb, Servant, Father, Lord, Lover. These are not literal descriptions of God; rather, each is a metaphor that sheds light on an aspect of God. But some of these (like Shepherd, King, or Lover) are beyond the range of modern children's experience. Others (like Lord or Father) are so familiar that they may not have power to reach children. In any case, Christians in every age are faced with the task of finding ways to talk about—to imagine or to *re-image*—God that speak to our unique time in history.

Three images of God are especially fruitful for mothers and children: Mother, Guide, and Friend. These three images grow out of a child and mother's frame of reference, their daily activity. They also focus on immanence and closeness in such a way as to promote an awareness of God's presence in ordinary day-to-day-life—the glory of the ordinary. And finally, all three focus on the *active response* of the individual. While God is all-powerful, humans have power too. Our society might try to tell us that we are merely passive consumers or victims, but in fact we possess freedom; we are free to make choices. With God we cocreate the world, no matter what our age, because we make choices about how to live.

God as Mother

God-as-Mother is an evocative metaphor; it not only connotes tenderness and nurturing, it also suggests creativity, person making, and protection. One aspect of God-as-mother is the way She mothers us, whether we are adults or children. When novelist Madeline L'Engle was born in 1918, her mother was sick and unable to hold or cuddle her baby much. Instead, L'Engle as an infant was often placed in a wire basket on a shelf, comparable to the plastic cribs used in hospitals today. L'Engle feels she was damaged by her prolonged early separation from her mother. Throughout her life (even into her eighties), L'Engle spoke of God as "Amma" (her counterpart to Abba; similar to Mama or Nana). This proved to be a very healing name for God. "When I am feeling down on myself, inadequate, clumsy, worthless, I need the Mother to pull me back on her lap, fold the protective wings about me, rock me, tell me that it will be alright," she writes. "I need the Amma God to rock me, to tell me that I am infinitely valuable, God's child, loved exactly as I am" (*Penguins and Golden Calves* 129). Whether we imagine God holding us in her lap, braiding our hair, rocking us to sleep, or tenderly feeding us, the effect is to affirm God's personal love and nearness.

Another aspect of God-as-mother is the way she shares mothering with us; she is our "co-madre" or "other mother" as we nurture and guide our children and others in our care. With our bodies—our brains, hearts, hands, wombs, and breasts—we mothers cocreate the world with God. This creation happens dramatically in gestation and physical birth as we create a new human being out of our very flesh. Less dramatic but just as important is the ongoing "person making" that mothers continue day after day through changing diapers, reading stories, bathing, feeding, and resolving disputes.

In a book called *Maternal Thinking,* philosopher Sara Ruddick writes about the preservation (protection), training, and nurturing that are universal components of child rearing; all these are part of the ongoing formation of a child, the person making, that mothers continue as long as children are in their care. In her view, these are all forms of mothering that need not be carried out by biological mothers. All the caring professions—such as teaching, nursing, social work, medicine—are arenas where women can cocreate with God.

Such creating is not limited to the fields of health care and education. Mothering can also be a metaphor for all life-giving, creative action. Human beings (men, women, *and children*) are cocreating with God as we "mother" all things into existence, through imaginative ventures in science and technology, the arts, the discovery of new ideas and new worlds. From Madame Curie to Sally Ride to J. K. Rowling (whose Harry Potter series has helped so many discover reading), women partner with God to create the world anew.

As we are ourselves mothered, so we mother the world, and our relationship with God is a central part of the process. In my own experience, viewing myself as God's "co-madre" made it easier for me to share mothering my son with other caregivers. It also helped me to forge a collaborative relationship with Bill's ex-wife, as we worked together to guide four teenagers into adulthood. In a time when we need to find new ways to connect with others—in stepfamilies, day-care centers, and neighborhoods—the image of God-as-Mother can help us. By affirming our connections with God-as-Mother, we can also help our children believe in an intimate, powerful, and benevolent God.

God as Guide

God is also a guide, mentor, teacher, or coach. All these are relationships that children understand readily because, at their best, they are extensions of the motherly role. Because a guide has more experience and knowledge, she is able to help the younger person grow toward equality.

As a child's world grows larger, she acquires more coaches and mentors who can equip her with needed skills.

Such guides are also important for mothers, too. As mentioned in an earlier chapter, in many cultures, it is common for a birthing woman to have a *doula,* an older woman who stays in her home while she recovers from childbirth and establishes a new relationship with her children. Today such a role might be filled by a woman's mother or an older neighbor or friend[1]. It is more common to associate *mentors* with the workplace, where a mentor is a seasoned professional who unselfishly assists a younger person. Mentors are important not just in the early years but throughout life. Such guides might be found in a pastor, spiritual companion, older friend, confessor, or even a favorite saint.

Whether we speak in terms of *doula,* mentor, or confessor, a guide is a powerful image of God because it connotes caring, helpfulness, and generosity. Sophia is a guide who invites all beings to a banquet, who calls us to follow the path of life, who promises intimacy, peace, and delight. Elizabeth Johnson explains, "Sophia comes toward human beings, tests and challenges them. She is a beneficent, right-ordering power in whom God delights and by whom God creates" (*She Who Is* 88). Like a caring mother, a guide communicates with us, giving encouragement and support. She also invites us to grow into more; she "tests and challenges" us.

This image of God as Guide is common in the teachings of Alcoholics Anonymous and various Twelve-Step recovery groups. Such groups speak of God as their "Higher Power," a force that is both personal and transcendent, who guides them toward healing. Turning to a "Higher Power" has enabled millions of people to salvage lives wrecked by addiction, bringing dramatic healing to themselves and their families.

God as Friend

A third fecund image for God is that of friend. Sally McFague, a theologian, points out that friendship, of all human relationships, is the most free. Mother, spouse, worker, and siblings are all roles created by necessity, while a friend alone is freely chosen. Friendship connotes mutual respect, pleasure in each other's company, shared interests, a commitment to trust and loyalty, and the sharing of meals and other basic needs.

Friendship is characterized by companionship and familiarity. A companion is literally one who is "with bread" (from the Latin *com-pan,* meaning "together with bread"). L'Engle describes family and friends as "the people we are committed to, the people we treat with love and respect, and eat our meals with…the people we forgive" (Chase 103).

Friendship is also a remarkably resilient and versatile kind of relationship. Deep friendships endure through many phases of life in ways that other relationships may not. Think of the ten year old who is discovering the difference between a buddy and a true friend, the college student who finds her first kindred spirit in a new place, the spouse who grows into a trusted friend, or the widow who enjoys traveling with dear friends. Friendship endures throughout the various stages of life.

Because of the intimacy of friendship, it is similar to what L'Engle describes as "the flash." As an awkward, lonely child, she first experienced God's presence as an intuitive "flash…[a sense of] love all about her and around her, breathed out from some great, invisible, hovering Tenderness" (*Trailing Clouds* 18). The biblical name for God's presence in darkness and struggle is *Shekinah* (pronounced SHEK-in-ah or shek-KI-nah). Shekinah connotes "the dwelling" or "the one who dwells" close to her beloved people, just as a friend offers refuge and comfort during good times and bad. Shekinah is often associated with light, luminosity, or insight, much like L'Engle's "flash." Perhaps the most familiar manifestation of Shekinah was the pillar of fire by night (and pillar of cloud by day) that guided the Israelites through the desert wilderness. Just as a friend can communicate through a knowing glance or a nod, humans also experience the presence of God as a flash of awareness. I like the literary term for this flash—an *epiphany* (or showing forth).

Matthew and Dennis Linn and Sheila Fabricant Linn conduct healing workshops around the world, helping people to heal from past hurts and traumas. The focus of these workshops is changing people's image of

God. "We encourage people to ask for healing. If you don't have—consciously or unconsciously—a good image of God, you can't do that," says Sheila Fabricant Linn. They encourage an image of a loving God, present in all life experiences, good and bad, sometimes using a notion of God as mother and nurturer. Their workshops have helped people who have experienced torture, war, abuse, or the loss of a loved one. "One of the easiest ways to receive healing is to change your image of God," says Dennis Linn. (Schuck-Scheiber 13–14).

Beside the Waterfall

Female metaphors have helped me be more attuned to God's presence in unexpected places. One summer afternoon I took Gabe to an unfamiliar park. The weather was 95 degrees, so we were both delighted to discover a wide creek, enclosed by tall cottonwoods on either side. Upstream from where we stood, a shallow waterfall spanned the creek, reaching perhaps thirty feet from bank to bank, and no more than two feet high. Despite the scorching heat, the water in the creek was several inches deep, cascading over the broad waterfall with a constant quiet splash.

Downstream from the waterfall, a group of young children played. Two girls were constructing a dam with rocks and sticks. One little boy sloshed through the water in soaked tennis shoes and shorts, his hands dipping for minnows. A few yards away, two other children launched sailboats made from leaves and twigs. A woman in a tank top and shorts lounged on the bank, keeping an attentive eye on the kids.

This occurred when Gabe was five, when he was withdrawn and had a hard time playing with other children. It had been just a few months since his teacher at the Flower School had labeled him "troubled," and I felt like a loser as a mother.

One girl approached Gabe. "You wanna help us with this dam?" I held my breath, waiting to see how he'd respond.

He joined in readily, disarmed by the coolness of the creek and the friendly offer of the other child. The children played for the next few hours—building, sailing, soaking. The smell of damp earth, the shade of the trees, the steady whoosh-whoosh of the waterfall, the children's voices—all combined to make the creek into a cool, moist tunnel amid the heat, a world apart. The other mother and I smiled at each other a few times, both enjoying the respite from the heat and the delicious sight of children playing harmoniously. All afternoon I had that sense of God close at hand, ministering to my weary soul, a great hovering Tenderness.

By suppertime, other women arrived at the creek to retrieve their children. Only then did I figure out that the first woman was caring for the children of *several* families. The mothers all departed with content, muddy children in wet clothes. When Gabe and I finally left, I was comforted with the hope that Gabe was capable of friendship. Maybe his future wasn't so grim after all.

Now, years later, I look back on that afternoon as one of my favorite memories. The coolness of the creek, the easy acceptance of Gabe by the other children, the playful mood—all conveyed to me the spirit of Sophia. I was especially impressed by the open spirit of the woman tending all those other children, some hers and others not. Her ease in comothering put the children at ease, which in turn allowed them to welcome Gabe and me. The afternoon spoke to me of Sophia present to us as guide, mother, and friend. Sophia ministered to us, dwelling with us, giving us hope in the midst of a dark time. It was as if Sophia herself were leaning over us, tenderly reassuring us that all would be well, indeed that *all was well.*

Notes

1. Some women find help by employing a *doula*. The term *doula* is used in two ways. One is a birth attendant who encourages and coaches a woman through labor and birth. A broader meaning is a person, usually female, who comes to a woman's home for a period of time to help her and her family adapt to the new circumstances created by the birth. Such a doula would help with child care, housework, cooking, and such. In the past older women—neighbors and extended family members—served as doulas.

15

Everyday Mystics
Spiritual Practices for Mothers and Kids

A Lively Flame: Everyday Mysticism

A wise Franciscan nun named Rosie said to me, "The most important influence on a child's faith is her parents' faith—*you teach who you
are.* That's why it's so important to tend to your own spiritual life." As the
person who sets the tone for the family, I came to appreciate the words of
Mother Teresa: "How does a lamp burn? Through the continuous input
of small drops of oil. These drops are the small things of daily life: faith-
fulness, small words of kindness, a thought for others, our way of being
quiet, of looking, of speaking, and of acting. They are the true drops of
love that keep our lives and our relationships burning like a lively flame"
(quoted in Kenison 173). For my child to develop a strong spiritual life, an
enduring faith, I realized I had to keep own spiritual life strong. But
how?

My adult faith had been influenced by Catholic tradition, whose
model for spiritual growth was geared to vowed celibates, mostly males.
As a childless adult, I fed my spirit with time-honored practices like daily
"quiet time," study of the Bible and other spiritual reading, frequent
church services, and yearly individual retreats. As an overwhelmed
mother, I could no longer manage these. By necessity, I searched for ways
to "experience God *with my children*" (from Kathy Coffey's book by that
name). More than ever, I needed to find God in the middle of the messiness of ordinary days. Sister Miriam called this "everyday mysticism."
She'd approve of this definition of mysticism as an "emphasis on immedi-

ate awareness of relation to God, on direct and intimate consciousness of the Divine Presence. It is religion at its most acute, intense, and living stage" (Borg 39, citing Quaker scholar Rufus Johnson). Others speak of it as experiences "the numinous" or "theophanies"—manifestations of the sacred as God (Borg, *The God We Never Knew* 37).

Certainly, caring for a young child is not at odds with spirituality— far from it. A friend recently related this Japanese saying, "Up till age seven, the child belongs to God." Young children can help us to "experience God" in new ways. At the same time, if we reinforce in young children a sense of God's presence, they will be better able to build on that spiritual base as they grow older and their vision isn't quite so clear.

Consulting many other parents, especially mothers, I've tried the following suggestions. They are especially suitable to mothers of younger children (seven and under) because such youngsters are so attuned to the spiritual world and their mothers are especially needy. Yet these practices can be adapted to parents and children of any ages.

1. Sleeping with bread.

Earlier I described the Ignatian *examen of consciousness* in terms of "sleeping with bread." Like the refugee children who sleep with a piece of bread, we can wrap up the day with a nightly reflection on its events. The beauty of this approach is that it can be adapted to any child old enough to talk. Every day at bedtime (or dinner time) a parent helps a child review the day, asking, "What was the best part of your day? The worst? Where was the Spirit most present? Least present?" To promote a sense of ritual, the Linns suggest passing out pieces of bread as you ask these questions, or perhaps lighting a candle. You, the parent, take your turn at saying where God was most present and least present. The daily examen can build intimacy within a family, even as it teaches children the habit of daily reflection on God's presence in ordinary life.

When children and parents share the practice of "sleeping with bread," both come to appreciate the importance of their own relationship with the Spirit. Children see that adults face struggles, questions, and uncertainty as well as joy and certainty. Adults have the chance to be intimately known by their children, as well as to know them. For example, for a time my "desolation" was dealing with a coworker who tried to intimidate me. Gabe, as an eight-year-old, readily made the connection between the bullies he faced on the playground and the bullies I faced at work. By "sleeping with bread" we enlisted God's help in dealing with difficult people.

Like mothers who listen to their hearts, children who grow up "sleeping with bread" can better trust their own perceptions and are less vulnerable to peer pressure. The Linns give the example of Beth, a fifteen-year-old girl invited to a party by a handsome and popular boy. Beth turned him down because she knew there would be a lot of drinking and sexually promiscuous behavior. The boy was so impressed by Beth's sense of herself that he left the party early to be with her. Her father remarks, "I think Beth's inner strength has come from all these years of doing the examen and learning to trust that she knows what gives her life and what doesn't" (Linn 26).

The Linns offer other examples of children and teenagers who, in the context of "sleeping with bread," speak candidly with their parents about struggles associated with a school, a dying friend, or sexual feelings. Parents value the way it promotes such candor, helping the family stay emotionally connected despite busy lives. The children know the parents better and the parents know the children better and all come to see God as part of their day-to-day lives.

2. Cultivating laughter.

Too often Christians focus on sin, suffering, and work, while neglecting the lighter, more joyful aspects of faith. One great grace of family life is the way my husband and children have taught me how to laugh! My teenage stepsons especially taught me the necessity of laughing at life's absurdities. Humor adds pleasure to everyday life, helps people to get along, and acts as an emotional shock absorber, making difficulties easier to bear. I often think of the saying "Angels can fly because they take themselves so lightly."

Humor is one area where children know more than adults, and they are eager to enlighten us. Lawrence Shapiro, a specialist in child development, points out that children who are "skilled at humor" are likely to be happier and more successful at social interactions. The same could be said of grownups! Of course, it's important for adults to teach children not to use humor at others' expense. But then we adults can encourage children to *teach us* to notice the funny, whimsical side of life. Here are some ways we can promote humor:

• *Entertain each other.* We can develop an eye for humor by telling jokes around the dinner table, watching funny movies, acting goofy, and making up silly bed-time stories. Or we can have a bulletin board dedicated to jokes, riddles, and cartoons. The lunch packer can slip cartoons or jokes into a child's lunch bag. Parent and child can read the comics together. And how about *Calvin and Hobbes* cartoons?

• *Entertain others with humor.* A family could host an hour during which members take turns telling jokes or acting out a skit or singing karaoke. Shapiro suggests that a parent and child dress up as clowns and learn a few clown routines (perhaps even performing together at a local nursing home or hospital). The same could be done with puppets; a costume or a puppet can loosen up even the most bashful. Family members can perform skits, sing, or juggle. One mother told me that when her three children got head lice, she wrote a song about it: "We are little lice. We are very nice. Take us home with you from school. Itchy, itchy in your head. Itchy, itchy in your bed…."

• *Preserve funny memories* by making funny home videos or by keeping a humor scrapbook or log in which you record funny experiences or things the kids (or adults) say. Who would want to forget the time your eight-year-old told his teacher, "I never eat cafeteria pizza because my dad says pepperoni is made from cow testicles!"? One person who was going through a difficult time made a tape of other people laughing, including a best friend's belly laugh and a granddaughter's giggle.

• *Look for ways to add whimsy to your life,* like the neighbor who displays a life-sized statue of a leprechaun in her yard each March, or another mother who has a collection of funny hats and disguises. Children delight in stories of elves, talking animals, and tooth fairies.

When I asked ten-year-old Gabe what laughing had to do with God, he didn't hesitate to answer, "Everything!"

3. Affirmations and mantras for kids.

Living in a society that has little regard for spiritual values, I long ago learned the value of consciously focusing my thoughts on "whatsoever things are lovely, whatsoever things are good." Mornings I often recite an affirmation to set my attitude for the day—sometimes phrases from Sister Miriam, like "Each life is a unique work of grace" or "Trust God with the horizons." Memorizing particular Bible verses can be an especially valuable habit. I can do all things through Christ who strengthens me" has gotten me through many challenges. Children as well as adults can benefit from memorizing affirmations.

In kindergarten, Gabe had trouble with impulsive behavior. Another mother taught me the "STAR affirmation"—coaching my son to recite the words "stop, think, act, review" when he feels like acting out. Gabe formed the habit of repeating this phrase every morning and at other times when he was impatient (like standing in line). For years, every day at school drop-off, Gabe quietly repeated to me: "Stop, think, act, review." As a result of so many repetitions, it's been woven into my consciousness as well as his, helping the whole family. Our "STAR affirmation" has become a rudimentary mindfulness meditation—a frequent habit of stopping to think before acting. This "stop and think" habit has helped us avoid many arguments and harsh words.

Affirmations can easily lead to prayer in the form of mantras. While an affirmation is a short phrase repeated to reinforce a certain attitude or action, a mantra involves repeating a word or phrase in order to quiet the mind and turn it toward God. Jesus scholar Marcus Borg points out that mantras have a long and esteemed history in the Christian tradition as "a means of giving the mind something to focus and refocus on as it sinks into silence before God" (*The God We Never Knew* 126). Borg mentions as examples the rosary with its multiple repetitions, and the Eastern Orthodox "Jesus Prayer": "Lord Jesus Christ, Son of the Living God, have mercy on me, a sinner."

Mantras are especially valuable at times of intense emotion. During the aftermath of fear that followed the September 11 attacks on the World Trade Center, I found it a source of strength to often repeat the prayer, "Lord, make me an instrument of thy peace." Similarly, when a loved one was in hospital intensive care, family members often repeated the prayer, "Bring healing to our Uncle Billy." Mantras can help open our hearts to God and to the "peace that passes understanding."

Mantras and affirmations are equally suited to adults and children as a way of fostering an awareness of a deeper level of reality. In our family, we've developed our own child-friendly mantras:

- Come Holy Spirit, Love so fine—live within this body of mine.

- Jesus loves me, this I know.

- It doesn't have to be perfect! Help me accept myself, my work, my life.

- This little light of mine, I'm gonna let it shine.

- Angel of God, my guardian dear....Ever this day be at my side, to light and guard, to rule and guide.

4. Deeds of compassion.

Once when struggling with depression, I came across this spiritual advice from a source now forgotten: "The best response to a dark night of the soul is to give alms." At the time I was an overworked graduate student and didn't personally know anyone worse off than me. How had my world ever grown so small? This advice—"give alms"—led me to seek out an opportunity to teach a sewing class to inner-city women through a church program. Teaching other women to sew gave me a much-needed sense of perspective and began a cycle of positive energy. Direct contact with others in need enlarged my world as well as lifting my depression. For me, giving money or material possessions wasn't enough—I needed to have direct contact with real people.

When Gabe was born, I was determined that he too would be able to take part in this positive energy cycle. One summer when he was just a toddler, for example, he accompanied me to a weekly "story hour" during which I read to "at risk" children in a city recreation center. The kids enjoyed his baby-presence as much as they enjoyed my stories, and Gabe began to learn early that he could not spend his life in a middle-class bubble.

A young child may not be able to give money or things, but she can still enrich others through smiles or loving attention. Even preschoolers can find ways to "give alms" as part of the family. A mother can help a child develop an eye (and a heart) for others' needs. Of course, it works both ways—often the child can help adults to respond to needs, like Norvell Smith, a teenager who lived in a violent part of Chicago. After nearly being shot in a gang fight, she began speaking out against gangs and violence. Her efforts led to her urban school becoming a model of safety; many other schools have sought Smith's help to resist violence (Barron 18).

Some opportunities for "deeds of compassion" appear spontaneously. My parents-in-law lived for several years in an assisted-living home. With coaching from us, Gabe (then nine) and my teenage stepsons developed an ease in interacting with elderly residents. They learned not to shy away from people who are suffering, and they came to appreciate the value of a warm greeting, a joke, or a hug. On the home front, children can volunteer to rake or shovel for an elderly neighbor, take welcome gifts (like baked goods) to newcomers, or sponsor a child overseas through a relief organization (like the Christian Children's Fund). And they can help you pack up outgrown clothes or toys to give to others who need them.

Of course, children (like adults) may need to be reminded that deeds of compassion are important in their own right. But such actions also benefit those who carry out the deeds. Borg remarks, "Intentionally placing oneself in situations where people are struggling and need help, and *being present to that experience*...can soften the heart" (*The God We Never Knew* 127, italics mine). It can also strengthen the spiritual bond among family members and foster courage that children will need in their later lives.

Traditionally, Christian children memorized the scriptural "Works of Mercy." This practice has grown less common, but it's worth preserving.

The Corporal Works of Mercy: (1) Feed the hungry; (2) Clothe the naked; (3) Visit the sick; (4) Bury the dead; (5) Give drink to the thirsty; (6) Shelter the homeless; (7) Ransom the captive.

The Spiritual Works of Mercy: (1) Teach the ignorant; (2) Counsel the doubter; (3) Admonish the sinner; (4) Bear wrongs patiently; (5) Forgive offenses willingly; (6) Comfort the afflicted; (7) Pray for the living and the dead.

5. Car prayers.

For many adults, commuting in the car is one of the few times we are alone. The result is that cars have become a sort of modern-day hermitage, in which people listen to spiritual tapes, reflect on the day, or simply enjoy the quiet. It's also a perfect time for conversational prayer, a time to express to God daily needs, worries, and thanks. Borg observes that conversational (or informal) prayer "takes seriously that life is a relationship with God: that God is there to be addressed (and address us), that the sacred is a 'You' and not an 'It'" (*The God We Never Knew* 124).

On a similar note, car time may be one of the few occasions when a parent and children are alone together, so it can be a good chance to teach them the value of informal prayer. In our family we've formed the habit of turning the radio off so we can talk, which sometimes leads to spontaneous "Spirit-talk." When we pass an auto accident or a funeral procession, one of us might comment, "Holy Spirit, be with these people who are hurting right now." Setting out on a long road trip, we ask for "travel mercies," or running late, we might pray, "Spirit, help us find a place to park!"

Such informal prayer is both easy and versatile. The parent must take the lead, but children, especially younger children, will follow the parent's example. Once, we were driving through an unfamiliar slum when Gabe cried out, aghast, "Look at how ugly this neighborhood is! There aren't any trees or grass. How can the kids grow up without any trees?" In response I said, "Creator God, help these children to grow up healthy. Help them find some green trees and parks!" Another time Gabe and a friend were squabbling in the backseat and I intervened to say, "Let's ask God to help us get along and make peace with each other." (I've learned to do this only with children whose parents share our faith.) Many times, one of us has remarked, "Thank you, Spirit, for that beautiful sunset!"

Admittedly, as he's grown older, such car prayers have convinced Gabe that he has a weird mom, but they've also reinforced the belief that the Spirit is involved in our most mundane lives—even the search for a parking spot.

Patty, another parent I know, says she and her kids often sing along to spiritual music tapes in the car. Guided meditation tapes also work well with older children. (Our personal favorite is *Quiet Time with Jesus* by Carey Landry and Carol Jean Kinghorn). With older children and teenagers who squirm at direct "God talk," a parent might use car time to initiate conversations on topics like after-death experiences (or near-death experiences), what their friends think about religion, or ethical controversies. A mother of teenagers says that she uses car time with them to talk about song lyrics or news on the radio: "What does that mean? Do you ever feel like that? Do you agree with that?"

6. Parent and kid retreats.

In *Experiencing God with Your Children,* Kathy Coffey, author and mother of four, writes about how much she benefits from periodic silent three-to-five-day retreats at a retreat center near her home in Colorado. She describes the solitude and silence as "a fine wine that I sip slowly, eagerly....A retreat is a high priority because it guarantees that what I give my family, friends, and colleagues is genuine, not phony" (102). Her retreats give her vitality and peace that she brings back to her busy life.

Coffey also describes "parent and tot" retreat centers where a team of women spend a morning teaching children of ages three or four how to enter their "heart room" where they can find peace no matter how crazy life gets. They begin with right-brain activities like story telling, art, and an imaginary field trip; gradually they lead the children into a guided prayer: "With a little prompting, children then close their eyes and picture Jesus. They lie on the floor and talk with him for a few moments. Their lips move silently; clearly some important communication goes on" (103).

Meanwhile, down the hall, their parents make the same trip to their "heart room." A retreat leader reassures them, "Your child is having a special time with Jesus. Now it's time for your spiritual experiences too. If Jesus himself had to withdraw from the constant demands at times, isn't it logical that you should also?" Through such parent and tot retreats, both children and adults develop a common vocabulary for talking about God and about their "heart rooms."[1] Surely children as well as mothers need to learn the importance of periodically withdrawing from the busy swirl of life; retreats teach us how to "step-back-in-order-to-step-forward."

When Miriam's community, the Brown County Ursulines, opened a new retreat house on their grounds, I persuaded them to allow Gabe and me to make self-styled "parent and tot" retreats there, just the two of us. This led to a delightful yearly tradition of spending a long weekend each fall simply savoring the presence of God.

The two days we spend there don't involve anything particularly churchy. We keep time unscheduled so we can stay up, sleep late, and eat whenever we feel like it. I bring along books and a new box of Legos to occupy Gabe while I meditate, pray, and read nearby. Together we take hikes on the convent grounds, and I entertain him with tales of his "Grandma-Mimi" and the old stories that Miriam herself used to tell about pioneer nuns who founded the convent and the mound builder Indians who preceded them. We visit the nearby house where Miriam grew up, the chapel where she and I prayed for him long before his birth, and the graveyard with Miriam's stone. Gabe makes sure we have time to get outdoors to notice the box turtles in the creek, to search out deer tracks in the woods, and to launch leaf boats on the lake. As a mother, I find such retreats strengthen my spirit—and are a lot of fun too! Like Coffey, I invariably return from a retreat knowing "I am the beloved of God, whose arms enclose me, whose spirit buoys me, whose love encircles me always" (102).

7. Sharing questions.

All these suggestions for deepening spirituality point to the importance of taking children (and ourselves) seriously—listening to them with true respect. This respect should especially extend to their questions, including their religious questions. Gareth Matthews, a philosopher, has made a study of the valuable philosophical questions that children ask. He writes, "[A child] has fresh eyes and ears for perplexity and incongruity [and also] a degree of candor and spontaneity that it is hard for the adult to match" (85). These qualities make it easier for children to zero in on life's most fundamental questions, such as: Where was I before I was born? Where do people go when they die? Do animals go to heaven? Who created God? Did anything exist before the universe? Is time a circle or a line? Why are humans so much meaner to each other than animals? Why do people fight so much over religion? Is the Bible true? Why doesn't Tim's family believe in evolution? If we take time to listen to their questions, children can help us recover our own spontaneity and fresh perspective.

I often have found myself encouraging Gabe to ask questions that might not occur to him naturally, especially in regard to social justice issues. "Why do you suppose children who are poor have a harder time in school? Who do you think was the boss in that meeting (or that family)? What does it take for black and white children to get along better?" Such questions foster critical thinking and help us see the connection between faith and justice.

Similarly, many young children report spiritual experiences that adults find enviable. One child insisted he could remember life before birth. Another described her guardian angel in detail. Another reported a distinct sense of God residing in his heart area. As adults we can dismiss these experiences or we can respect them as—in the phrase of the poet Wordsworth—"intimations of immortality."

Spiritual experiences and questions should be taken seriously and remembered. When Gabe was young I formed the habit of jotting his questions down so I'd have a record; Hay and Nye argue that after age seven such fundamental questions are suppressed to the point where children insist that they never asked them. By listening to children carefully without imposing easy answers, parents can foster a tolerance for ambiguity and mystery. Parents can also supply some language and concepts as scaffolding for spirituality. In these ways we lay a spiritual foundation.

*   *   *

The above are some of spiritual practices that have been valuable for parents and children. Other possibilities include a home prayer space with a prayer gong, incense, holy water, or candles; dream work; nature or wilderness experiences; silent hours; guided visualization; art such as drawing or clay work; music; walking a labyrinth; and church camp.

My friend Susan offers even more possibilities: observing the liturgical year and the cycle of nature, including the solstices; making an Advent wreath; celebrating feast days for children's namesakes; learning about the lives of the saints; drawing pictures of what they're thankful for on Thanksgiving; acting out Scripture stories; a prayer spot in nature.

Depending on the individuals involved, each family will find practices and traditions that suit its own style. All these practices share an emphasis on the child's *experience,* not on abstract dogma or outward show. These practices also help the adult provide scaffolding for the child to deepen his or her natural spirituality—by offering a simple gesture, ritual, or prayer. These practices also reinforce an openness to Mystery in the here-and-now; the Sprit is an active, living force that meets us in our mundane lives, not only "in church." If we believe that Jesus is "the way," we must give children resources for continuing to seek and walk the path of faith.

Notes

1. Coffey credits *Parent and Child Retreats* by Maggie Pike et al. (Denver, CO: Living the Good News, 1997).

16

Embracing Mothers
What Women Want from Mother Church

"You said you'd had some new developments in your church search," said Susan. "I can't wait to hear the details." Susan and I were getting together for one of our tea parties to reminisce about Miriam and share our spiritual journeys.

"I told you we've been attending First Church for nearly a year. It's right in our neighborhood and is a hub for the whole area. Lots of Gabe's friends go there, they have a great music program, strong outreach, and a big majestic sanctuary. Gabe even learned to play hand bells!" I explained. Outside was a sweltering summer afternoon, but inside Susan's dining room, the air was cool. The tall ceiling and dozens of plants made it feel like a soothing forest hideout.

"What about *you*? Is it a woman-friendly church? You have a lot more patience for organized religion than I do." Susan handed me a ceramic plate filled with hummus and wedges of pita bread. Her dangling Celtic earrings caught the light.

"It has lots of women members—all ages—and a reputation for being really friendly. They're having a big membership drive this year. The associate pastor is a woman and so are several of the elders. I'm determined to find a church that views women as equals, not secondary members, so it's been a huge thrill to settle in there. But then a couple of encounters have given me second thoughts."

"What happened? Tell me they're not as bad as the Catholics." Susan refilled my iced tea, then leaned back in her chair so Maggie, her aged tabby, could leap into her lap. A cradle Catholic, Susan had left the church years ago, yet she was one of the most deeply spiritual people I knew.

"It's really important to be able to share my faith with others—to be able to worship. And I want a church home for my son too. First Church seemed to offer that." I went on to review the churches I'd visited over the past few years—Catholic, many Protestant groups, including Unitarian and Quaker. How First Church drew us like a magnet. How I especially liked the music and the children. We'd been worshiping with them for a year, and then after three months of membership classes, we were all set to join.

"Then at the very last meeting, an elder passed out a sign-up sheet with twenty or thirty ministries listed, from child care to visiting shut-ins to tending bake sales. Of course, being a teacher, I was eager to sign up to teach," I went on. "I'd already told several members maybe I could lead a workshop on prayer or spiritual growth for young moms."

"What a great resource you'll be for First Church!" Susan with her fair skin and attentive blue eyes was always quick to remind me of my talents, just like Miriam once did.

"But teaching wasn't on the list. In fact, *none of the public roles* were on the list! I asked Scott, the elder, 'How does a person get involved in teaching?' And he said, 'God raises teachers up. That's something our leaders *invite* members to do.'"

"I'm starting to smell a rat! It sounds like teaching-and-leadership service is a different tier from the keep-things-going service. It's like the 1950s—keep those women in the kitchen and the nursery! For any public roles they need gatekeepers." Susan was quick to notice a red flag.

"That's what I started to think. I'd already volunteered several times to teach, but no one had called me back. Gatekeeping would explain it. Anyhow, that day I went home and cried—I felt *so left out* and *so dumb*. But then I decided to give it more time. I kept praying for guidance."

"I agree with Mary Daly who says that a woman wanting to join the Christian religion is like a black person wanting to join the Ku Klux

Klan," Susan contributed. "You said there were two encounters—what else happened?"

I helped myself from the tray of fat strawberries. "A couple weeks later, someone called and asked me to lead a discussion. I thought, 'Terrific, God is opening a door.' I remember it was Mother's Day, because they were handing out carnations in the lobby. Only one other person showed up—an elder named Jim and me. We hit it off, so I got to telling him about my book and Sophia and God-as-mother. I also confided in him about the mixed messages from the church—how people seemed real friendly at first but then nobody returned my calls."

"Did Jim shed any light?"

"Did he ever! He told me he was invited to become an elder his very first year at First Church. He explained that all the elders are conservative professionals. The men have stay-at-home wives."

"But you said there were women elders and a female pastor!"

"There are, but they're all religiously conservative. None of them would ever talk about God-as-mother or about empowering women or challenging the status quo. Before they're invited to lead, evidently they're carefully screened to make sure they have *no trace of feminist consciousness.* If they press for inclusive language or female god-images or changes in policy, they're quietly encouraged to leave. That's my take, anyhow."

"They're afraid you might come in and rock the boat," said Susan.

"All I want is to be able to belong and use my God-given talents. I've always believed that the church is the body of Christ—that there should be room for all kinds of people. Doesn't Jesus talk about going out into the highways and byways and inviting *everyone* in? Church is one place we should embrace everyone. If I accept traditionalists, they should accept me—or at least hear me out." Suddenly I felt myself tearing up.

"They sound like hypocrites. They're talking out of both sides of their mouth. They're having a membership drive, but then they turn you away," Susan leapt to my defense. "I mean, here you are a working mom with a PhD who's *volunteering,* and they don't grab you? They put women in leadership but only *certain kinds of women.* Where does that leave you?"

"Jim said he *personally* thought I had good ideas but I'd be *more comfortable* somewhere else. He said, 'You don't fit the profile so you won't be seen as leadership material. Not for a long time, if ever. People will see you as a crusader, a troublemaker.'" I took a long sip from my iced tea and noticed its cinnamon scent. Maggie jumped to my lap and purred. Susan and I sat in silence.

"I guess churches are torn by so many controversies they want to keep a lid on," I said without conviction.

"Isn't that what the Pharisees told Jesus? 'Don't stir up trouble! We like things the way they are!' And he still rocked the boat *big time.*"

"I feel awful about this. The last time I joined a new church I was twenty-four and very needy and so grateful to be welcomed in. Now I'm wiser and more capable—with twenty more years of faith and Bible study and a higher income—much more to give! But I'm only welcome if I pretend to be a *trusting young thing.*"

"That was always true but you just didn't test it," said Susan.

"I guess I'll keep searching. But I feel bad for my son, not having a church home. He's missing out. A neighbor of mine has joined the church. She can't stand the male religiosity either, but she has three young sons who like the Sunday school and Scout troop at First Church, so she goes along. I just can't do that." I looked to Susan for understanding.

"Do you want Gabe in a church where his mom has to pretend to be something she's not? I say shake the dust off your feet and forget about them. What would Miriam say? 'You need to fortify yourself! Have a brownie, honey!'" We both laughed because Susan mimicked Miriam so well—a proper-nun-turned-grandma who always fed us goodies.

My conversation with Susan helped me to better understand my disappointment with First Church; I'd been visiting different churches out of a desire for a church-home for my whole family, especially for Gabe.

But I needed a place where I too would feel accepted and challenged. My local church didn't need to be perfect, but there needed to be a spirit of genuine acceptance and welcome. As an educated professional and also a mother, I needed to feel my work and talents would be respected. There needed to be room for questions, too!

With further thought and study, I began to realize that great numbers of other Christian women felt as if they were on the outskirts of their churches. Women had grown up in organized religion, had fallen in love with God, and naturally aligned themselves with Christianity, just as I had. Concepts like the family of God, all humans being made in the image of God, the reign of God held great meaning for us; they guided our lives. We believed that we were valued members of the church.

Then as we matured, our gifts and needs began to change. In chapter 4, I wrote about the dream where my menstrual blood leaked onto the white bedspread and my mountain man refused to help me. Instead he grew angry. Women today are undergoing big and important changes. Some are getting advanced educations and finding success in nontraditional career fields. A majority of us are facing a family-work crunch unknown to our foremothers. Moreover, most of us are living longer, which raises a host of new issues as we "mother" aging parents as well as our children, even as we hold down paying jobs and save for our own old age. A great many women today feel a deep spiritual thirst as well as a desire to be a transformative force ("leaven") in a society that is increasingly impersonal, bureaucratic, violent, and superficial.

All these are inescapable aspects of the times in which we live, bringing both danger and promise. Yet both our gifts and needs often seem as messy as menstrual blood leaking onto a white bedspread. Naturally we turn to our churches for help. In order to continue to travel with the mountain man, we need him to pay attention, to take our needs seriously. We don't ask for anything unreasonable—only for him to value and love us, as we love him.

Yet too often the church tunes us out, even in regard to issues that affect it deeply. The particular needs of mothers of young children are explored by Bonnie Miller-McLemore, a professor of religion, personality, and culture at Chicago Theological Seminary and also the mother of three young sons. In *Also a Mother: Work and Family as Theological Dilemma,* she challenges church leaders and theologians to "take seriously what mothers think, feel, desire, and know bodily" especially in regard to the multiple roles that women play today. She uses three helpful categories to describe the church, particularly local parishes ("congregations"): (1) a normative, or *prophetic* role ("this is how the Christian life should be"); (2) a descriptive or what I call *witnessing* role ("this is how life really is these days"); and (3) a programmatic *pastoral* role ("here are a few ways to get there"). These categories provide a good starting point to consider ways to help parents, specifically mothers.[1]

The Prophetic Role of the Church: Holding Up the Ideal

Fresh perspectives can be found in *The Church Women Want: Catholic Women in Dialogue* (edited by Elizabeth Johnson), an anthology of essays by prominent Catholic women. One essay specifically addresses the needs of mothers. In "The Challenge of 'Being Leaven' in a Secular Culture," Harvard Law professor Mary Ann Glendon considers two essential questions: "To what extent are we [Christians] being transformed by the culture, rather than transforming it? What can we do to increase respect in our society for women who want to give priority to the vocation of parenthood?"

Glendon reiterates the prophetic mission of the church to stand up for Christian values in the midst of secular culture. Today the dominant American culture is "saturated with attitudes and habits that are antithetical to core Christian beliefs...materialism, consumerism, secularism, and moral relativism" (113). These attitudes and habits are shared by those who wield the most influence in governments, political parties, corporations, mass media, foundations, and universities. Secular leaders, according to public opinion studies, are less likely than most other citizens to have strong ties to religion and family life. Our work is cut out for us!

Yet rather than challenging and transforming the secular culture, churches often mimic it by reinforcing extreme individualism, militarism, the subordination of women, and a preoccupation with property, wealth, and sexuality—all forces at odds with Christian family life. Glendon urges churches to "think carefully about the links among exaggerated individualism, extreme liberty, moral relativism, the breakdown of the family, and the feminization of poverty" (115).

Glendon is especially concerned about the needs of women who give priority to child rearing. Historically (and still today), the nurture and education of children has been one of the main ways that women have been a "transformative presence" in the world. "Who can doubt that [these tasks] are among the most influential determinants of the supply and quality of leaven in any society?" she asks (113).

And yet, despite unprecedented advances for women in the economic and political arenas, today women who choose to make family life a priority encounter tremendous difficulties. In chapter 3, I drew from Glendon's essay to outline "the dangerous Ds," which afflict many mothers in American society, things like disrespect, disadvantages in the workplace, vulnerability to divorce, and destitution. Glendon argues that the church should provide an alternative to the "dangerous Ds" rather than mirroring them. Churches should, for example, promote women's economic security and offer practical support for child rearing.

Church as Witness: Telling It Like It Is These Days

Our times are marked by a trend toward greater openness regarding subjects once considered taboo. Though still highly charged and stigmatized, many subjects are now part of public awareness in ways that were impossible even twenty years ago: subjects like child abuse, eating disorders, domestic violence, sexuality, racial bigotry, incest, substance abuse, rape, and mental illness. These issues have always existed, yet in earlier eras many believed that refusing to acknowledge them would make them disappear. Today they are out in the open, so there's a greater chance for us to understand and perhaps address them. It's worth noting that many of these issues concern women's sexuality and subordination;

one of the reasons they are out in the open is because women have given them voice.

Despite this growing openness, in churches many subjects are still considered taboo. The sexual scandals in the Catholic Church have forced the issue of child molestation into the limelight, yet churches in general continue to tiptoe around sexual issues and social problems once viewed as too private to discuss in church settings.

Miller-McLemore believes that churches should be a safe "holding environment" where members can be themselves, speak their minds, and truly *listen* to one another. It's one of the few places in our society that welcomes a wide range of ages and that seeks to welcome all. Unfortunately, the "forum for discussion" that people are most familiar with are TV talk shows that often promote mud slinging. Churches can provide an alternative approach where all voices are listened to; such an approach is part of being "leaven" in a secular society. To promote fruitful dialogue, leaders can set the tone by supplying good information (invited speakers, recommended articles or books), facilitating honest discussion, and fostering a respectful tone that welcomes divergent perspectives.

By being a holding environment, churches can help members support one another in the face of the plagues of modern life. It strikes me that in our grandmothers' generation, families faced enemies that were easy to recognize: the poverty of the Great Depression, communicable diseases like polio and influenza, uncertain crops. Most families agreed these were enemies and pulled together to combat them. Today the enemies are harder to recognize and thus harder to combat: the time famine that arises from the family-work crunch, substance abuse, domestic violence, pornography. Though the media asserts that these problems exist, in the middle-class churches I visited (mostly white), members conveyed the attitude that these problems afflicted the lower classes—the poor, minorities, perhaps immigrants, or lapsed Christians—but not our own members. Thus the problems are denied within the flock even as they are projected onto the larger culture.

Miller-McLemore believes that pastors and other church leaders can help determine which topics are "up for discussion." She gives the example of small-town church bulletins, which list members' "joys and concerns." Often these include only certain kinds of joys and concerns (anniversaries and weddings, graduations, acceptable diseases and problems). She believes bulletins should also include sensitive topics (like infertility, miscarriage, teen-parent conflicts, vocational conflicts) to bring them out in the open. Leaders could also address such issues in sermons, intercessory petitions (even anonymous ones), or discussion groups. If leaders set a respectful, open tone, members are likely to follow suit.

To serve their congregations, pastors and pastoral staffs should become knowledgeable about their needs. In addition to listening, this means professional education in areas such as addiction, anxiety, depression, the family-work crunch, and holistic health. Though needs will vary according to the local congregation, other areas of professional development might be reproductive health, family planning, mother loss, eating disorders, recovery from childhood trauma, sexual identity, the unique needs of minority mothers, and hysterectomy (or mastectomy) and women's identity. In earlier centuries, religious communities and Christian reformers took the lead in starting hospitals and schools; Christians today should be in the vanguard addressing the social plagues of our time. These should be part of seminary training and religious formation, supplemented by professional education and reading. As leaders grow more knowledgeable, they will find ways to pass their insights on to others. Pastoral workers should also learn to be at ease in interacting with and listening to women of all ages and backgrounds.

Of particular concern to Miller-McLemore is the "family-work crunch." Though we tend to regard it as the problem of the individual woman, it is in fact an important social and spiritual issue. The solution is not simply for the individual to learn to manage her time better; it is for us as a church to change expectations and the resources available to mothers. We should sponsor gatherings to discuss the family-work crunch in ways that look for solutions. Topics related to this are the generation gap, gender roles in marriage, teenage sexuality, and concern for health and wellness.

Sometimes people can speak openly but get stalled at the venting stage ("My husband works too much! He won't help out at home!"). It's important to press further and look at these personal issues within a larger cultural framework. A handout, article, or book could be used as a starting point to help frame the "family-work crunch" in a larger context.[2]

The Pastoral Role of Church: Getting from Here to There

At my university, I recently taught a summer course on children's religious education. It attracted a mix of people, mostly teachers and parents of all ages, united by a commitment to helping children develop healthy spiritual lives. As part of the workshop, we had a spirited discussion of the participants' own church experiences.

Pam spoke first. "What I value most in my church is the emphasis on human rights. I'm committed to Amnesty International and to working for nonviolence, and many people in my church are too. But sometimes it seems ironic that we talk so much about the rights of people overseas while there are kids and mothers in our own community that are really oppressed. I don't mean just poor women either—I mean young moms who are lonely and overwhelmed and feel like the church has no place for them."

A woman named Peg added her comments. "In the Catholic tradition we believe that every person is made in God's image. I was a pastoral worker in my thirties when I began to come to terms with being a lesbian. When I opened up to my husband, our marriage eventually fell apart and I lost my job soon after. Within a matter of months I went from a model citizen—a Catholic mom with four great kids—to an outcast in search of a job. Now I'm in a solid relationship with another woman, but we aren't part of any church. The kids go to mass when they visit their dad. They ask, 'Are we still part of God's family, Mom?' I don't know what to say."

"My church experience has been mixed," said Trisha, a mother of three. "When my first son was born my husband and I were living in an intentional Christian household with another couple. It was a joy to share Michael's early years with three other adults. By the time my second was born, the other couple had moved out, so then it was two adults and two babies—whew, was that ever an awakening! I really missed living with other believers! Ever since then, I wished we could find a church that valued communal living for young families."

"My four kids are all grown now, but I can relate to what Trisha said," added Terry. "I was divorced and had four young kids and little money. An older woman in my church community offered us a house at very low rent so I could stay home with my kids. Her help made a *huge* difference in my life! Later I invited another single mom to live with me for six months with her newborn till she got on her feet. We all felt that being part of God's family meant offering concrete help—including financial help!"

Trisha spoke again. "Once my kids reached their teens, our experiences were more positive. We joined a Society of Friends [Quakers] meeting where the adults took an interest in my children. One man tutored my son in advanced calculus. The kids have also been serving in a soup kitchen every Friday night. I wish we'd known these Friends when they were little—we might not have been so overwhelmed!"

"I'm just nineteen and I don't have any kids yet," remarked Ebony, "but when I do, I'm going to be open with them about sex. My mom was totally open and it saved me from a lot of mistakes. If they don't get information from home or church, they'll get it from their friends and that can be *big trouble*!"

Our discussion continued for some time, touching on a wide range of topics. As the teacher, I tried to find common threads in our discussion. "I'm impressed by how strongly all of you feel about your churches! It's remarkable that so many of you have hung in there, even when you've felt you weren't being taken seriously. On the one hand, the church preaches high ideals that you value."

"For ourselves as well as for our children! We need noble values to live for," said Pam.

"Yet it sounds as if the reality falls short of the ideals," I said.

"It's not just that they fall short. Of course, we all fall short. We're all human," said Peg. "What's troubling is when church leaders talk as if they *aren't even interested in including us,* don't even want to hear what we have to say."

"So why do you hang in there?" I asked.

"Because we need a spiritual community. We can't let the secular culture be the only influence on our kids," said Pam. "Besides, the church needs us! Our churches are part of who we are, and we want to make them better for our kids and grandkids."

A week later, my workshop met again, and I asked if we could take some time to brainstorm practical responses to the needs of mothers, what I'm calling the pastoral role of a congregation. This pastoral part tries to bridge the gap between "how life should be" and "how things really are today." It's one thing to point out problems, but how about ideas for solving them?

"The most important thing is to get the adults involved in their own spiritual growth. If a woman is to be a good mother, she needs to be rooted in God herself," said Vicki. "I'm preparing second graders for their first communion this year, and I plan to insist that the parents play an active role."

"To do that, you have to know what their spiritual needs are, and their practical needs too," insisted Susan. "We need a place where women can speak candidly about what's really happening in our lives!"

"Where people listen without getting defensive!"

"Why couldn't you have a discussion at church just like the one we're having here?" I asked. "I know many churches coach volunteer leaders to be good listeners. Couldn't they be trained to facilitate dialogue in light of Christian values?"

"I could never be this open at church. They'd kick me out!" said Ebony.

"But just pretend you could: What sort of suggestions would you make?" I asked. "Can we compile a wish list for mothers?"

In the next two hours, the ideas flew fast and furious. I wrote as fast as I could on huge sheets of newsprint, filling several pages. Only afterward did I begin to sort them out, and to add examples from my own research. What follows is a list of our ideas. This list is meant, of course, to be suggestive rather than exhaustive. The pastoral application will vary from one congregation to another.

1. Adult Formation and Christian Education

• *Offer retreats or study groups with a spiritual focus for women.*[3] Schedule such events at times when "working moms" as well as "at-home" moms can attend. Provide child care and transportation and keep costs low. This might take the form of a single day (or afternoon) of prayer and recollection, a weekend getaway, or even longer retreats. Some church-sponsored camps have begun offering week-long "mom and tot" camps that offer spiritual enrichment for all ages, all in a rustic setting.

• *Help teenagers and young adults learn more about parenting,* both the difficulties and the joys. Youth groups, Sunday school classes, and Scout troops could teach young people about child development and parenting, perhaps with a service component in a day-care center or church nursery. Delve beyond the obvious things (like diaper changing and CPR) into subjects like gender conflicts, priority setting, and burnout.

• *Address parenting concerns as part of marriage preparation.* Include topics like gender roles, spiritual needs, discipline, mothering traps (such as the "the dangerous Ds"), costs of child care, and power issues within marriage.

2. Worship, Music, Preaching

• *Use inclusive language.* In *The Church Women Want,* Johnson summarizes the things women want in worship: "...inclusive language for humans as well as for the images and names of God; women's liturgical leadership in preaching and celebrating the Eucharist; and women's participation in decision making in all areas of church governance" (9).

- *Include women's experiences in public worship.* Invite women and young adults to lead worship and singing and to offer their reflections on Scripture readings.

- *Develop special rites to bless new parents,* such as the "blessing ceremony" held for me during my high-risk pregnancy (described in chapter 4).

- *Develop special rites to bless girls at key junctures in their lives.* Groups of women might honor a girl's menarche, for example. The church could also place a greater emphasis on confirmation's many facets; since it often occurs in early adolescence, confirmation could address and celebrate the many different aspects of this exciting stage, including the physical and psychological as well as the spiritual. The Jewish tradition has developed the bat mitzvah as a public celebration of the emerging woman. High school and college graduations are other important milestones.

- *Choose or adapt music so that it reflects women's experience.* In *The Church Women Want* (mentioned above), Miriam Therese Winter offers an intriguing adaptation of a beloved song:

Rocka a my soul in the bosom of She-Who-Is,
Rocka a my soul in the bosom of She-Who-Is,
Rocka a my soul in the bosom of She-Who-Is,
Oh Rocka my soul.

Oh, I know I come from Her.
Oh, I know I go to Her.
Oh, I know I live in Her.
Holy is She who is God. (26)

Winter asks, "Have you ever asked yourself how it happened that Abraham ended up with a bosom?" (26). According to the *Oxford English Dictionary,* the original meaning of *bosom* is associated with the womb as well as the breast; it connotes an embrace or abode.

• *Celebrate various holidays with an eye to their relevance for women.* Many people don't realize that Mother's Day originated as a way to honor mothers who resisted war. Similarly, speeches or ceremonies around Labor Day, Memorial Day, Thanksgiving, or various saints' days might include the roles women have played in our common history.

3. Buildings and Facilities

• *Consider whether the church's physical facilities welcome mothers.* A glassed-off "cuddle room" (what's usually called a "cry room") makes communal worship easier for nursing mothers or parents of preschoolers or others who can't sit quietly.

• *Equip the church with furniture that is welcoming.* Anyone who has ever tried to keep toddlers still in hard, immovable wooden pews can relate to this suggestion. Sturdy, movable chairs are more practical for young children or those holding infants. How about rockers or beanbag chairs in a section of the sanctuary? If this is not feasible, they could at least be made available in a cuddle room or balcony.

• *Consider the needs of stroller-pushing parents* when designing parking lots, sidewalks, and entranceways. I once visited a funeral home where each restroom was not only equipped with a diaper-changing table, but also with a basket containing lotion, disposable diapers, and sanitary products. This made a very strong statement about the respect accorded women and children.

• *Install playgrounds and protective fences on church property.* Devoting a portion of the budget to good nursery equipment, books for children, and the best available religious education materials will also enhance the lives of parents.

4. Stewardship

• *Promote equality.* Help adults be good stewards of their God-given talents by welcoming all adults into all aspects of church life. Miller-McLemore argues that talent and interest, not gender or age, should be the criteria for participation in various church ministries. Men in the nursery and women on the finance committee could be signs of a healthy congregation.

• *Encourage personal growth.* In fact, the church can nurture adult growth by actively encouraging gender bending, that is, by inviting members to choose ministry on the basis of their gifts, not on the basis of stereotypes. Pastoral leaders can model this behavior.

• *Mentor young parents.* Encourage retirees to mentor younger adults in the areas of child care, fund-raising, and community involvement. I think for example of my father, Bill Thomas, who, in his seventies, helped his small church develop a cookbook (including his own favorite recipes)!

• *Sponsor opportunities to learn about personal finance.* This is an area of some urgency for women because of our longevity and mothers' uneven employment patterns and vulnerability. Issues addressed could include the usual "stewardship" topics of tithing and philanthropy, but also budgeting, credit, investing, and retirement planning.

5. Outreach and Mission

• *Provide social and learning opportunities* so that mothers in the local community (as well as those in the church) can get to know both their peers and older women who have already raised their families; sponsor speakers, support groups, and workshops. Those reluctant to attend Bible studies or Sunday school may be attracted to weekday or Saturday events with a broader focus such as personal health (nutritious cooking, meditation, weight control, yoga, overcoming depression, CPR), communication skills (advocating for your child in school, conflict resolution, anger management, coping with teens, etc.), or a local social justice concern (race relations, recycling, vegetarianism, school quality).

• *Make the church building available for meetings* for support or education groups such as La Leche League, Alcoholics Anonymous, the National Alliance for the Mentally Ill, parenting (or stepparenting) classes, prenatal classes, and so forth. Such groups serve diverse types of families.

• *Sponsor groups such as Mothers' Day Out* (a once-a-week child-care program that gives mothers a half-day without children) or MOPS (Mothers of Preschoolers—an educational gathering that provides child care while mothers attend a class/discussion in the church on a topic of common interest). Keep fees low.

• *Sponsor a parents' night out.* When my son was a preschooler, our local Salvation Army offered "parents' night out" a few times a year on a Friday night for a minimal fee—one in December so parents could Christmas shop, another, near Valentine's Day for a "date with your sweetheart." On a similar note, to combat child abuse, a local social service agency uses a renovated house as a getaway for frazzled moms, providing child care on a drop-in basis so that a woman can have an hour alone to take a bubble bath or read a book on site. A church could sponsor a "Women's Escape Center."

• *Consider convenience.* For any of these programs to reach the needy, they must be scheduled at times when mothers can come, and they must include child care. For example, Vacation Bible school often serves as a form of outreach to parents as well as children. If a congregation wants to reach a larger population through a VBS, offer it during weekday evenings rather than mornings, when many parents are at work.

6. Social Justice and Public Witness

• *Address injustice.* Take the lead in addressing the injustices faced by young families, especially mothers. Seek to influence the decisions, policies, and proposed legislation that support children, parents, and a variety of current family forms. Proposals include family-friendly workplaces (with family-leave policies, child-care services, flexible schedules, and flexible definitions of promotion); schools that design their programs to affirm shared parenting and respond to the constraints of dual-income families, single-parent families, blended families, etcetera; male participation in schools and day-care centers; changes in the tax and Social Security laws, divorce laws, and other policies that impact women who give priority to raising children. Just as some churches have challenged militarism and slavery, churches today can challenge political, economic, and other institutional policies (including church policies) that undermine women and their families.

• *Endorse parent-friendly practices.* The National Parenting Association has conducted extensive research nationwide to come up with an agenda that a great majority of parents support, despite difference in race, politics, and income level. These include: passing laws to keep guns away from children; flexible hours in parents' jobs; raising wages so that all full-time workers are above the poverty level; increasing tax deductions and breaks for parents with children at home; and making the school day and year more in sync with the workday and year. (For details, visit www.parentsunite.org.) All these suggestions merit thoughtful discussion by people of faith.

• *Promote the well-being of children and families in society.* In a book called *Children First: What Our Society Must Do—and Is Not Doing—for Our Children Today,* child-development expert Penelope Leach offers an intriguing discussion of ways society could be more "child friendly" and thus more "mother friendly": change zoning laws so that different housing types, industry, and day-care centers could all exist in proximity; give mothers of young children a special card (similar to a student ID) that entitles them to special discounts and privileges; designate certain parks only for those adults accompanied by a child, and more. Another excellent resource for practical suggestions is *The War Against Parents* (Hewlett and West).

7. Governance

Because my students were most concerned about mothers' immediate practical needs, we didn't come up with many fresh ideas for governance, except the idea that mothers' voices needed to be heard. This subject is the topic of lively discussion in many churches, including the Roman Catholic Church. My own position is that gender should not be a consideration in church leadership; both genders should have equal access to all church ministries and roles.

Today's Vision, Tomorrow's Reality

Every May I attend my university's commencement ceremony. This year I had a front-row seat, with a close-up view of all the graduates as they marched past, one by one, to receive their diplomas. I watched especially for seniors I taught this past semester: There went Elizabeth—a straight A student who's already been admitted to a competitive doctoral program in physics; then Lisa, who's been eagerly sending out résumés for elementary teaching jobs; later came Linda, a recently divorced single mother who's prepared for a career in public relations. I know the obstacles they've overcome on their path to graduation day.

I also know that the greatest obstacles are still ahead. Every one of these young women hopes to have a happy family *and* a worthwhile career. My university—a religious institution—has equipped them with valuable intellectual and professional tools. Their college educations have the potential to make them intelligent mothers and competent professionals. But this potential won't be realized unless they also find creative ways to navigate the family-work crunch that will likely be most challenging in their twenties and thirties. In this effort, they need the help of their larger society.

As Glendon mentioned earlier, it is the calling of all Christian churches to be a transformative presence ("leaven") in the secular world. Churches must take seriously our *prophetic* role—our call to uphold values and ideals that are at the core of Christianity. We stand at a unique juncture in history; never before have so many women (including the mothers of young children) been in the paid workforce. Born largely out of economic necessity, this trend over the past thirty years shows no sign of reversing. It brings with it tremendous potential as well as great spiritual needs on the part of women, as we try to compose lives that harmoniously combine work, home, and various kinds of relationships. Just as the Christian tradition has contributed so much in the education of young people, we now have an opportunity to help them prepare spiritually for (and endure) the family-work crunch and the other challenges that come with child rearing. We need to adapt our theology, our worship, and our general worldview to the times we live in. Only in this way can we truly be a "leaven" in the larger culture.

Notes

1. Miller-McLemore observes that liberal churches tend to be stronger in articulating "how things are these days" but may fail to uphold the ideals of "how things ought to be." Conversely, conservative churches may focus great energy on "how things ought to be" but pay scant attention to "how things are" and thus be out of touch with the real needs of people.

2. Some good possibilities are *The War Against Parents* by Sylvia Hewlett and Cornell West; *In the Shelter of Each Other* and other books by Mary Pipher; *A Mother's Work* by Deborah Fallows. I could also imagine a fiction reading club that selected novels portraying contemporary mothering, such as books by Sue Miller, Barbara Kingsolver, Elizabeth Berg, Anita Diamant.

3. Readers should exercise discrimination in choosing books for discussion. Specifically, an outmoded worldview is promoted by the so-called "Christian Living" genre, which includes books such as *The Total Woman* (which has sold over three million copies), *Fascinating Womanhood* (by

Helen Andelin), *The Christian Family* (Larry Christenson), and the best-selling *Dare to Discipline* and *The Strong-Willed Child* (by James Dobson, famous for his arch-conservative "Focus on the Family" books). Marketed primarily to women, these books accept a divinely ordained "chain of command" that cuts across all cultures and times. This "chain" is nearly identical to the static medieval concept of the patriarchal "order of creation": as God rules over men, men should rule women and children. Woman is "created" to be submissive to men, yet (so the thinking goes) she is also responsible for the success and happiness of all family members and for maintaining her own subordinate status. These conflicting messages contribute to women's stress, codependency, and low self-esteem. Linda Coleman argues that the "chain of command" is based on bad theology and a skewed use of biblical texts. For further discussion see her article, "Forging the Chains of Command" (in *The Wisdom of Daughters,* edited by Reta Finger and Kari Sandhaas, Philadelphia: Innisfree Press, 2001, pp. 210–14). Far better than the Christian Living books are those with a more experiential and theological base, such as *Motherhood: A Spiritual Journey* (by Ellyn Sanna), *Experiencing God with Your Children* or *Hidden Women of the Gospels* (both by Kathy Coffey), *The God We Never Knew* (and others by Marcus Borg), or *Clothed with the Sun: Biblical Women, Social Justice, and Us* (Joyce Hollyday).

Readers can learn from Peggy Comella, a Kentucky woman who offers retreats specifically for mothers. Contact her, or find out more, at www.mothersnurture.info.

Epilogue
Ten Years into Motherhood

When the next October rolled around, Gabe and I packed up the car for our yearly pilgrimage to the retreat house in Brown County. By now Gabe was almost ten and accustomed to visiting "Grandma Mimi's place." Though she died when he was four, he was aware of her as a guiding force in the life of our family. Through stories and snapshots, he knew her as the looming figure who helped his mother become a woman, who prayed for him before he was even conceived, who continued to watch over us from infinity.

The weather promised to be warm and clear, and we were both eager for a carefree weekend near woods and water. We talked about our plans as I left the interstate for State Route 32.

"Look at all those pumpkins, Mom! There's a cauldron, and a scarecrow with a pumpkin head! Can we stop?" In front of Shaw's Pumpkin Farm was a vast display of pumpkins.

"The nuns are expecting us, and we still have an hour to drive." I promised we'd stop on our way back, and we continued our drive and arrived safely at Brescia in time for dinner. Later we settled into the retreat house nearby.

The next morning I awakened at dawn. I checked on Gabe, still asleep clutching his stuffed gorilla, "Gilly." His shaggy blond hair needed trimming, and a calloused foot stuck out from under his quilt. His feet have grown as big as mine, I marveled. What happened to those soft baby feet that once fit in my palm? I rejoiced in my new freedom to actually leave him alone for thirty minutes while I went for a walk.

The route out to the nuns' cemetery was familiar: Past the champion oak and the big stone chapel, across Chatfield's grassy campus, down a lane of trees. Nestled beside the woods I found the cemetery where gravestones commemorated Sister Miriam, her beloved foundress Julia Chatfield, Sisters Mary John, Dorothy, Elizabeth, Imelda, Regina….Women I knew well, they lived long and blessed lives, spending fifty, sixty, or seventy years "in religion."

On one side of the cemetery lay the woods; on the other, a sunlit field. Across the field was Brescia, where the elder nuns were probably singing the morning psalms—known as Lauds. Last night I delivered my gift of homemade bread. They "oohed and ahhed": "How thoughtful! However do you find the time? It smells so good!" Maybe even now the cook was slicing my loaves for breakfast.

As I strode along the woods, my thoughts rambled. Like walking, baking bread is a luxurious escape from more tedious work—a sensual, satisfying task that lends itself to musing. Sometimes I ponder the parallels between the spiritual life and baking bread. When I was twenty, growing in faith seemed akin to following a fixed recipe. Certain ingredients were required: daily quiet time, Scripture, right living, and "fellowship." If combined in the right mix, they would lead to unquestioning faith, a successful life, and a harmonious church community. Just as important was clearing away the wrong ingredients, like carnality, pride, doubts, disagreements.

Now at fifty, I believe that growing in faith is a process more like baking bread. Long ago my old friend Bob gave me his favorite recipe for honey-whole wheat bread. I've probably baked hundreds of loaves and now know the steps by heart. First you mix yeast with honey and warm water and wait for it to bubble. Combine eggs, oil, salt, and wheat flour and mix to form a wet, spongy dough. Next comes more flour and add-ins.

As the dough takes on a life of its own, you turn it onto your table and knead, adding more flour as you go, then set it aside and turn your attention elsewhere till it doubles in size. Then knead again, and divide the dough into pans and soon they're ready for the oven!

What I love most about Bob's recipe is the marvelous flexibility. There are, of course, some essentials—warm water, yeast, and wheat flour. In the same way, in the spiritual life there are basics: openness to the infinite, deep respect for human experience, willingness to love. The "water" is openness to grace—the expectation to be loved and led. Flour includes whatever human experience you bring to the table—your own culture, temperament, struggles, and questions. The yeast of love is the force that activates the other ingredients, mixing with experience to create reverence for self and God and others, even strangers.

Once dough begins to form, there's freedom to add more ingredients. At this stage, you can add more wheat flour or substitute wheat germ, soy flour, rolled oats—whatever is available. You can add extras, too—like raisins, walnuts, or dried apricots. In spiritual life, one's culture influences the mix. Sister Miriam's life included a convent education, coming of age in the 1920s, and living through the Great Depression and two world wars. Mine offered a Methodist upbringing, public education, and maturing in the midst of Vietnam and women's liberation. I brought to the table a belief in women's equality, concern for my female body, a secular career, motherhood, and my doubts and questions. Once I would have viewed these as impurities, but I learned to add them in.

The next step is to turn the dough onto your counter and knead by hand. No bread machines allowed—the best bread comes from hands-on kneading! By some alchemy, yeast mingles with wheat gluten to make the sticky dough adhere, and then give way to a stretchy, satisfying texture, warm as flesh. It takes muscle to work it—punch down, turn, roll, and turn again. Hands learn to recognize and savor the feel of dough growing stretchy and smooth as they distribute air evenly throughout.

Kneading is the vigorous human effort of praying, thinking, feeling, practicing, and spiritual disciplines. The form varies according to the language, images, and devotional practices of your time. In kneading, the Spirit works through repeated turning to God. There is movement and muscle involved in this process—intention and steady effort. Sometimes the mood is playful, others—serious or fierce.

Miriam fell in love with God when she was young and chose the spiritual disciplines available then—a cloistered monastery, vows of obedience and chastity, praying the Divine Office, religious garb. My choices were different: Bible studies, Christian community, and daily "quiet time." Not only did our cultures change over time, but our own needs changed too. After nearly forty years in the convent, Sister Miriam's spirituality took new forms with Vatican II; she began to promote interfaith dialogue, direct retreats, and work with the poor. None of these were part of her life as a young nun. Retreats led to mentoring a host of protégés with children and secular careers. As I matured, my mix came to include advanced study, a spiritual director, and prayer walks.

Of course, there are spiritual practices beyond the ones we've used. I think of Helen, a deeply spiritual woman who has attended the same small-town church her entire adult life, faithfully singing in the choir and visiting shut-ins. Or Sunny, whose mix includes a Twelve-Step program and daily meditation. Though outward lives and practices differ, the essence remains the same: love, respect for human experience, and openness to grace. In each case, kneading is essential—the sustained effort of turning to God, living in tandem with the Spirit. As when the baker sets the dough aside to rise, spiritual practice is always accompanied by waiting and other tasks. This takes patience and trust as the Spirit works and life takes on new dimensions.

Finally there's the shaping as you divide the dough into pans, place them in the hot oven, and wait. In the same way that dough is divided into loaves, we face our human limitations—our choices and finiteness. The yeasty fragrance of warm bread slowly permeates the house, and an hour later the bread emerges—crusty and nourishing!

As I continue on my walk between field and woods, I think back over the years of writing about mothers' spirituality. Mothers' experiences offer compelling metaphors: dilation, birth, training, protecting, nurturing. What if each Christian experimented by imagining God for even a day as a birthing woman? If we imagined the Holy Spirit as a seasoned, loving grandmother? How might our priorities and churches be different if we placed mothers and children at the center for even one single year? What if we imagined the Holy Spirit as a seasoned midwife? If every childless adult decided to become a caring "other mother" to one needy child? If all of us Christians made a conscious effort to "dilate" our hearts, what changes might result in congregations and individuals?

My exploration has led to a preliminary lexicon: matrescence, bonding, kything, composing, co-madres (or other mothers), cottonhead, tiger love, the Dark Mother, and more. Few of the phrases originated with me; I've searched and brought them together as a starting point—the beginning of a framework for understanding mothers' spiritual lives. Such language provides common ground between those in the "mother zone" and those beyond. Such a lexicon can help mothers survive difficult years, as well as enhancing our family lives and our larger culture.

I made a final stop back in the cemetery. We'd left buckeyes and army guys on Miriam's headstone. Gabe's love offerings were still there. She was the Holy Spirit incarnate, kneading the leaven of hope, kindness, questions, and laughter into my sticky life. Through decades of friendship, she'd passed on images, attitudes, language, and spiritual practices that gradually became second nature. Now she'd left her body, but I was still very much alive, and so were my son, my family—and so many newcomers to our lives. As the morning sky grew bright, I felt lighter too.

Comparing faith to bread baking helps me appreciate new aspects of spiritual growth. At twenty I believed that the right mix of spiritual "ingredients" would lead to a strong faith, a successful life, and a harmonious church community. In my earlier church, we tried to get back to the purity of the community of believers as described in the Book of Acts, reaching back over two thousand years of human history. We tried to mix the practices of the earliest Christians with the needs of the 1970s.

Now as a mature woman, I see looking backward as escapism. As Christians, we must focus our attention on the present—using only those aspects of the past that will help us create a better future. Now a "successful life" is harder to define. And a harmonious church community? While desirable, it must not be an end in itself. The goal of religion is literally *turning back* to God, not necessarily fitting in with a church. Even Mother Teresa was criticized by her order for ministering to dying Hindus without evangelizing them. If Jesus and Mother Teresa sometimes ran afoul of religious leaders, why should it be different for the rest of us?

The metaphor of bread baking allows for change and hope. As our culture evolves, instead of running away from change, Christians can move *toward it*. It makes sense that we'd develop new language, images, and forms of devotion, not simply retreat into the old. Even the stations of the cross and the rosary were brand-new once!

Like yeast dough, spirituality grows by a living process, not a fixed recipe. It is unpredictable. Sometimes the yeast won't rise properly, and it's hard to know why. More often, as you knead you can feel the dough taking on a warm life of its own. "You know when it's ready," Bob explained long ago, "when the dough feels like a baby's bottom, or like a firm breast." (In monastery kitchens, do bakers think of firm breasts?)

Once baked, the bread is broken, passed on, eaten—just as our lives give life to others. "Blessed is…the work of human hands. It will become our spiritual food." The freedom of mixing and kneading seems so basic to faith. Of course spirituality will grow and change—it is alive! Yet wars have been fought and people martyred over disagreements. Even now, when we pay so much lip service to diversity, often we are quick to judge unfamiliar religious practices.

Making my way back toward the retreat house, I noticed the sun lightening the treetops in the distance. I've always loved the way trees light up from the top down as the sun climbs the sky. Breathing the chill air, I remembered all the times my dad said, "Get outside and get the stink blown off ya! Get your blood circulating!"—as he pushed me, his bookworm daughter, out-of-doors. As a child, I resented Dad's intrusion, but now I see his wisdom.

It's been a full decade since Sister Miriam placed her hands upon the mound of my pregnant belly. It's hard to explain, but the past ten years has brought a growing lightness. They call it "lightening" when the baby drops into the pelvic cavity, giving the mother more room to breathe. It signals that birth is near.

I sensed lightness most intensely the weeks following Gabe's birth; I'd been confined to bed for six weeks with fifty extra pounds. In contrast to all that heaviness, my baby seemed so light—a small, buoyant creature in my arms!

As the sky became a deeper blue, I hurried back toward the retreat house. For a long time, I'd pictured Sophia kneading our spirits through all the events of our lives. As I learn to trust her more, she brings lightness.

By the time I let myself back into the retreat house, Gabe was stirring. I filled our bowls with cereal.

"Hurry up, Mom. It's already time for 'Yu-Gi-Oh!'" Gabe and Gilly nestled into the couch by the small television. Ten years ago, who would have dreamed that I'd be watching Japanese cartoons during a retreat?

*　　*　　*

For the rest of the weekend Gabe and I explored the woods, shared a dinner with the nuns, and took turns reading aloud. A snapshot shows him posing with a feather-and-leaf boat beside the shining blue lake. Both sky and lake shone so blue that Saturday!

At night we hiked the convent grounds by flashlight, awed by the hoot of an owl and the blazing stars we can never see in the city. Although I enjoyed many retreats in the years before Gabe was born, they've taken on a whole new dimension as he pulls me outdoors to explore God's handiwork. He gives me a sense of the circle of life and the Creator alive everywhere in the tangible world.

On Sunday evening on our way home, Gabe and I stopped at Shaw's Pumpkin Farm. After a sunny weekend, the weather turned rainy, so we ran to the open-air shelter where tables of gourds and Halloween trinkets were on display. Huddling together to escape the rain created an intimacy among the browsers and the proprietors.

"What brings you folks out to the country?" asked the bearded man behind the counter. Judging by his wrinkled face, he was maybe seventy.

"We've been on retreat with the Brown County Ursulines near Fayetteville. We go out there every fall."

His face lit up. "I know the Ursulines. When I was a boy, I attended their day school for fifth and sixth grade. They made a lasting impression on me. They taught me to enjoy the fine things of life, like art and music, and the sisters were so kind." Sixty years later he remembers the Ursulines!

A browser spoke up. "The Ursulines—isn't that Sister Miriam's group? I remember back in the sixties when she first started Chatfield College. Then for the longest time she ran that free store. Many people from these parts turned to her when times were hard."

"Some other Ursulines run the free store now," I explained. "It'll be six years next month since Sister Miriam died. She was a dear friend to me, a second mother." Even after so much time, my eyes teared up.

"She's sort of a legend around here! She was a great woman!" said the browser.

Gabe and I paid for our pumpkin and climbed back in the car.

"Did you hear them talking?" I asked, accelerating along Route 32. "We're fifty miles away and they all remember Grandma Mimi. Isn't it amazing that our grandma made such an impression?"

Sunday night I returned home filled to the brim with peace, that feeling of lightness and hope—ready to face life's challenges. And so the process continues. The same Spirit of Wisdom spoke in ancient times. "[Wisdom has] set her table. She has sent out her servant-girls, she calls from the highest places in the town…'Come, eat of my bread and drink of the wine I have mixed. Lay aside immaturity and live, and walk in the way of insight.'" (Proverbs 9:2–6).

Her invitation found new expression in the Gospel of Luke, when a stranger joined the disciples on the path to Emmaus and later dine them: "When he was at the table with them, he took the bread and broke it, and gave it to them. Then their eyes were opened, and they recognized him; and he vanished from their sight. They said to each other, 'Were not our hearts burning within us while he was talking to us on the road, while he was opening the scriptures to us?'" (Luke 24:30–32).

And Sophia continues today to invite us to fullness of life.

Acknowledgments

The most pleasant aspect of finishing a book is the chance to look back and take note of all the generous souls who have accompanied me along the solitary path of writing. I am grateful to many.

My dear friend Susan Mueller has attended every page of this book in its birthing stage and contributed her own creative intelligence and humor. She has taught me much about women's body images and attitudes toward reproduction. I regard Susan as a personal emissary from Sister Miriam and an important contributor to this book.

My mother, Helen Klingensmith Thomas, has taught me so much about resiliency and hope in God, especially this past year.

Various members of my writing group have provided a steady stream of insight, especially Sheree Brown, Maureen Conlan, and Patty Houston. Josephine (Pipin) Miranda has been my son's first and *favorite* caregiver, and has become my "adopted sister." For as long as we've been friends, "Aunt Lucy" Schultz has taken a lively interest in my writing and offered consistent encouragement. Barbara Sis Elekes has been a soulmate since age six.

Kevin di Camillo, my editor at Paulist Press, brought both candor and a poet's sensibility to our collaboration. Publisher Lawrence Boadt saw potential in my early manuscript, and hard workers in production, marketing, and sales at Paulist Press brought it to fruition.

At key moments I received valuable advice from Joan Chittister, Peter Elbow, Maria Harris, Brennan Hill, David Kushner, John Tallmadge, and Joe Wessling—all scholars whose work has nourished mine. Brennan Hill is a mentor and a vibrant example of the kind of person I hope to become by age seventy!

Xavier University provided me with faculty development leaves in spring 1997 and summer 1999 for the early stages of my research. Secretary Linda Loomis, consummate copy editor and friend, has been "the woman who knows what's going on" in my department. Generous friends agreed to read the manuscript in its almost-final stage and to offer suggestions: Laurie Henry, Linda Maupin, Elizabeth Resnick, and Ruth Thomas. I appreciate the warmth and open-mindedness of my dean, Janice Walker.

I've sensed the guiding presence of several dear ones who have died in recent years: Sister Miriam Thompson; Bob McMahan, Sr.; Bill Thomas, my father; and Ida McMahan. All modeled generativity in their long lives.

I am deeply grateful to the many mothers who agreed to be interviewed for this project, and to the students who offered responses to my ideas over the years. May my project be worthy of their trust and openness.

Finally, I thank my mate, Bill McMahan, and our son, Gabriel ("Vegi-man") who continually tug me by the hand, out of my study and into the big wide world. They give me so many reasons to laugh and savor the sweetness of life.

Works Cited, Resources Consulted, and Further Reading

Albert, Susan W. 1992. *Work of Her Own: How Women Create Success and Fulfillment off the Career Track.* New York: Tarcher.

Aron, Elaine. 1998. *The Highly Sensitive Person: How to Thrive When the World Overwhelms You.* New York: Broadway Books.

Baldwin, Rahima. 1989. *You Are Your Child's First Teacher.* Berkeley, CA: Celestial Arts.

Barron, T. A. 2002. *The Hero's Trail: A Guide for a Heroic Life.* New York: Philomel Books.

Bateson, Mary C. 2000. *Full Circles Overlapping Lives: Culture and Generation in Transition.* 1st ed. New York: Random House.

Bechtel, Stefan, and Laurence R. Stains. 1998. *A Man's Guide to Sex.* New York: Berkley Books.

Borg, Marcus J. 1998. *The God We Never Knew: Beyond Dogmatic Religion to a More Authentic Contemporary Faith.* San Francisco: HarperSanFrancisco.

———.1995. *Meeting Jesus Again for the First Time: The Historical Jesus and the Heart of Contemporary Faith.* San Francisco: HarperSanFrancisco.

Carson, Rachel. 1998. *The Sense of Wonder.* New York: Harper Collins.

Chase, Carole F. 1998. *Suncatcher: A Study of Madeleine L'Engle and Her Writing.* 2nd ed. Philadelphia: Innisfree Press.

Chester, Laura, ed. 1989. *Cradle and All.* Boston: Faber and Faber.

Chopin, Kate. 1976. *The Awakening: An Authoritative Text: Biographical and Historical Contexts Criticism.* Edited by Margo Culley. New York: Norton.

Christ, Carol P., and Judith Plaskow. 1992. *Womanspirit Rising: A Feminist Reader in Religion.* San Francisco: HarperSanFrancisco.

Coffey, Kathy. 1997. *Experiencing God with Your Children.* New York: Crossroad.

Coleman, Linda. 2001. "Forging Chains of Command." In *The Wisdom of Daughters: Two Decades of the Voice of Christian Feminism.* ed. Reta Halteman Finger and Kari Sandhaas. Philadelphia: Innisfree Press.

Conn, Joann W. 1996. *Women's Spirituality: Resources for Christian Development.* 2nd ed. New York/Mahwah, NJ: Paulist Press.

Crittenden, Ann. 2001. *The Price of Motherhood: Why the Most Important Job in the World Is Still the Least Valued.* 1st ed. New York: Metropolitan Books.

Daly, Mary. 1994. "After the Death of God the Father: Women's Liberation and the Transformation of Christian Consciousness." In *Feminism in Our Time,* ed. Miriam Schneir. New York: Vintage.

Diamant, Anita. 1998. *The Red Tent.* New York: Picador.

Erdrich, Louise. 1996. *The Blue Jay's Dance: A Birth Year.* New York: HarperPerennial.

Finger, Reta H., and Kari Sandhaas. 2001. *The Wisdom of Daughters: Two Decades of the Voice of Christian Feminism.* Philadelphia: Innisfree Press.

Gill-Austern, Brita L. 1996. "Love Understood as Self-Sacrifice and Self-Denial: What Does It Do to Women?" In *Through the Eyes of Women: Insights for Pastoral Care,* ed. Jeanne Stevenson Moessner. Minneapolis: Fortress Press.

Glendon, Mary A. 2002. "The Challenge of Being 'Leaven' in a Secular Culture." In *The Church Women Want,* ed. Elizabeth A. Johnson. New York: Crossroad.

Goldsmith, Judith. 1990. *Childbirth Wisdom: From the World's Oldest Societies.* Brookline, MA: East West Health Books.

Hay, David, with Rebecca Nye. 1998. *The Spirit of the Child.* London: HarperCollins.

Heilbrun, Carolyn G. 1988. *Writing a Woman's Life.* New York: Norton.

Hewlett, Sylvia A., and Cornell West. 1998. *The War Against Parents: What We Can Do for America's Beleaguered Moms and Dads.* Boston: Houghton Mifflin.

Hochschild, Arlie R. 1997. *The Time Bind: When Work Becomes Home and Home Becomes Work*. New York: Metropolitan Books.

Hochschild, Arlie R., and Anne Machung. 1989. *The Second Shift: Working Parents and the Revolution at Home*. New York: Viking.

Jackson, Marni. 1992. *The Mother Zone: Love, Sex, and Laundry in the Modern Family*. New York: H. Holt and Company.

Johnson, Elizabeth A. 2002. *The Church Women Want: Catholic Women in Dialogue*. New York: Crossroad.

———. 1993. *Women, Earth, and Creator Spirit*. New York/Mahwah, NJ: Paulist Press.

———.1992. *She Who Is: The Mystery of God in Feminist Theological Discourse*. New York: Crossroad.

Kabat-Zin, Myla and Jon. 1997. *Everyday Blessings: The Inner Work of Mindful Parenting*. New York: Hyperion.

Kenison, Katrina. 2000. *Mitten Strings for God: Reflections for Mothers in a Hurry*. New York: Warner Books.

Kenison, Katrina, and Kathleen Hirsch. 1996. *Mothers: Twenty Stories of Contemporary Motherhood*. New York: North Point Press.

Kephart, Beth. 1999. *A Slant of Sun: One Child's Courage*. New York: Quill/W. Morrow.

Kerr, Barbara A. 1985. *Smart Girls, Gifted Women*. Columbus, Ohio: Ohio Psychology Publishing Company.

Kidd, Sue M. 2002. *The Secret Life of Bees*. New York: Viking.

———.1996. *The Dance of the Dissident Daughter: A Woman's Journey from Christian Tradition to the Sacred Feminine*. San Francisco: HarperSanFrancisco.

Landry, Cary, and Carol J. Kinghorn. 1997. *Quiet Time with Jesus*. audiotape. Portland, OR: OCP Publications.

Lapp, Cynthia A. 1998. "There's Power in the Blood: Women, Christian Ritual, and the Blood Mysteries." Master's thesis, Wesley Theological Seminary.

Leach, Penelope. 1995. *Children First: What Society Must Do—and Is Not Doing for Children Today.* New York: Vintage.

L'Engle, Madeleine. 1996. *Penguins and Golden Calves: Icons and Idols.* Wheaton, IL: Shaw.

———.1991. *Two-Part Invention: The Story of a Marriage.* New York: Walker.

L'Engle, Madeleine, and Avery Brooke. 1985. *Trailing Clouds of Glory: Spiritual Values in Children's Literature.* Philadelphia: Westminster Press.

Lerner, Harriet G. 1985. *The Dance of Anger: A Woman's Guide to Changing the Patterns of Intimate Relationships.* Perennial Library ed. New York: Perennial Library.

Levinson, Daniel. 1978. *The Seasons of a Man's Life.* New York: Ballantine.

Levinson, Daniel, and Judy D. Levinson. 1996. *The Seasons of a Woman's Life.* New York: Knopf.

Liedloff, Jean. 1975. *The Continuum Concept.* London: Duckworth.

Linn, Dennis, Sheila F. Linn, and Matthew Linn. 1995. *Sleeping with Bread: Holding What Gives You Life.* New York/Mahwah, NJ: Paulist Press.

———.1994. *Good Goats: Healing Our Image of God.* New York/Mahwah, NJ: Paulist Press.

Matthews, Gareth B. 1980. *Philosophy and the Young Child.* Cambridge, MA: Harvard University Press.

Maushart, Susan. 1999. *The Mask of Motherhood: How Becoming a Mother Changes Everything and Why We Pretend It Doesn't.* New York: New Press.

Miller, Jean B. 1976. *Toward a New Psychology of Women.* Boston: Beacon Press.

Miller-McLemore, Bonnie J. 1994. *Also a Mother: Work and Family as Theological Dilemma.* Nashville: Abingdon Press.

Milner, Marion B. 1981. *A Life of One's Own.* Los Angeles and Boston: J. P. Tarcher; distributed by Houghton, Mifflin.

Moessner, Jeanne S. 1996. *Through the Eyes of Women: Insights for Pastoral Care.* Minneapolis: Fortress Press.

Nemiroff, Greta H. 1994. "Reflections on Motherhood." In *Mother Journeys: Feminists Write about Mothering,* ed. Maureen Reddy et al. Minneapolis: Spinsters Ink.

Northrup, Christiane. 1998. *Women's Bodies, Women's Wisdom: Creating Physical and Emotional Health and Healing.* New York: Bantam Books.

Norton, Mary, Beth Krush, and Joe Krush. 1953. *The Borrowers.* New York: Harcourt Brace Jovanovich.

Orenstein, Peggy. 2000. *Flux: Women on Sex, Work, Kids, Love and Life in a Half-Changed World.* New York: Doubleday.

Park, Clara C. 1972. *The Seige: The First Eight Years of an Autistic Child.* Boston: Little, Brown.

Pike, Maggie. 1997. *Parent-Child Retreats.* Denver: Living the Good News.

Pipher, Mary. 1996. *The Shelter of Each Other: Rebuilding Our Families.* New York: G.P. Putnam.

Raphael, Dana. 1976. *The Tender Gift: Breastfeeding.* New York: Schocken Books.

Reddy, Maureen T., Martha Roth, and Amy Sheldon. 1994. *Mother Journeys: Feminists Write About Mothering.* Minneapolis: Spinsters Ink.

Roiphe, Anne R. 1996. *Fruitful: A Real Mother in the Modern World.* Boston: Houghton Mifflin.

Ruddick, Sara. 1989. *Maternal Thinking: Toward a Politics of Peace.* Boston: Beacon Press.

Saiving, Valerie. 1979. "The Human Situation: A Feminine View." In *Womanspirit Rising: A Feminist Reader in Religion,* ed. Carol Christ and Judith Plaskow. New York: Harper and Row.

Savary, Louis M., and Patricia H. Berne. 1988. *Kything: The Art of Spiritual Presence.* New York/Mahwah, NJ: Paulist Press.

Schneir, Miriam. 1994. *Feminism in Our Time: The Essential Writings, World War II to the Present.* New York: Vintage Books.

Stern, Daniel N., MD, and Nadia Bruschweiler-Stern. 1998. *The Birth of a Mother.* Boston: Basic Books.

Thurer, Shari. 1994. *The Myths of Motherhood: How Culture Reinvents the Good Mother*. Boston: Houghton Mifflin.

Trelease, Jim. 2001. *The Read-Aloud Handbook*. New York: Penguin.

West, Melissa. 1992. *If Only I Were a Better Mother: Using the Anger, Fear, Despair and Guilt That Every Mother Feels at Some Time, as a Pathway to Emotional Balance and Spiritual Growth*. Walpole, NH: Stillpoint Publishing.

Wolfteich, Claire E. 2002. *Navigating New Terrain: Work and Women's Spiritual Lives*. New York/Mahwah, NJ: Paulist Press.

Wootan, George, MD. 1992. *Take Charge of Your Child's Health*. New York: Crown.

Young-Eisendrath, Polly. 1992. *Women and Desire*. New York: Harmony Books.